Palgrave Studies in Economic History

Series Editor
Kent Deng
London School of Economics
London, UK

Palgrave Studies in Economic History is designed to illuminate and enrich our understanding of economies and economic phenomena of the past. The series covers a vast range of topics including financial history, labour history, development economics, commercialisation, urbanisation, industrialisation, modernisation, globalisation, and changes in world economic orders.

More information about this series at
http://www.palgrave.com/gp/series/14632

María Vázquez-Fariñas
Pedro Pablo Ortúñez-Goicolea
Mariano Castro-Valdivia
Editors

# Companies and Entrepreneurs in the History of Spain

## Centuries Long Evolution in Business since the 15th century

palgrave
macmillan

*Editors*
María Vázquez-Fariñas
Department of Economics
University of Jaén
Jaén, Spain

Pedro Pablo Ortúñez-Goicolea
Faculty of Economics and Business
University of Valladolid
Valladolid, Spain

Mariano Castro-Valdivia
Department of Economics
University of Jaén
Jaén, Spain

This book has been evaluated by the double-blind peer-review system.

ISSN 2662-6497 ISSN 2662-6500 (electronic)
Palgrave Studies in Economic History
ISBN 978-3-030-61317-4 ISBN 978-3-030-61318-1 (eBook)
https://doi.org/10.1007/978-3-030-61318-1



This Palgrave Macmillan imprint is published by the registered company Springer Nature Switzerland AG.
The registered company address is: Gewerbestrasse 11, 6330 Cham, Switzerland

# Preface

The aim behind the establishment and dissemination of the subject of the History of the Company is to encourage the spread of entrepreneurial culture among scholars of the subject and readers in general. Its emergence as a teachable subject, the setting in which it appeared, the students to whom it was addressed, as well as the main bibliographical contributions made by the great teachers who taught it, all make it a fundamental tool for developing entrepreneurial spirit among all those who are interested in founding companies and in building their professional careers along the path of entrepreneurship.

For these reasons, analyzing and learning about the life trajectory of businesspeople allows the incorporation of their experiences into the business organization. This set of actions enriches the decision-making process in the company, since people take them in very complex concrete circumstances, regardless of the organizational variables or structures. Likewise, immersing yourself in the biographies of the people who run companies offers an introduction to economic realities, since understanding success and failure in the business world means accepting the ups and downs of the commercial activity. This approach is intended to provide those interested in the subject with a dynamic view of the economic process and the commercial enterprises, however large or small they are.

The interest in Economic History especially arose from the 1970s onward, and the History of the Company has been closely linked to the development of it. This may be one of the reasons for the late incorporation of these studies in Spanish universities. On the other hand, the idea of

Spain's economic and industrial backwardness throughout the nineteenth century had been the focus of research by distinguished historians for many years, and issues considered more tangential, such as companies, were overlooked.

The influence of American universities (especially the pioneering Harvard) in the introduction of the History of the Company, directly influenced its development in Spain. The methodology for the study of current business situations was based on case studies, which allowed students to learn business organization techniques. The starting point was a very basic proposal: to study cases of companies from the past that would allow the analysis of situations that could arise in the direction, management and organization of a company in the present. This is the usual practice developed by business schools in Spain: IESE, ICADE, IE, ESADE and ESIC, among others.

To bridge the gap, the final aim of the compilation and "succession of cases" included in this book is to foster a better understanding that enables effective decision-making in the business world. At first, the use of this methodology was merely descriptive, but more recently, researchers have begun to explore new procedures in order to achieve greater conceptual precision that allows generalizing the evolutionary processes of companies. This trend has fostered comparative analysis—such as those of Chandler and Cole—and the application of economic theory, highlighting the role of the company and the entrepreneur in economic development and industrialization. Many of the studies presented here are largely a response to these approaches.

The cases selected in this book aim to show a broad panorama and respond to the multiple studies that have been carried out in Spain in recent decades. Advances in the knowledge of Spanish companies and entrepreneurs have been considerable and represent a relevant approach in the field of Business History. The topics covered reveal the different conceptions and focal points of Spanish companies and entrepreneurs in recent centuries. Cases have been sought from regions of Spain that have traditionally had less business activity, such as Andalusia, and Castile and León. Other cases correspond to marginal areas from a geographical point of view, such as Minorca. On the contrary, cases from the Madrid area have also been selected. The objective of the selection has been to carry out a "positive discrimination," presenting companies and entrepreneurs from lesser known areas, both from the regional and sectoral point of view.

Some chapters cover more general sectors such as water supply, rail transport, tourism and the changes during the political transition from dictatorship to democracy.

After an initial introductory work where the figure of the entrepreneur and the historiographic advances in the History of the Company are analyzed, several studies on companies and businessmen in the pre-industrial period are included; for example, the commercial companies in Castile during the fifteenth and sixteenth centuries, and a brief overview of the businessman Simón Ruiz as an example of advanced business management. Among these, the figure of a great modern capitalist, Jakob Fugger, has been inserted. Although it is true that he was not Spanish, his multiple relationships with the Spanish crown in the sixteenth century, as well as his actions and variety of businesses, establish him as a clear reference in the institutional concomitance between the business world and the political power.

A second block is made up of several studies focused on the nineteenth century and the first decades of the twentieth century, such as commercial activity on the Reinosa route, the wine business in Cádiz and the vicissitudes of the Antequerana Sugar Company. In this part, a work focused on the analysis of commercial bankers, banking houses and large national banks also appears.

The third group of works is under the auspices of two large sectors that converge in the field of public services: drinking water supply companies and railway companies.

The fourth block of studies is characterized by the analysis of relevant entrepreneurs in various branches of the economy: Eusebio Cafranga in the travel agency business, Santiago Pons and Jaime Mascaró in footwear, and Pedro Montañés in food. These contributions culminate in the chapter on the possible keys to the success of the leading company in the insurance sector (MAPFRE), as well as a sharp reflection on the role of Spanish businessmen in the face of the regime change from the Franco dictatorship to the democracy, with its respective challenges, difficulties and hopes. Finally, this book closes with a novel contribution of the Valladolid company Lingotes Especiales, which in a few years has undergone the transition from a small company to a major multinational.

All these cases, and this book as a whole, are intended not only as a manual for the History of the Company courses, but also as a text to be studied and consulted by professionals. The works found within, in a rigorous and systematic way, aim to illustrate the diverse business panorama existing in Spain. In essence, these have been the main reasons behind the preparation of this book.

Finally, it is essential to thank the Springer Nature Switzerland AG group for the publication of this project. On the one hand, we thank the anonymous evaluators who have supported this work with their comments. On the other hand, we thank the effort, interest and help provided by Ruth Jenner, and her excellent disposition as Economics Editor of Palgrave Macmillan.

Jaén, Spain — María Vázquez-Fariñas
Valladolid, Spain — Pedro Pablo Ortúñez-Goicolea
Jaén, Spain — Mariano Castro-Valdivia

# Contents

# Notes on Contributors

**Pablo Alonso Villa** is an associate lecturer at the University of Valladolid. He holds a degree in Economics, a master's degree in Economics Research and a PhD in Economics from this university. He made a research stay at the Institute of Social Sciences, University of Lisbon. He has published numerous articles in indexed journals and a book chapter. His research focuses on the industrial history of Castilla y León and especially on the metallurgical sector and its connections with the automobile industry.

**Rafael Barquín** is an associate lecturer at the Universidad Nacional de Educación a Distancia, Madrid. His main lines of research focus on railroads, integration of cereal market, and processes of literacy in nineteenth-century Spain. Some of his publications are "El consumo urbano en Andalucía Oriental a mediados del siglo XIX", *Investigaciones de Historia Económica*, 2019; "La influencia del ferrocarril en el desarrollo urbano español (1860–1910)", *Revista de Historia Económica/JILAEH*, 2012; and "Analysis of Spanish wheat prices (1765–1855)", *Histoire et Mesure*, 2011. He is editor-in-chief of *Transportes, Servicios y Telecomunicaciones* (TST).

**Leonardo Caruana de las Cagigas** is on tenure at the University of Granada (Spain). His research is on insurance and reinsurance history. He has published *From Mutual to Multinational, Mapfre, 1933–2008* with Gabriel Tortella Casares and José Luis García Ruiz; *The Internationalization of the Spanish Insurance: The Case of Mapfre in ICE* with José Luis García

Ruiz; *The History of Spanish Insurance* with Gabriel Tortella Casares, Alberto Manzano Martos, Jerònia Pons Pons and José Luis García Ruiz; and *Corporate Forms*, edited by Robin Pearson and Takau Yoneyama. Recently, he has published with André Straus (eds.) *Highlights on Reinsurance History* (2017). He also did research on economic warfare with Hugh Rockoff and has had it published in the *Journal of Economic History* and in the *European Review of Economic History*.

**David Carvajal** is a graduate in History and in Business Sciences (University of Valladolid, 2007 and 2009). In 2008 he was granted with a National Fellow—University Teachers Training Program (FPU) scholarship, and in 2013, he finished his PhD dissertation titled "Private Credit and Debt in Castile 1480–1520." He enjoyed two academic international research stays at the University of Cambridge—Queens' College (2009 and 2011)—and was awarded with the PhD National Award on Humanities (Real Academia de Doctores de España) and the University of Valladolid PhD Prize. His research lines include premodern economic history and topics like credit, banking, merchants and trade, networks and institutions, on which he has published many publications in prestigious editorials and journals.

**Hilario Casado-Alonso** is Professor of Economic History at the University of Valladolid (Spain). He has held visiting professorships at the universities of Bari (Italy) and Oporto (Portugal) and at the Ecole des Hautes Études en Sciences Sociales (Paris). He is a member of the Giunta Esecutiva della Fondazione Istituto Internazionale "F. Datini" de Prato (Italy) and is the director of the "Simón Ruiz Chair in the History of Commerce and Finance" at the University of Valladolid, financed by the Banco de Santander.

**Mariano Castro-Valdivia** holds a PhD in Economics from the University of Jaén and is an associate lecturer in History and Economic Institutions Area (Department of Economics) at the University of Jaén. He has been a coordinator of several research projects, member of the Jaén Applied Economics Research Group and secretary of Agua y Territorio / Water and Landscape (AYT / WAL). His research work has focused on the teaching of Economics at the Spanish University and on the dissemination of classical economic thought in Spain, on which he has published several works. He has conducted research stays of more than three months at the Universita degli Studi di Roma "La Sapienza", University of Salamanca and University of Michel de Montaigne

Bordeaux III. He has been a participant and coordinator of several teaching innovation projects at the University of Jaén, with publications such as *La investigación histórica a través de la TIC: una experiencia docente*.

**Mercedes Fernández-Paradas** is Head Professor of Contemporary History at the University of Málaga. She has specialized in Economic History and public services, especially business history, gas and electricity. She is the principal researcher of the Research and Innovation Project of Excellence of the Government of Spain "*La industria del gas en España: desarrollo y trayectorias regionales* (1842–2008)". She has carried out several research stays, including at the London School of Economics and Political Science. She has won several awards, including the *Premio Extraordinario de Doctorado en Filosofía y Letras* [Extraordinary Doctorate Award in Philosophy and Arts] for the History Department, University of Malaga.

**Francisco José García Ariza** is affiliated to the University of Málaga. He has specialized in Economic History, Business History and Agroindustrial History. He has published several researches on the Sociedad Azucarera Antequera, related to the construction of the sugar factory, its founders, shareholders, sugar production and so on, and among them, with Mercedes Fernández-Paradas, "La Sociedad Azucarera Antequerana: una respuesta a la crisis finisecular (1890–1906)", in J.M. Matés (coord.), *Empresas y empresarios en España. De mercaderes a industriales* (2019).

**Agustín González-Enciso** is chair-holding Professor of Early Modern History and Emeritus Professor at the School of Philosophy and Letters, University of Navarra. He has also been a professor at the universities of Valladolid, Autónoma de Madrid and Murcia, and research associate in several universities of the United States, Peru, Argentina and Guatemala. He is a correspondent member of the Royal Academy of History. Specialized in the Economic History of the Early Modern Era, he has studied Spain's seventeenth and eighteenth industrial centuries and commercial and financial history. He is a member of the Contractor State Group-Imperial Network. His line of work is the mobilization of warfare resources. His latest book is *Power and the Economy. Mercantilism and State Formation in Eighteenth-Century Europe* (2017).

**Juan Henández Andreu** holds a PhD in Economic Sciences and is Professor Emeritus of History and Economic Institutions at the

Complutense University of Madrid. He is a visiting scholar at the universities of Texas at Austin and California at San Diego. He has been a professor at the University of Paris X in Nanterre and La Sapienza in Rome and a recipient of a Fulbright scholarship awarded by the Joint Hispanic-North American Committee and Jean Monnet Action. He has been the vice-rector of Complutense University (1995–1997) and the first founding director of the Complutense Institute for International Studies (1997–1999). He was also rewarded the Complutense University Honor Medal (1997). He is the author of numerous books and articles on economic thought and economic history.

**Jorge Lafuente del Cano** is Lecturer in Economic History at the University of Valladolid. He holds a degree in History, a degree in Journalism and a PhD in History. He made a research stay at the University of Oxford and at the University of Roma-La Sapienza. He is a member of the "Studies on Economic History" Research Group and the "Studies on Recent History" Research Group as well. Lafuente has published two books and numerous articles on entrepreneurship, economic history of Spanish transition to democracy, negotiations for Spain's entry into the European Economic Community and the figure of former Spanish prime minister, Leopoldo Calvo-Sotelo.

**Carlos Larrinaga** is Associate Lecturer in Economic History at the University of Granada (Andalusia, Spain). His research is in the history of tourism, railways in the nineteenth century and the service sector. He is currently leading an interdisciplinary project on the history of tourism in Spain and Italy in the twentieth century, funded by the Spanish Ministry of Science, Innovation and Universities and the European Regional Development Fund (ERDF).

**Juan Manuel Matés-Barco** is Professor of Economic History and Business History at the University of Jaén. He holds a bachelor's degree from the University of Zaragoza and a PhD from the University of Granada. He has made stays at the Università degli Studi di Firenze, European University Institute (Italy) and University Michel de Montaigne Bordeaux III. He has been a member of the Group of Historical Studies on the Company and researcher for the Permanent Seminar Water, Territory and Environment. He is part of the Editorial Board of the journal Transportes, Servicios y Telecomunicaciones (TST). He is director of Agua y Territorio / Water and Landscape (AYT / WAL), edited by the

University of Jaén and promoted by the Permanent Seminar Water, Territory and Environment (Escuela de Estudios Hispanoamericanos from Seville-CSIC: Superior Council of Scientific Investigations). His research is focused on the public water supply service, and he has published studies on the economy of contemporary Spain.

**Miguel Muñoz Rubio** holds a PhD in History. He has specialized in railway history, having researched widely on the Spanish railways. He was director of the Railway History Archive and the National Railway Museum, and Professor of Economic History for ten years at Madrid Autonomous University. He has published more than 50 books and papers, and was the founder and editor of the academic journal *Transportes, Servicios y Telecomunicaciones* (TST) between 2001–2009 and 2013–2015. He also was a member of the High Commission for Administrative Documentation Rating of the Spanish Government, vice chairman of the International Association for Railway History (IRHA), curator of several exhibitions and secretary of the Eighth International Congress of the International Committee for the Conservation of the Industrial Heritage (1992).

**Pedro Pablo Ortúñez-Goicolea** holds a PhD from the University of Valladolid, 1999. He is Senior Lecturer in Economic History at the University of Valladolid (Spain). His research interests include the Spanish railway system and the public sector before nationalization of the railway, and regulation and business history. He has published his research in books (on editorials of first quartile like Oxford University Press, Ariel, Pirámide, Comares, etc.) and specialized journals (indexed in JCR or Scopus) and has participated in conferences in these fields. He has undertaken research on several stays at the London School of Economics and at the École des Hautes Etudes en Sciences Sociales (Paris).

**María Vázquez-Fariñas** holds a PhD in Social and Legal Sciences at the University of Cádiz (Spain) and is Lecturer in History and Economic Institutions Area (Department of Economics) at the University of Jaén (Spain). She has been actively involved as a component of the Esteban Boutelou Historical Studies Research Group and Lean Management of Production and Hyperconnected Universal Integrated Logistics Research Group, both at the University of Cádiz. She did a pre-doctoral research stay at the School of Hispanic American Studies (CSIC, Seville) and a post-doctoral stay at the University Michel de Montaigne Bordeaux III. Her lines of research focus on the economic and business history of

Cádiz in the nineteenth century, the wine industry of the region, and the development of commerce and the port of Cádiz between the mid-nineteenth and mid-twentieth centuries, on which several works have been published in books and specialized journals.

**María José Vargas-Machuca** has a degree in Economics and Business Administration and is an associate lecturer in the Department of Economics at the University of Jaén, where she teaches the subjects of Spanish Financial System and World Economy. She belongs to various research groups and teams related to her area of knowledge. Her research has focused on the history of the financial system, especially at the local level. She has published several articles in specialized journals on this topic. Her doctoral thesis deals with "La Caja Rural de Jaén: 60 years at the Service of the Province of Jaén."

# List of Figures

# List of Tables

CHAPTER 1

# The Influence of the Entrepreneur as a determining factor in the History of the Company

*Mariano Castro-Valdivia*

## 1.1 Introduction[1]

A country's economic growth is increasingly linked to the success of its companies. In this context, studying the figure of the entrepreneur and/or businessperson is essential. As the professors José Manuel Menudo Pachón and José Maria O'Kean Alonso (2019) point out, one would

[1] This work is the result of the reflections which originated within the Teaching Innovation Projects at the University of Jaén and the University of Málaga. The former has been focused on the study of "*Las TIC's y su influencia en la enseñanza de la Historia*." The latter deals with the "Nuevas metodologías y contenidos aplicados a la práctica docente: el Archivo y el Museo como base para la innovación docente y la investigación histórico artística en la Era Digital, PIE 15–67." A first version, which is more extensive and detailed, of this work has been published in Matés-Barco Juan Manuel and Mariano Castro Valdivia (2017). To facilitate reading, the detailed footnotes have been removed from the original text.

M. Castro-Valdivia (✉)
University of Jaén, Jaén, Spain
e-mail: mcastro@ujaen.es





M. Vázquez-Fariñas et al. (eds.), *Companies and Entrepreneurs in the History of Spain*, Palgrave Studies in Economic History,
https://doi.org/10.1007/978-3-030-61318-1_1

expect to find various epigraphs devoted to this subject in Economics textbooks. The reality, however, is quite different, since references to the entrepreneur—their characteristics and functions in economic theory—are rather scarce.

The figure of the entrepreneur has become a pertinent factor when explaining economic development and the growth process. Likewise, growing rates of unemployment have generated, among both institutional and private agents, a significant interest in promoting entrepreneurship as a formula which could eradicate the social scourge of unemployment. In all areas, political, educational, social, and economic, the active promotion of policies that encourage the culture and initiative entrepreneurship brings are being encouraged. In academia, research on *entrepreneurship* has multiplied (De la Torre and García-Zuñiga 2013; Díaz Morlán 2013; Espinosa and Miranda 2013; Caruana de las Cagigas and Mates-Barco 2016; Fernández-Paradas and Matés-Barco 2016; Castro-Valdivia and Matés-Barco 2017; Castro-Valdivia et al. 2019). The term entrepreneurship has a triple meaning: the figure of the entrepreneur, the entrepreneurial function and the creation of companies. This polyvalent meaning needs to be supported by a consistent theory on the company and the entrepreneur.

In order to understand the idea of the modern entrepreneur, as it has progressed since the end of the eighteenth century, it could prove useful to explain how the concept has advanced. For this reason, the perception great economists had of the figure, various texts at the formation process of the current notion of entrepreneur and how a company should function have been analysed. All this, while bearing in mind the ethical, economic and social aspects, which allow for a more equitable society, one which minimises the problem of economic inequality.

This has all given rise to an academic discipline, the History of the Company. The knowledge of the historiographic development of this subject, at both the international and the national level, is essential in order to promote a business culture which is able to generate entrepreneurship in society. Without this, it is clear that a country or territory will not be able to maintain sustainable economic growth.

## 1.2 The Figure of the Entrepreneur

It is difficult to determine in which direction the entrepreneurial factor acts: whether it was entrepreneurs who promoted development or whether it was development that stimulated their emergence. Most likely, the influence was circular (González González 1995). In economic theory the role of the entrepreneur in economic development was not paid much attention. Tortella and Quiroga (2012) has masterfully summarised the interpretations provided by economists such as Cantillon (1755) or Say (1819, 1828–1829). The former used the expression entrepreneur and described their actions as arbitrage favouring the equilibrium of the markets while assuming the risks of market fluctuations. For this reason, their income was variable and insecure and sometimes caused their collapse. Richard Cantillon (1680–1734), of Irish origin, was the first to establish the theory that the entrepreneur is linked to the concept of uncertainty, assuming that the risk of a given activity determines whether an economic agent is an entrepreneur or not. His economic ideas are outlined in his posthumous work *Essai sur la nature du commerce en général*, published in London in 1755. In chapter XIII of the first part of this book, titled *La circulation et le troc des denrées et des marchandises, de même que leur production, se conducisent en Europe par des Entrepreneurs, et au hasard*, he argues that there is both a total and an individual structural uncertainty that prevents knowledge of demand. In this way, the entrepreneur is the economic agent who, by assuming risk, makes it possible to cover the needs of society through the market. Cantillon, makes a distinction between an entrepreneur and a capital provider, since the profit of the former came from the difference between the foreseen and what actually happened, and the risk assumed by the entrepreneur would determine the level of profit. For the capital provider or capitalist, however, profit occurs at an interest rate previously agreed by the parties with guarantees in place in the event of non-payment. This signifies that they have a different profile to that of the entrepreneur, who assumes the market risk.

For his part, the French economist Jean-Baptiste Say (1767–1832) furthered Cantillon's approach and broke with the ideas put forward by the classic English economists, who did not distinguish between capitalist profit and business profit.[2] For Say, the retribution of capital is not business profit, since it is the profit obtained by assuming the risk of a commercial activity. Defending this position from the fourth edition of *the Traité*, published in 1819, and in *the Cours*, published between 1828 and 1829, a work in which he compiled his economic thought. He deals with this subject in Chapter 7 of Book II of *the Traité*, titled *Des revenus industriels*, in particular, and in Chapter VIII of the fifth part of *the Cours*, titled *Des profits que font les entrepreneurs d'industrie en particulier*. Say's

[2] Adam Smith, *The Wealth of Nations* in 1776.

approach brought about yet another idea to the theory of the entrepreneur. He posits that the entrepreneur is the main agent of production, one who combines the productive factors and is introduced as a new actor into the traditional trilogy of those involved in the productive process: landowners, workers and capitalists (Castro-Valdivia 2015a, 2015b). Without entrepreneurs the new industry, of which Say was an example, would not exist. It should be remembered that his confrontation with Napoleon forced him into exile from Paris between 1804 and 1813. During this period the French economist set up and managed, together with a partner, a cotton spinning mill in D'Auchy les Hedin, a place in the French municipality of Pas-de-Calais, where he employed more than 400 workers. In short, Jean-Baptiste Say gave the entrepreneur a key role in the economic activity.

Classic economics scarcely developed this train of thought and the company and entrepreneurs became almost irrelevant. It is only worth mentioning the popularisation of the term *entrepreneur* by John Stuart Mill (1806–1873). The English economist was the only one of Adam Smith's followers who understood the particular role of entrepreneurship. However, although he introduced risk and uncertainty into the equation of entrepreneurial profit, he was not able to abandon the Smithian position totally and continued to consider the function of the capitalist and the entrepreneur as going hand in hand.

Neoclassical economics did not pay much attention to entrepreneurship either, but Alfred Marshall (1842–1924) did highlight the role of the entrepreneur in economic activity. Both Marshall and John Bates Clark (1847–1938) tried to introduce the entrepreneur into their models of economic growth. The English economist Marshall proposed that the entrepreneur is an essential agent for development, considering that their ability to organise business is a specific productive factor. However, he continued the tradition of classic British economists by not distinguishing between the role of the entrepreneur and the capitalist, as if to echo Cantillon and Say. Marshall, however, did not exclude the possibility that the distinguishing factors could affect profits, which he described as extraordinary. He also argued that the desire to accumulate wealth is not a bad pursuit; on the contrary, he saw it as a symbol of business success, as an incentive to become an entrepreneur, which fosters competitiveness. The American economist Clark continued Marshall's postulates, but he did distinguish between the profits of business, as those that come from the work of the administration of the company, which he considered as a type of salary, and those which for him are ordinary profit and those which he deemed the extraordinary, where he intuited that risk and uncertainty were a determinant factor.

Joseph Alois Schumpeter (1883–1950) went a further step, noting the innovation factor of the entrepreneur and their relationship with the degree of development of an economy. The Austrian thinker placed the entrepreneur at the centre of economic activity. In his model, the economy tends to be in a situation of equilibrium, so that the world is neither uncertain nor profitable; therefore, in the long term there is no development and the stagnation of society. Periodically, however, innovations emerge that unbalance the economy and produce development. Therefore, in order to increase the well-being of humanity we need to innovate. For Schumpeter the agent of innovation is the entrepreneur. In short, the author associated entrepreneurial activity and innovation as mechanisms of economic growth. This addresses the problem of the nature of the entrepreneur's profit, although he did not offer a contrastable explanation. Furthermore, his model does not feature the element of risk or the option of failure, implying the union between business activity and innovation always generates success.

For his part, Frank H. Knight (1885–1972) highlighted the risk and uncertainty in which the entrepreneur moves. The American economist, after publishing his doctoral thesis in 1921—*Risk, Uncertainty and Profit*—, explained that the entrepreneur is the only factor of production, since the rest of the factors—land, work and capital—are only the means of production. On the other hand, he pointed out that the main function of the entrepreneur is to assume the risk of an activity and that their profit will depend on it. As he states in his thesis, his business model is indebted to the work of the German economists Johann Heinrich von Thünen (1783–1850), Hans von Mangoldt (1824–1868) and the American Frederick Barnard Hawley (1843–1929). In his model, Knight gives order to and enhances the postulates of these authors, who collated the seminal ideas of Cantillon and Say. In particular, he defines risk as an objective uncertainty, which can be estimated and therefore measured, that is, that it has a cost and can be insured. He introduces the idea of subjective uncertainty to explain the role of the entrepreneur. He points out that subjective uncertainty is the result of limited rationality and is conditioned by the expectations of the entrepreneur, the lack of certainty of what the entrepreneur expects, that is, having imperfect information about the future is what distinguishes a manager from an entrepreneur or businessperson. However, uncertainty, as well as, an individual's own capabilities accompany human beings from birth. This leads to a specialisation of people, meaning that those individuals with the greatest capacity to manage uncertainty will be society's entrepreneurs. For Knight, entrepreneurial abilities are innate, although they can be improved through education and experience, and specifically for this reason, they are not susceptible to commercialisation. The entrepreneur's remuneration cannot therefore be taken as a type of salary, but rather as profit.

Later, Keynesian and neoclassical economists, in the years following the Second World War, dismissed protagonism in the company or the entrepreneur. Finally, the Austrian School, with Israel Kirzner at its helm, began to outline the value of entrepreneurial function, and almost immediately, studies began to emerge which breathed new life to the contributions of Schumpeter and Knight. Other authors such as Casson and Shane have enhanced this by reaffirming the role of the entrepreneur in economic theory, combining Suchempeterian doctrine with aspects of Kirzner. Casson, for example, points out that entrepreneurial function is based on making decisions in conditions of incomplete information. For Shane however, entrepreneurship not only relies on the presence of enterprising individuals with initiative, but rather responds to the confluence of it together with the existence of business opportunities. Studies on this issue have highlighted some elements that should be taken into account such as geographical framework, political and institutional regime, financial system, economic context, as well as educational, scientific and cultural model.

At times, the theory of the company and technical change, raised by evolutionary economics, has played an important role for a large number of researchers in the history of business. The ascendancy of the evolutionary theory of biology can be seen to a large extent, as well as the weight of Schumpeter's contributions, which have led to the work of Rosenberg and Basalla. Some characteristics of this theory are eluded to in the work of Richard Nelson and Sidney Winter. For them, the strategy of a company is marked by its "natural trajectory" and is a characteristic and persistent feature of it. This is acquired through experience and is performed hereditarily, although it is evident that in the decision-making process there are elements of uncertainty.

On the other hand, some authors have developed a history of the company that extracts hypotheses from the theory of transaction costs, which is demonstrated in the studies of Alfred Chandler and Oliver Williamson in particular. Their study and application of the theory has proved controversial in its interpretation. For some, the theory of transaction costs, derived from Coase's work, has considerable nuances in its adaptation to the current situation, and although it contributes to the analysis of business organisation, it has limitations which other theories rectify. In light of this, Williamson's work responds more to a theory of the company or industrial economy than to the history of the company itself; while Chandler, who develops an eminently historical method, does not provide a selection of data to contrast or validate general theories. However, for others, the history of the American company has been seen as a process of growth that culminates in the great multi-divisional and multinational corporation. For this reason, the theory, focused on the determinants of company size, allows for interesting relationships with the history of the American company. Which is why Chandler is one of the most emblematic examples of this type of work, especially with his work *The Visible Hand*. The history of American business is characterised by an excessive reduction to its own country and to the period after American independence, issues that sometimes make it less valid when trying to expand these assumptions to other times or other territories. In any case, the dissemination of studies on American companies and entrepreneurs has been enormously abundant and perhaps superior to those carried out in Europe.

Spanish business history has sometimes been blamed for excessive empiricism and scarce theoretical analysis. It is therefore necessary to analyse the reality that drives companies, the historical context in which they were born and developed, the aspects that mark their size and organisational form, as well as the particularities that determine the degree of vertical integration of an activity, internal organisation or the characteristics of contracts. The history of the company allows us to contrast the analysis to which theory has been pointing with reality. The power of the businessperson is limited on many occasions. It should be said that they cannot be given an excessive role and that their actions are generally determined by the social and economic conditions of the environment in which they perform their role. Here lies the importance of the history of the company developed in the United States which frames the performance of the entrepreneur in the context of economic history, and does not deny the existence of a personal element but also does not exaggerate its presence.

In recent years, a large number of works have been published that aim to unravel the role of the entrepreneur and its determining factors in economic activity. In a context where technical-economic progress is indispensable for the growth of welfare, the figure of the entrepreneur is a referential element to achieve this objective. The history of the company should not be restricted to the confirmation of economic theories, or to trying to assert one theory over another, but rather should highlight that previous approaches determine the questions posed which can then be answered in further given research.

## 1.3 The History of the Company as an Academic Subject

The 1990s gave rise to an extensive debate on the need for studies on the history of the company. But we can go back more than a hundred years to find the first studies that expressed an interest in the company and the figure of the entrepreneur. The first works on the history of the company appeared in Germany, throughout the nineteenth century. Their influence would eventually go on to be noted in British and American historiography. The first historical work on the company dates back to 1825 with the publication of the monograph on the *Lauchhamer Iron and Steel Industry* in Saxony on its centenary celebration. The publication shows the long tradition, methodological and consolidated orientation of the company's history and its subsequent expansion into the United States and Europe. The subjects dealt with in these early works address questions relating to the structural evolution experienced by the English markets with the emergence of commercial capitalism, the use of company archives as a source for understanding the British textile industry during the years of the Industrial Revolution and, among others, the intervention of the respective American governments in monopolistic activities.

The first journal on specific issues of Business History appeared in the *Harvard Journal of Economics and Business History*, which has made it an obligatory point of reference for this type of study. In 1948, the Research Centre for Business History was created at Harvard University, which through the new publication, *Explorations in Entrepreneurial History*, promoted studies on companies. In 1954, as a continuation of *the Bulletin of the Business Historical Society* (1926), *the Business History Review* was first published at Harvard. Another focal point in the history of business is Great Britain. The University of Liverpool began publishing the magazine *Business History*, in 1958, which has been an important focus for the dissemination of research in this discipline.

The company and the entrepreneur were seen to be economic agents capable of confronting competitiveness and all its challenges, on a global scale. The change in centrally planned economies practised by political regimes and the complexity and the speed of changes caused by new technology, as well as the setback that the public sector has experienced in some countries, are some of the reasons for the promotion of a change in perception.

There are several reasons for the growing interest in the study of the company and the role played by the figure of the entrepreneur. Firstly, because of its weight as a historiographic tradition in the late nineteenth and early twentieth centuries. In those years, an extensive group of English and American historians—Toynbee, Hobson, Webb, Veblen, among others—, described the entrepreneur as a symbol of exploitation, selfishness and excessive profit. While, in Germany, at the same time, another group of historians applied an inductive methodology to the analysis of different social segments, particularly, towards the emergence and evolution of local companies and the changes experienced in business organisation. It is worth mentioning that Gustav Schmoller, Karl Bucher and Werner Sombart promoted studies on individual companies and the development of entrepreneurship, as a means to explain the expansion of capitalism.

Secondly, the propensity for studying the history of the company is due, largely, to the enormous field of exploration that the subject encompasses within the sphere of economic history. In recent decades, the importance of company archives has been highlighted, many of which still remain to be studied. There has also been an emphasis placed on the need to use a methodology that combines economic theory with a detailed description of specific case studies through sources. It is important to link theoretical analysis with empirical data and to carry out a reflection that allows the discovery a company's evolution.

On the other hand, studies on the industrial revolution, in its different phases, have shown the importance of the figure of the entrepreneur in the process of economic development. Publications on specific companies, sectors and biographies of entrepreneurs, as well as the factors that explain their growing relevance acquired in the process of product quality control or of vertical integration of large corporations, have been frequent. Likewise, other fields related to the company such as the institutional framework in which it operates or the social and legal problems to which it could be subject have also attracted the attention of researchers. In short, the need to use historical perspective to explain the evolution of companies and their importance in economic development seems obvious.

## 1.4 The History of the Company in Spanish Universities

The interest in studying the history of the company in Spain has been long-standing and has had wide repercussions in the academic world. At the beginning of the 1990s, seminars, conferences and debates in scientific forums were held. This trend led to the production of works on company histories, biographies of entrepreneurs, sectorial and regional studies. Studies by historians such as Carreras and Tafunell (1996), Coll and Tortella (1992), Comín and Martín (1996), Fraile (1993), García Ruiz (1994), Núñez and Segreto (1994), Tortella and Quiroga (2012), Tortella et al. (2011), Valdaliso and García-Ruiz (2013) and Valdaliso and López (2007), among many others, are good examples and have marked a clear path for research. *The Catalogue of Publications on Spanish Business History in the 19th and 20th Centuries*, which was once compiled by Eugenio Torres Villanueva (1993), indicates that interest in the subject became more evident from the 1980s onwards. The progress of the discipline in subsequent years, despite its initial delay, has been more inclined to take an interest not only in company histories, biographies of entrepreneurs or sectorial and regional studies, but also in other issues such as the organisation of the Spanish economy, its size and the degree of vertical integration, to name but a few.

For various reasons, the history of the company has had difficulty in making its way into the academic world. Pedro Fraile (1993) explained the reasons for this in his documented work and showed the legacy left by the historiography after the Second World War. Coll and Tortella (1992) eluded to the negative prejudice which existed for a large number of researchers when dealing with issues related to the discipline. In the same vein, Luciano Segreto agrees in his comments on this aspect and points out that it is necessary to speak of a "lack of business culture" or "lack of industrial culture". It should be remembered that a country like Spain, where the economy has been predominantly marked by excessive dirigisme, is inclined to play down the role of the company and disregard the social function of the entrepreneur. In short, it is important to distance oneself from both "servility" and "denunciation", that is, to abandon the deep-rooted prejudice that the only legitimate wealth is inherited and not to take on the polar opposite role by writing a business hagiography.

The development of Economic History took place in particular from 1970 onwards and the History of the Company has developed under this umbrella. This may be another reason for the late incorporation of these studies in Spanish universities. On the other hand, the idea of the Spain's delay throughout the nineteenth century in terms of industrialisation was, for many years, the focus of Economic History studies and issues which were considered more tangential, such as companies were not taken into account. In this slow process of incorporation of company studies, the distrust of business people towards researchers, for varying motives, cannot be ignored either. This has meant that studies have had to be carried out solely using the documents which companies publish themselves, such as Reports of the Shareholders' Meetings, and summaries of profit and loss accounts for legal or publicity reasons.

As a result, many publications are of a journalistic nature—with little rigour—on current economic figures, which do not have the documentary and critical basis that allows development of in-depth analysis. These have even included stories about companies produced on the anniversaries of their foundation, which have little scientific value, and on many occasions, businesspeople themselves have taken the initiative of having company studies carried out on them or their companies in order to improve their image or as a form of advertising. This does not prevent important work from being undertaken on public (INI, Banco de España, Tabacalera) and private companies (Banco Herrero, Banco Zaragozano, Sevillana de Electricidad), certain sectors (gas, tramways, railways, textiles) and, more recently, regional analyses, despite it being prompted by the entrepreneurs themselves (Germán 2009; Garcia-Cuenca and Ángulo-Tejada 2010; Parejo 2013).

It is worth highlighting the need to bring company archives into consideration. It is true that many entrepreneurs are reluctant to show the internal workings of their companies publicly, for fear that some discoveries might tarnish their image. It should be pointed out however that, on many occasions, the archives reflect on the era rather than on the individual's behaviour and that, on occasion, they have served to revive the image of the businessperson. Coll and Tortella (1992) cite the cases of Alfonso XIII, branded as corrupt and amassing his wealth through ill-gotten gains, the opposition of businessmen to the Second Republic and, finally, the "fabulous profits" obtained by the Minas de Río Tinto Company and the "scarce rent" it paid. Various research has shown that the amassing of the king's wealth occurred legitimately, that among businessmen there was support and respect for the republican regime, and that the profits from the mines were not so exaggerated nor the payment of rent insufficient.

Nor can we ignore the great conceptual and methodological diversity that exists in the study of the History of the Company which causes rejection of or adherence to models promoted from other geographical or academic viewpoints. The model of American universities, for example, developed by Chandler and Williamson in particular, has been controversial. On occasions this perspective has been accused of being reductionist because the business structure studied—large North American companies—does not fit with the predominant model of small- and medium-sized enterprises in Spain. Along similar lines, studies have emerged that highlight the importance of small companies during North American industrialisation. These studies prove a direct relationship between economic situation and business success, which undermines the lead role that has sometimes been given to the companies themselves.

The influence of American universities in the implementation of these studies, particularly the pioneering Harvard, has directly influenced their development in Spain. The methodology for the study of current business situations was based on case studies which provided an understanding of organisational techniques of a business. This was based on the very elementary approach: studying company case studies allowed the analysis of the direction, management and organisational structure of a company and was able to shed light on how the present situation could have arisen. This is the usual practice performed by business schools in Spain: IESE, ICADE, IE, ESADE, ESIC, among others. The ultimate objective of this "succession of case studies" is what the compilation of works presented in this book aims to achieve. At first, the use of this methodology was merely descriptive, but then researchers began to explore new ways of achieving greater conceptual precision that allows them to make generalisations about the evolutionary processes of companies. This trend has prompted comparative analyses—such as those of Chandler and Cole—and the application of economic theory which outlines the role of the company and the entrepreneur in economic development and industrialisation.

It should be remembered that both the research and the teaching of the history of the company must have a dual perspective. Firstly, by not simply reducing the study to accounting or organisational issues, since many problems of a company cannot be fully understood without analysing the social coordinates. In other words, it is necessary to approach the study of dominant values, the workforce, business and trade union organisations, and so on. Secondly, placing the company within the context of the evolutionary phases of capitalism, in order to understand whether it is a consequence of growth or a factor thereof.

Despite the differences in the characterisation of the discipline, the use of a particular economic theory and the explanatory causes of the delay in development of this subject in Spain, it is clear that the progress made in recent decades is palpable and notorious. Progress has been made not only in the curricula, subject programmes, manuals or specific research on the subject, but also in the leading role acquired by the figure of the entrepreneur and the company at social, political and economic levels.

## 1.5 Conclusions

The dissemination and establishment of the subject of History of the Company facilitates the understanding of an entrepreneurial culture among students. The explanation of its birth as an academic subject, the scope of its appearance and the students to whom it was addressed, as well as the main bibliographical contributions made by the important scholars who taught it, make it a fundamental tool for developing entrepreneurship among students of the various degrees in faculties of Economics and Business Administration.

Similarly, understanding and analysing the trajectory of entrepreneurs allows for the incorporation of experience in business and location of business organisation. These factors enrich decision-making within a company, since people are working in very specific and often complex circumstances, independent of variables or organisational structures. On the other hand, the immersion in the biographies of entrepreneurs facilitates an approach to the economic reality as the understanding of successes and failures, which means that the ups and downs of specific business activity should be taken into account. This prevents the student from having a static vision of the economic process and of commercial companies, however large or small they may be.

On the other hand, the study of companies and their creators provides a knowledge with which to integrate the theoretical reflections of economists and the experience developed in specific areas. In turn, it is necessary to analyse not only the general theoretical framework, but also the organisational structure of companies, the different geographical locations and the innovations experienced throughout their existences.

Finally, the subject of the History of the Company, with all its multiple and varied endeavours, provides an indispensable critical sense in the exercise of the professional task. All the variables of experience—biographies, colloquies with businesspeople, conferences of academic experts and so on—signify an indispensable development of the capacities of the student in the procellous business world.

## References


Cantillon, Richard. 1755. *Essai sur la nature du commerce en général. Traduit de l'anglois*. London: Chez Feltcher Gyles.

Carreras, Albert, and Xavier Tafunell. 1996. La gran empresa en la España contemporánea: entre el Mercado y el Estado. In *La empresa en la historia de España*, ed. Francisco Comín and Pablo Martín, 73–90. Madrid: Civitas.

Caruana de las Cagigas, Leonardo, and Juan Manuel Matés-Barco. 2016. La necesidad de transmitir las nuevas investigaciones en los manuales. In *Nuevas perspectivas en la Investigación docente de la historia económica*, ed. Miguel Ángel Bringas, Elena Catalán, Carmen Trueba, and Lorena Remuzgo, 38–53. Santander: Editorial de la Universidad de Cantabria. https://doi.org/10.22429/Euc2016.003.

Castro-Valdivia, Mariano, and Juan Manuel Matés-Barco. 2017. Innovación educativa y fomento de la cultura emprendedora en la Universidad. In *La didáctica de las Ciencias Sociales ante la necesidad de nuevas narraciones en el siglo XXI: Digitalidad, nuevas tecnologías y competencias documentales*, coordinated by Antonio Rafael Fernández-Paradas and Mercedes Fernández-Paradas, 241–257. Granada: Comares.

Castro-Valdivia, Mariano, Carlos Larrinaga-Rodríguez, and Juan Manuel Matés-Barco. 2019. La enseñanza de la Historia de la Empresa en la Era Digital. In *Educación y felicidad en las Ciencias Sociales y Humanidades. Un enfoque holístico para el desarrollo de la creatividad en la Era Digital*, coordinated by Antonio Rafael Fernández-Paradas, Mercedes Fernández-Paradas, Luis Tobar Pesántez, and Rafael Ravina Ripoll, 469–488. Valencia: Tirant lo Blanc.

Castro-Valdivia, Mariano. 2015a. La difussion mondiale de l'œuvre de Jean-Baptiste Say. Traductions précoces et impacts sélectifs. In *Et Jean-Baptiste Say… créa l'Entrepreneur*, ed. Société Internationale Jean-Baptiste Say, 219–245. Bruxelles: Peter Lang. https://doi.org/10.3726/978-3-0352-6525-5.

———. 2015b. Money and Finance in the Wealth of Nations: Interpretations and Influences. *Journal of US-China Public Administration* 12 (5): 415–429. https://doi.org/10.17265/1548-6591/2015.05.007.

Coll, Sebastián, and Gabriel Tortella. 1992. Reflexiones sobre la historia empresarial: estado de la cuestión en España. *Información Comercial Española* 708–709: 13–24.

Comín, Francisco, and Pablo Martín, eds. 1996. *La empresa en la historia de España*. Madrid: Civitas.

De la Torre, Joseba, and Mario García-Zuñiga. 2013. Instituciones y 'empresarialidad' en el norte de España, 1885-2010. *Revista de Historia Industrial* 51: 141–171.

Díaz Morlán, Pablo. 2013. Cómo han obtenido su capital inicial los empresarios británicos y españoles (c. 1800–c.1939). *Revista de Historia Industrial* 51: 19–41.

Espinosa, Mónica, and José Antonio Miranda. 2013. Germaine de Capuccini: iniciativa empresarial y entorno socioeconómico en el desarrollo de la industria cosmética española. *Revista de Historia Industrial* 51: 79–105.

Fernández-Paradas, Mercedes, and Juan Manuel Matés-Barco. 2016. Un recurso para la docencia y la investigación: la biografía empresarial. In *Nuevas perspectivas en la Investigación docente de la historia económica*, ed. Miguel Ángel Bringas, Elena Catalán, Carmen Trueba, and Lorena Remuzgo, 111–117. Santander: Editorial de la Universidad de Cantabria. https://doi.org/10.22429/Euc2016.003.

Fraile, Pedro. 1993. La historia económica de la empresa como disciplina independiente: una perspectiva histórica. *Revista de Historia Económica* 11: 181–192.

García Ruiz, José Luis. 1994. *Historia económica de la empresa moderna*. Madrid: Istmo.

Garcia-Cuenca, Tomás, and María del Carmen Ángulo-Tejada. 2010. *Empresarios de Castilla-La Mancha*. Madrid: LID.

Germán, Luis (coord.). 2009. *Grandes empresarios aragoneses*. Madrid: LID.

González González, Manuel Jesús. 1995. La empresa en la historia del pensamiento económico. In *De empresas y empresarios en la España contemporánea*, coordinated by Moisés Llordén Miñambres, 13–28, Oviedo: University of Oviedo.

Matés-Barco, Juan Manuel, and Mariano Castro-Valdivia. 2017. La Historia de la Empresa: herramienta para fomentar la cultura emprendedora. In *Educación Histórica. Patrimonios olvidados y felicidad en la Didáctica de las Ciencias Sociales*, coordinated by Antonio Rafael Fernández-Paradas, Mercedes Fernández-Paradas, and Guillermo Antonio Gutiérrez-Montoya, 123–150. San Salvador: University Don Bosco.

Menudo, José Manuel, and José María O'Kean. 2019. El mercado de empresarios en la historia del pensamiento económico. Historia de un fracaso. *Investigaciones de Historia Económica – Economic History Research* 15 (2): 69–77. https://doi.org/10.1016/j.ihe.2017.11.001.

Núñez, Gregorio, and Luciano Segreto. 1994. *Introducción a la historia de la empresa en España*. Madrid: Abacus.

Parejo, José Antonio (coord.). 2013. *Cien empresarios andaluces*. Madrid: LID.

Say, Jean-Baptiste. 1819. *Traité d'économie politique, ou Simple exposition de la manière dont se forment, se distribuent et se consomment les richesses, 4e édition, corrigée et augmentée, a laquelle joint un épitomé de principes fondamentaux de l'économie de principes fondamentaux de l'économie politique*. 2 tomes. Paris: Chez Deterville.

———. 1828–1829. *Cours complet d'économie politique pratique, ouvrage destiné à mettre sous les yeux des hommes d'État, des propriétaires fonciers et des capitalistes, des savants, des agriculteurs, des manufacturiers, des négociants et en général de tous les citoyens, l'économie des sociétés*. 6 vols. Paris: Chez Rapilly.

Smith, Adam. 1776. *An Inquiry into the Nature and Causes the Wealth of Nations*. 2 vols. London: W. Strahan and T. Cadell.

Torres Villanueva, Eugenio. 1993. *Catálogo de publicaciones sobre la historia empresarial española de los siglos XIX y XX*. Documento de Trabajo 9301. Madrid: Fundación Empresa Pública.

Tortella, Gabriel, and Gloria Quiroga, eds. 2012. *Entrepreneurship and Growth. An International Historical Perspective*. Houndmills, Basingstoke: Palgrave Macmillan.

Tortella, Gabriel, Gloria Quiroga, and Ignacio Moral-Arce. 2011. El empresario nace o se hace? Educación y empresarialidad en la España contemporánea. *Revista de Historia Económica. Journal of Iberian and Latin American Economic History* 29: 123–153.

Valdaliso, Jesús María, and José Luis García-Ruiz. 2013. El espíritu empresarial en la historia económica española. *Revista de Historia Industrial* 51: 15–18.

Valdaliso, Jesús María, and Santiago López. 2007. *Historia Económica de la empresa*. Barcelona: Crítica.

CHAPTER 2

# Castilian Companies: Between the Medieval Model and Modern Business (Fifteenth and Sixteenth Centuries)

*David Carvajal*

## 2.1 Introduction

In the late fifteenth and early sixteenth centuries, the Castilian economy underwent a period of intense economic growth based on the expansion of production as well as mercantile and financial activities. This new situation forced economic agents to improve their organisational skills as well as the way in which they managed production resources. In response to these needs, Castilian companies were key players in promoting and expanding economic activity. Such an institution, which was founded on the basis of a practice that was well known and widespread throughout the whole of Castile, proved vital when boosting the flow of goods and capital in Castile as well as in other European centres. Companies played a crucial role in the rise of local markets, where small corporations grew to be

D. Carvajal (✉)
University of Valladolid, Valladolid, Spain
e-mail: david.carvajal@uva.es



M. Vázquez-Fariñas et al. (eds.), *Companies and Entrepreneurs in the History of Spain*, Palgrave Studies in Economic History,
https://doi.org/10.1007/978-3-030-61318-1_2

organisations that were able to compete on an equal footing with the leading overseas companies (Casado 2003, 2012).

Although there were various types of company at the time, this work seeks to explain different aspects linked to the "life cycle" of Castilian companies. In particular, we look at the most important organisational aspects, from companies' foundation to their dissolution, spanning the choice of company structure, how funding was obtained or how the company organised its economic and work management, whilst not overlooking other issues such as the internal problems and conflicts that arose. In sum, our aim is to provide an overview of the Castilian "firms," showing how far they developed during a crucial period that was marked by the start of the economic and financial expansion of the Iberian Peninsula, Europe and the Americas.

## 2.2 Castilian Companies: Business and Strategy

The company was a free and voluntary association of two or more people who opted to pool their economic resources. As an institution it was similar to those which had been operating in other European centres, in particular, in Italian cities, since the thirteenth century (Le Goff 2004). Nevertheless, in Castile it was not until the fifteenth century that such a business structure was to become widespread. This did not prevent the legal bases governing the foundations of the companies from sharing the same chronology as their European neighbours (De Ruysscher et al. 2017). Roman law and *Las Partidas* (Castilian Statutory Code), which formed the cornerstone of Castilian law between the thirteenth and nineteenth centuries, offer us an early definition of the company, perceiving such associations as ones "which merchants and other men create with one another in order to make profit."[1] This definition remained virtually unchanged for centuries, and placed trade at its centre.

### 2.2.1 *The Mercantile Company as a Model*

The level of development of the Castilian economy and the range of commercial and financial activities they were involved in meant that Castilian companies stood out thanks to their ability to adapt to any kind of business. Nevertheless, when speaking of companies, it is first necessary to

[1] *Las Partidas*, Part V, Title X.

refer to the best-known model: the large mercantile companies. These companies, which were able to mobilise material, financial and human resources between various points of Castile and Europe, provided the benchmark for companies at the time. Smaller corporations sought to emulate and adapt this model to all kinds of business.

Trading (of raw materials, finished products etc., at local, regional, and international scales) was the main activity the major Castilian companies engaged in. These larger companies tended to focus their interests on the products that proved to be most profitable for export (wool or iron) and import (quality fabrics or luxury products). Another key business for the companies revolved around transport, linking markets and creating opportunities in coastal towns for seafarers such as Juanico de Cotillos from Guipuzkoa, a shipmaster, who set up a transport company through a charter agreement with Juan de Ansogarlo, who was also a shipmaster, to dispatch 150 barrels of wine from Bordeaux to Flanders around the year 1490.[2] Despite the appeal of international trade, the major companies did not ignore the potential of domestic trade and, in particular, the business that could be conducted in places such as Seville, Toledo, Valladolid or Burgos, and at the main fairs throughout the kingdom. Thanks to this broad array of interests, the primary characteristic of these major companies was their geographical dispersion. A second feature was their family nature. Important families of merchants from centres such as Burgos, Seville or Toledo were behind their setting-up and running (Caunedo 1993; Otte 1996; Casado 2000). Thirdly, mention might be made of a complex organisation, grounded on the creation of intricate networks of factors (mercantile agents or managers) and representatives, as well as a wide-ranging financial network.

In addition to the large companies, the bulk of Castilian mercantile activity lay in the hands of hundreds of small- and medium-sized corporations that operated in nearby markets, trading in raw materials, livestock, fabrics, food and other products related to activities such as supplying the towns and villages. In this regard, we know of the important role that companies played in supplying meat to major towns such as Valladolid or Burgos, as well as to small towns like San Martín de Valdeiglesias (Bonachía 1992; Carvajal 2020). Much the same was true of fish, although its transport and distribution meant organising more complex companies, located

[2] Archive of the Royal Chancellery of Valladolid—Archivo de la Real Chancillería de Valladolid—(hereinafter ARChV), *Registro de Ejecutorias* (RE), box 64, 3.

throughout the country, and linking the coast to the hinterland. One example may be found in 1524–25, in the company run by Lope de Medina, and which was entrusted with supplying the markets and fairs inland with fish from Galicia (Herrero and Díaz 2009).[3]

Beyond what was merely trade, many entrepreneurs decided to set up companies linked to other businesses such as finance. When speaking of finance companies, we are broadly referring to two types of businesses: those founded by moneychangers, whose activity was based on offering credit and financial services, and tax farming companies. The former first came to prominence in the late fifteenth century, when a process of specialisation commenced that would convert such institutions into something akin to modern-day banks. These companies proved key when it came to maintaining the financial network—involving businesses and fairs—during the sixteenth century (Al-Hussein 1986; Carvajal 2019). Families such as the Santa María, the Cocón or the Castro family were well known for the exchange and financial services they provided during the first half of the sixteenth century. Tax farming was the other major financial business. Leasing the right to collect revenue or other benefits became a source of income for some companies (Vítores 2011; Ortega 2012; Ortego 2012). Their structures varied depending on their interests and on the kind of revenue in question: royal revenue or municipal revenue, not forgetting revenue from the church or the nobility. Towards the end of the fifteenth century, the system of royal tax farming was an important business for many financiers, prominent amongst whom were the Jews or Jewish converts, whose large corporations dominated said business for decades. After 1496, the transformation of the system for administering revenue, which gradually shifted from tax farming to *encabezamiento* (whereby a town was committed to an annual lump sum payment for a period of time), led to the emergence of smaller local corporations that were commissioned with the levying and collecting of royal and municipal revenue. Changes in the system, coupled with the need to have financial resources available, meant that new families, such as the Santa Cruz, were able to gain a foothold in a business which in the late fifteenth century was dominated by families such as the Coronel. The

[3] Valladolid Municipal Archive—Archivo Municipal de Valladolid—, Fondo Hospital de Esgueva, box 404–78.

family network acted as a lever that enabled these new corporations to emerge, founding their businesses on the tax farming of small holdings (Carretero 1999, pp. 159–162).[4]

### *2.2.2 Diversification as a Strategy*

One of the most characteristic features of Castilian companies was their versatility. Under such a generic formula, many businessmen, producers, craftsmen and other people interested in joining together were able to operate in order to engage in a wide range of undertakings. In addition to trade, banking or other financial activities, there were many other businesses they could become involved in, ranging from companies dedicated to raising livestock[5] to those dedicated to leasing out inns and other establishments.[6] It was even common to find companies engaged in the "spiritual business", through preaching and charging for the papal bulls and indulgencies granted in different bishoprics.[7]

This business versatility was linked to corporations' ability to diversify. Broadly speaking, companies tended to specify the nature of the business they were to engage in from the outset, although some were not very clear on this point or later expanded their interests as fresh opportunities arose. In fifteenth and sixteenth century Castile, it was common to find large corporations involved in a wide range of enterprises: trade, credit, tax collection and so on. One good example may be found in the company founded by Pedro del Campo, Gonzalo de Segovia and Álvaro de Soria, whose company deed cites some of the main transactions: "purchasing bread and wine, livestock, fabrics, silks and any other goods of whatever quality, and for purchasing bills of exchange or tax farming of any revenue derived from sales taxes and tithes, taxes and obligations, as well as any other revenues from their majesties [...] and any other revenue from the church and laypersons."[8] The interests of these partners, who hailed from centres like Segovia or Medina del Campo, extended throughout the whole of the peninsula and, on the one hand, focused on trading in wool and textile products and, on the other, on administering revenue such as

[4] An agreement which enabled them to take control of handling revenue valued at 34.5 million maravedís in 1519.

[5] ARChV, RE, box 46, 49.

[6] ARChV, RE, box 51, 11.

[7] Valladolid Provincial Historical Archive—Archivo Histórico Provincial de Valladolid—(AHPV), Protocolos Notariales (PN), leg. 8434, ff. 70–72 (1517).

[8] ARChV, Pleitos Civiles, Pérez Alonso (F), box 103, 1.

the export duties levied in Seville (1495–97) as well as the sales taxes from districts like Osma or Jerez de la Frontera (Casado 2000, pp. 135–156). These companies, which were able to move several million maravedís, provide a good illustration of Castilian merchants' ability to diversify.

## 2.3 The Life Cycle of Castilian Companies

### 2.3.1 *The Foundation: Objectives and Types*

The main aim of the corporation was to make a profit by engaging in one or more business activities. With the exception of the leading commercial companies, which were highly specialised or which held commercial interests abroad, most companies confined themselves to limited business opportunities, which they sought to exploit over a short period of time. As a result, the corporation was not built to last. It was more of a flexible formula which adapted to the challenges posed by an ever-changing economy.

Although there are no clearly defined types of companies, law and actual practice do allow us to draw certain distinctions. According to the law, there were two kinds of company, bearing in mind, on the one hand, the involvement of the partners and, on the other, the purpose for which the companies were set up. The first type was the *comunal*,[9] wherein partners held a share in the social capital from its creation until it was dissolved. This meant that the partners shared the losses or profit obtained, and were bound to respond jointly to any unforeseen or unexpected circumstances. The second type of company was set up *sobre cosa señalada* (on a specified thing); in other words, its life cycle was linked to a specific business. In line with other classification criteria based on how it was run (Caunedo 1993, pp. 42–43), we may speak of companies administered by a main partner who also acted as the principal manager, who was the visible part of the company and who negotiated on its behalf. Such a format was common amongst merchants dedicated to the wool trade or amongst the major tax farmers. In contrast to this hierarchical and vertical company structure, we find other more horizontal structures where, in addition to putting up capital, the partners shared the management responsibilities. This was the most common type of association. One final criterion to be

[9] Companies could be made up of free men, except those subject to severe handicaps, and those under 14 years of age. *Las Partidas*, Partida V, Title X, Law I.

borne in mind when classifying companies concerns the nature of the business for which they were created. The versatility of these organisations made it possible to set up a vast array of companies, prominent amongst which were those dedicated to trade, finance as well as tax farming and administration.

Distinguishing the type of corporation or company was important for the partners, since the way they were run varied depending on their legal status as well as on the business or management model. These and other aspects were reflected in the founding deed: the *capitulación* (agreement). This document, which was sometimes endorsed or countersigned before a notary, set out, amongst other matters, the following details: the partners involved and the capital put up, the aim and/or purpose, the duration, as well as details concerning administration. It also tended to detail particulars regarding how any profit or loss would be shared. The *capitulación* could also contain certain details as to the type of goods, the markets at which they would be traded, specific tasks to be undertaken or clauses concerning the corporation's extension or renewal. The *capitulaciones* were characterised as being short and binding documents, whose legal validity was fully recognised by the civil and mercantile authorities.

### 2.3.2 *The Duration of the Company*

Most companies were founded on the basis of specific business areas and for the short term only—they did not tend to operate for longer than a year, given the uncertainty that characterised many activities of the period—. A good example of this situation is to be found in companies dedicated to providing supplies to those trading in raw materials, and who organised their activity in annual cycles. This was related to the cyclical nature of food, wool or wood production itself, for example. The cyclical component of such activities helped with company relaunch, an issue which tended to be broached once the partners had settled the accounts and concluded the period in question. Relaunching a corporation could be envisaged within the *capitulación* itself, although the issue could also be raised subsequent to the agreement of the partners, who, in general, took into consideration factors such as how successful the previous company had been, future business prospects and the absence of any internal conflicts. In this way, companies such as the one supplying meat at San Martín de Valdeiglesias were reconstituted on at least one occasion in 1517–18, or the company which shipped wood along the river Tagus, which resumed activity on at least two occasions between 1496 and 1500 (Carvajal 2015, 2020).

Companies dedicated to fiscal matters were particularly subject to the seasonal nature of business. This was true of the tax business, which was renewed each year through procedures like auctions. In the larger domains of tax collection, namely at the local-municipal and royal levels, annual companies were the norm, coinciding with the period established by the authorities for collecting revenue in the form of taxes, although many were restarted almost automatically if the business had proved to be successful. In some cases, they would eventually come to hold a monopoly over certain areas of tax revenue.

In contrast, the major trading companies were governed by the cycles imposed by the market, in particular by when the various fairs were to be held. The periods when fairs took place at Medina del Campo, Medina de Rioseco, and Villalón were used as a reference to set up the company as well as to dissolve or restart it. These markets and the institutional framework which surrounded them generated a certain degree of confidence among businessmen when it came to conducting transactions, seeking partners, obtaining credit, having notaries present and, ultimately, proceeding to the final settlement and closure of their companies. In contrast to others, these large companies tended to last longer, with the lifespan of the leading trade corporations and tax farming companies stretching over a number of years. This was understandable given the financial outlay required to arrange their activity and to set up a complex organisational and managerial structure. For example, the Burgos company Pesquera-Silos, whose main business was trading wool with Florence, was operational from its foundation in 1513 until 1525, although it was dissolved in 1519 (Casado 2015, pp. 76–77).

### 2.3.3 *Dissolving the Company*

One the period established for the company had concluded or after its particular business had ended, the partners finally closed the company. The corporation could be dissolved before this point in one of the following cases: the death of a partner, unless otherwise stated in the *capitulación*; if one of the partners was banished, which the law interpreted as *civil death*;[10] over-indebtedness by one partner, who would then be forced

[10] *Las Partidas*, Partida V, Title X, Law X.

to hand over his goods in order to settle his obligations and cede his share in the company; and, finally, if the reason for which the corporation had been created were to disappear or to radically change. Nevertheless, we should again highlight the prevalence of the *capitulaciones* and their clauses which could, amongst other matters, specify which instances might give rise to the cessation of the activity.

Generally speaking, the *capitulaciones* specified when and where the settlement should take place. There was no established procedure governing company closure, and this depended on the type of corporation, its turnover and so on. It was common for those running the company to present the related documents: accounts books, lists of income and expenditure, lists of creditors and debtors, stock inventories and so forth. During this process, it was essential to present a balance sheet drawn up on the basis of the daybooks and the general ledgers detailing the company's rights and obligations with third parties, any expenses related to the activities undertaken, as well as the income obtained and an estimate of total profit or loss.

Based on the financial information gathered from the partners and the balance (Table 2.1), the company was wound up and the profit/loss generated was shared, in accordance with what was stipulated in the *capitulación*. The partners shared out the surplus stock amongst themselves, as well as the corporation's rights and obligations and remaining capital, thus winding up the association. If no such distribution were specified, the law

**Table 2.1** Balance of the Cota-de las Cuentas company (1507)

| *Assets* | | | *Liabilities* | | |
|---|---|---|---|---|---|
| *Item* | *Value (maravedís)* | *% Total* | *Item* | *Value (maravedís)* | *% Total* |
| Stock | 151,743.5 | 4.7% | Interests (profits) | 414,060 | 12.8% |
| Companies | 781,135 | 24.2% | | | |
| Revenue, payment rights | 303,000 | 9.4% | Revenue, payment obligations | 6395 | 0.2% |
| Others | 573,030 | 17.7% | Others | 9500 | 0.3% |
| Debtors | 1,396,381.5 | 43.2% | Creditors | 2,801,420 | 86.7% |
| Doubtful debts | 26,085 | 0.8% | | | |
| Total assets | 3,231,375 | 100.0% | Total liabilities | 3,231,375 | 100.0% |

*Sources*: Author's own elaboration with data from ARChV, Pleitos Civiles, Pérez Alonso (F), box 664, 8

established, as a general rule, proportional distribution and forbade practices such as an *abusive company*, wherein one partner could accumulate all of the profits without taking his share of the losses, or the opposite, when one partner was forced to shoulder all of the losses without being able to obtain his fair share of the profits.[11]

However, it did not always prove easy to reach an agreement amongst the parties vis-à-vis settlement. Any differences which emerged within a company, whether when winding it up or in the event of more serious cases such as bankruptcy, were dealt with through the various jurisdictions to which both Castilians and foreigners alike had recourse. Partners in mercantile companies tended to resort to mercantile jurisdiction, represented by guilds, brotherhoods and other institutions such as the Consulates of Burgos or Bilbao. These institutions contained a court made up of judges-arbitrators, and merchants with the capacity and technical knowledge to understand such conflicts. For example, merchants like Diego de Aguilar, Alonso de Medina, Pedro de Alcor and Rodrigo de Cieza sat as judges in lawsuits concerning company closures such as that of Fernando de Encinas and Pedro de Encinas, who clashed over a difference of 135,000 maravedís when winding up their company.[12] Cases could be taken to an appeal submitted to royal justice, before the Royal Chancelleries, where the judges would be presented with various kinds of evidence, accounting documents, expert opinions and testimonies in order to then rule on the liquidation of the company.

The final distribution was set out in an agreement known as the "letter of settlement". At that time, some companies, taking advantage of the success of their business venture, would decide to renew their commitment or would opt to found a new corporation. The company might be set up as a continuation of the previous one, undertaking the same commitments as in the original *capitulación*. In other instances, the newly formed company might differ in terms of the number of partners, the capital that was put up, or the share of responsibilities and so on.

[11] *Las Partidas*, Partida V, Title X, Law IV.

[12] ARChV, RE, box 48, 24.

## 2.4 Running the Company: The Partners and Funding

In addition to actively founding companies, merchants and financiers brought about deep-rooted changes in organisation and administration thanks to improvements in accounting, information networks and other aspects. In the late fifteenth century, many of the companies already displayed a significant level of expertise and knowhow, which was the result of dynamic professional activity that had embraced the knowledge and models from overseas into their management and administration techniques.

### 2.4.1 *The Partners*

Setting up a company was linked to the common interest of a group of people who had the capacity to engage in contracting, who freely decided to share a business venture and who jointly assumed the benefits and risks involved. Aside from this, the diversity in terms of partners was immense, although, as pointed out before, they all shared a desire to engage in a common economic activity.

Each partner played a role in the company following what was established in the *capitulación*. A partner could contribute work, capital or both and, depending on their contribution, the share in the profit or loss could vary. In addition, being a partner in a company entailed a series of rights, such as access to information on the company's business, although in corporations dominated and run by a principal partner, this right was to a certain degree restricted, and lay at the discretion of whatever said partner might decide (Caunedo 1993, p. 45).

The number of partners in Castilian companies varied, although it tended to be between two and four. Partner participation in the initial capital also varied enormously. Being the majority partner was important, since the company was usually associated to his name. This was the case, for example, amongst the leading merchants such as Diego de Soria from Burgos (Caunedo 1985), or the lessors rabbi Mayr and Luis de Alcalá (Ortego 2012), or Luis Cocón, the moneychanger from Valladolid (Carvajal 2019). However, as pointed out, if there was one outstanding feature of companies it was the cooperation that existed between the members.

As regards the companies dedicated to tax farming, the situation was somewhat more complex, since the *capitulaciones* system was by no means commonplace, or at least we do not have the same type of documentation available as we do for mercantile companies. On occasions, the term company was not clear, although sources do contain numerous references to the term *compañeros* (Ortega 2012, pp. 268–269), both at a national level and between corporations dedicated to farming local taxes (Carvajal and Bonachía 2014, pp. 187–188). One distinguishing feature of these companies was the need to present backers, since it was necessary to ensure the lessees were paid. The emergence of these figures led to the appearance of a complex network around companies based on relations with family, professionals and neighbours.

There were many different types of secondary partners; in other words, minority partners, ranging from investors, who were only keen to make a profit, to others who assumed all kinds of responsibilities such as representing the company at national and overseas markets, involving themselves in the day-to-day running, helping to convey information, seeking out and negotiating with clients, suppliers, moneylenders, and money-borrowers, and so on. Such tasks were set out in the *capitulación* or were recognised through powers granted for such purposes. In this way, many Castilian companies were able to efficiently pool their financial resources and available human capital so as to conduct their business in the best possible conditions and in such competitive centres as Italy and Flanders (Casado 2003) or other like the Portuguese (Medrano 2007).

Partners could request to leave the company, provided that they notified their colleagues of the decision, assuming the possible costs, and provided that the *capitulación* allowed them to do so. The law envisaged at least four acceptable instances for leaving the company. The first concerned the issue of harmony and concord. It was possible to opt out of the company if there was a lack of understanding or if a partner was felt to be so "aggressive or such a bad partner" that his continuing in the corporation would pose a problem. The second case involved a partner entering the service of the monarch or taking up public office. Third, a partner could ask to leave if they felt that the conditions or clauses included in the *capitulación* were not being met and that this could be proved. Finally, the partner could leave the company if the product which the company had been set up to trade in was embargoed; for example, if a company dedicated to exporting wool had its stock embargoed.[13]

In general, partners tended to be already linked in some way prior to the company being set up. Family ties proved crucial at centres like Seville, Toledo or Burgos, where many merchants were neighbours or shared interests in urban institutions—the local council and University of Merchants—. The company was a powerful vehicle that was able to strengthen strategic alliances amongst the large families-unions, which in the best cases ended up being crystallised through marriage (Carvajal 2014; Carvajal and De la Torre 2019). In financial companies, the situation was similar, and it was common for partners to share family links, a local neighbourhood and the same trade (Ortega 2012, pp. 275–276). In addition to the cooperation, it should be remembered that rivalry and competition between families/companies was a feature of the mercantile world in Castile and exerted a decisive influence on the formation of trade alliances.

Previous relations between partners were also a vital element amongst the more modest companies; with family ties, the neighbourhood and the trade proving to be key features. It was common to find cases such as that of Catalina de Escobar, a resident of Trujillo, who ran a "livestock company" with her brother, Álvaro de Escobar, whose death triggered a lawsuit between Catalina and her sister-in-law.[14] Other factors such as mutual acquaintance—through having shared a business or having dealt with one another in the past—coupled with a good reputation also helped to forge alliances such as the one established in 1520, by the merchant Alonso de Palenzuela and the cobbler Sebastián de Villamayor, to engage in the salt business in Medina de Rioseco.[15] In sum, we see a wide range of relations which, through social capital, enabled many to form part of a company—even those who lacked the reputation and skills to be great merchants—.

### 2.4.2 Capital and Funding

When setting up a company, it was necessary to have sufficient funding for a business venture that would be beyond many people were they to undertake it alone. Theoreticians at the time advocated the idea that the greater

[13] *Las Partidas*, Partida V, Title X, Law XIV.

[14] ARChV, RE, box 46, 49.

[15] AHPV, PN, leg. 8434, 299r–300r.

the capacity to raise capital, the greater the profit, and encouraged people to invest in companies (Mercado 1569). The contributions made by the various partners was vital, since it meant injecting credit and liquidity into the company.

Partners' contributions enabled initial expenses to be met: acquiring a lease or a right, the financial outlay, purchasing and procuring goods, paying travel expenses or the first salaries. The initial investment could be made in at least one of three ways: furnishing a sum of money, providing goods to an amount proportional to the share in the company or by actually working for the company and giving over part of the salary.

The initial contribution could vary substantially and mainly depended on the type of business. The financial needs of an international trade company were not the same as those of a small company focusing on the local market. The initial worth of the major companies, such as those of Francisco de Orense and other similar enterprises, could reach 10–12 million maravedís (Caunedo 1993, p. 53), or close to the 8,695,556 maravedís held by the Pesquera-Silos company (Casado 2015, p. 79). More modest companies, like the Cota-de las Cuentas corporation in Toledo (Fig. 2.1), would have been set up for something approaching three million maravedís (Carvajal 2012, p. 62). Lower down the scale, there were enormous variations, ranging from the company founded in the town of San Martín de Valdeiglesias to supply meat, which began with 130,000 maravedís; or the company that shipped wood along the Tagus, in 1500, founded by three partners who put up a total of 30,000 maravedís (Carvajal 2015); to corporations with a value of barely 13,600 maravedís, such as the one formed by the previously mentioned Alonso de Palenzuela and Sebastián de Villamayor for trading in salt.[16]

However, a company's financial requirements did not end once it had been set up-quite the opposite. Throughout its life cycle, a company's financial needs could increase considerably, and the Castilian economy offered a wide array of possibilities for securing funding. In the case of mercantile companies, for example, the most common formula was to purchase goods on credit. Thanks to such transactions, companies were in a strong position to enhance their business capacity, since they could boost their stock without having to pay for it until it was sold. Other finance methods were based on loans or transactions involving bills of exchange

[16] AHPV, PN, leg. 8434, 299r–300r.

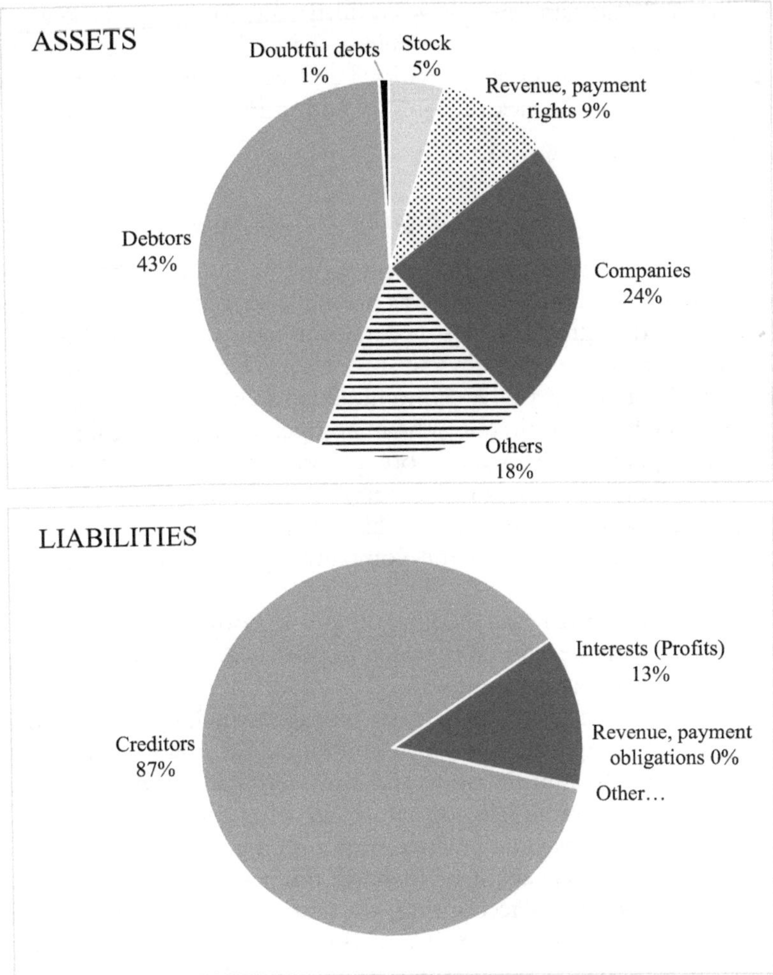


**Fig. 2.1** Balance distribution of the Cota-de las Cuentas company (1507). (Source: author's own elaboration with data from ARChV, Pleitos Civiles, Pérez Alonso (F), box 664, 8)

and other such mechanisms. These credit transactions played a key role in companies' balance books. Nevertheless, the difficult and dangerous juggling act between payment obligations and collection rights was one of the main causes of the lack of liquidity and ultimate bankruptcy of some companies.

### 2.4.3 *Managing the Company*

Running a company meant controlling tasks that required the daily attention of the partners. Such a duty was normally set out in the *capitulación*, which specified in greater or lesser detail the tasks that needed to be carried out to ensure the company ran smoothly. We can mention three such tasks: (1) taking charge of the economic-financial management of the corporation, which meant directing the main operations, stocks, finances and so on; ( 2) organising the work, in other words, the staff as well as the various tasks to be dealt with; and (3) representing the company by contracting and negotiating on its behalf. This was paid work, either through a salary or through a share in the company's profits, depending on the *capitulación*.

Managing a company was a demanding task, both because of the workload it entailed and because of the need to possess a knowledge of mercantile techniques and accounting skills. The model of mercantile companies provides us with an insight into what management involved. Merchants were at an advantage because since childhood they had been acquiring basic knowledge (reading, writing and arithmetic) and during their youth had gained further training as apprentices in other companies. During this stage, learning was based on practice, although their training did not overlook theoretical aspects acquired through the manuals on trading and by studying matters such as accounting, starting by embracing the principles of double-entry bookkeeping (Caunedo 2012). Such knowledge was required if a company's business was to be run with any degree of skill.

In addition to the skills inherent to a merchant, the manager needed to have a knowledge of financial and mercantile legislation. He needed to be able to draw up documents related to administering his business and to conveying information through letters. Probably the greatest demands placed on the managers concerned accounting matters. Managers were entrusted with compiling, updating and keeping the main books: the daily book—daybook, the ledger, the cash book—and, in certain cases, supplementary books that contained the minutes, accounts, inventories of documents and goods, and so on. The managers were also in charge of drawing up other documents such as the company's balance sheets and provisional accounts, which were used when winding up the company. In short, the manager's job involved attending to a wide range of duties yet was one which required dedicating a great deal of time and work and, above all, a certain degree of specialisation and knowledge.

Small-scale merchants and craftsmen also made for efficient managers. For instance, in the *capitulación* of his salt trading company, the cobbler Sebastián de Villamayor agreed to keep the books in which he would note down the people, days, amounts and prices of the company's operations in addition to keeping a record of the profits or losses.[17] Martín Ruiz, a butcher, was able to handle his company's financial affairs through the accounts book and other documents which were fully recognised before the authorities who were to rule on a case concerning the results of the company (Carvajal 2020).[18]

With regard to organising the work, we know that in mercantile companies this task meant controlling the times and deadlines needed to gather the stocks and to sell them, and which required a knowledge of what nowadays might be termed logistics. The managers contacted the suppliers, taking into account the production periods of the raw materials or goods they aimed to sell, and also made sure these were available on time at the markets and fairs where their products were to be offered, such as those at Medina del Campo, Villalón or Medina de Rioseco. Information networks proved vital in this system, and thanks to the correspondence between the company's partners and workers, managers were able to keep up to date with demand and prices, the most sought-after products as well as other unforeseen issues (Casado 2008).

This latter function, representing the corporation, was key in commercial companies, where, in addition to the partners, the factor (mercantile agent) played a leading role. This employee represented the company at various national and European centres, where the company needed to be constantly present. The profile of the mercantile agent was that of a young merchant who was seeking to gain further training through a unique experience which, in addition to endowing him with knowledge, would provide him with a salary and the chance to earn a share of the company profits, and even to become involved in future enterprises (Caunedo

[17] AHPV, PN, leg. 8434, 299r–300r. Agreement.

[18] ARChV, Pleitos civiles, Fernando Alonso (F), box 13, 14.

1998). Although the figure of the factor was confined to a known young person from a merchant family, discrepancies were not uncommon and the relations with the partners could spark conflicts. Such was the case between the Burgos merchants Diego de Castillo and Francisco de Santa Cruz and their shipping clerk in Flanders, Álvaro de Aguilar, who was denied payment of 50,000 maravedís for five years' service.[19]

In financial companies, the work of the mercantile agent was different: exchange companies needed hardly any staff, whilst the tax farming companies, who stood out because of their geographical dispersion, made use of sub-leasing collection rights in order to manage their interests. These companies developed complex organisation systems involving many people who served the company either directly or indirectly: lower-ranking lessors and collectors charged with directly collecting the taxes (Ortega 2012; Ortego 2012).

For the other small and medium-sized companies, organising and managing the work could prove to be a real challenge. Certain businesses were particularly labour intensive and required painstaking work management. The three partners of the company of Martín and Juan Marroquín, and Juan Sánchez de Toledo, dedicated to the wood trade along the river Tagus, took charge of running the company, in addition to employing their servants—who acted as messengers—and as many as 22 labourers, who undertook a wide range of jobs: transporting the wood, controlling the flow of the river by setting up and removing weirs and mills, and so on (Carvajal 2015).

## 2.5 Conclusion

Between the fifteenth and sixteenth centuries, the Castilian business world experienced a time of development and splendour. Companies evidenced their enormous capacity to adapt to ever-changing economic conditions. From the leading commercial and financial companies down to the smaller corporations that were devoted to supplying local markets, it can be said that it was a time of progress on a wide range of fronts.

Companies formed the backbone of local, regional and national mercantile activity in addition to fostering the internationalisation of Castilian trade towards Italian, Flemish, French or English centres. Companies were an example of cooperation between partners, and showed the

[19] ARChV, RE, box 51, 40.

potential of business collaboration. Likewise, companies became instruments for investing capital, thereby encouraging the flow and movement thereof.

From the organisational perspective, companies developed rudimentary management and administrative structures which, at least in basic terms, call to mind modern-day practices. Partners in Castilian companies, particularly the mercantile companies, displayed an admirable knowledge of mercantile techniques, which were learnt through theory and practice. For their part, the managers had certain clear priorities, such as the economic-financial control of the company through the accounting and by safeguarding the company's mercantile documentation, not forgetting other aspects such as providing information. Finally, mention should be made of the partners' other main priorities: such as work management (processes and employees).

In sum, the ability of Castilian companies to adapt and diversify led to these structures becoming a solid pillar on which one of the periods of greatest business success in the history of Castile was founded.

## References


Al-Hussein, Falah Hassan Abed. 1986. Las compañías o asociaciones de mercaderes. In *Historia de Medina del Campo y su tierra*, ed. Eufemio Lorenzo, vol. 2, 191–220. Valladolid: Ayto. de Medina del Campo – Excma. Diputación Provincial de Valladolid – Consejería de Educación y Cultura.

Bonachía, Juan Antonio. 1992. Abastecimiento urbano, mercado local y control municipal: La provisión y comercialización de carne en Burgos (Siglo XV). *Espacio, Tiempo y Forma, Serie III. Historia Medieval* (5): 85–162.

Carretero, Juan Manuel. 1999. Los arrendadores de la hacienda de Castilla a comienzos del siglo XVI (1517–1525). *Studia Historica. Historia Moderna* 21: 153–190.

Carvajal, David. 2012. Crédito y préstamo entre mercaderes castellanos a fines de la Edad Media. In *Los negocios del hombre. Comercio y rentas en Castilla. Siglos XV y XVI*, ed. Juan Antonio Bonachía and David Carvajal, 53–76. Valladolid: Castilla Ediciones.

———. 2014. Merchant Networks in the Crown of Castile Cities Between Medieval and Early Modern Age. In *Commercial Networks and European Cities, 1400–1800*, ed. Andrea Caracausi and Christoff Jeggle, 137–152. London: Pickering & Chatto.

———. 2015. Compañías y comercio de la madera en Castilla a fines del siglo XV e inicios del XVI. *Espacio, Tiempo y Forma. Serie III* 28: 201–219.

———. 2019. ¿Sobre la fragilidad del capital? cambios y quiebras en Castilla (ca. 1471–1547). In *Comercio, finanzas y fiscalidad en Castilla (siglos XV y XVI)*, ed. Hilario Casado, 199–215. Madrid: Dykinson.

———. 2020. Los carniceros y sus negocios en el mundo rural castellano a fines del siglo XV e inicios del XVI. In *Los carniceros y sus oficios. España-Francia siglos XIII–XV*, ed. Catherine Verna, Sandrine Victor, 279–301. Valencia: University of Valencia.

Carvajal, David, and Juan Antonio Bonachía. 2014. Financieros locales en los primeros encabezamientos castellanos: Valladolid, 1496. In *Agentes de los sistemas fiscales en Andalucía y los reinos hispánicos (siglos XIII–XVII)*, ed. Mercedes Borrero et al., 169–192. Madrid: Arca Comunis.

Carvajal, David, and Sandra de la Torre. 2019. Los Daza: mercaderes aragoneses en Medina del Campo. *Revista de Historia Jerónimo Zurita* 95: 153–175.

Casado, Hilario. 2000. Comercio, crédito y finanzas públicas en Castilla en la época de los Reyes Católicos. In *Dinero, moneda y crédito en la monarquía hispánica*, ed. Antonio Miguel Bernal, 135–156. Madrid: ICO–Marcial Pons.

———. 2003. *El Triunfo de Mercurio. La presencia castellana en Europa (Siglos XV y XVI)*. Burgos: Caja Círculo.

———. 2008. Los flujos de información en las redes comerciales castellanas de los siglos XV y XVI. *Investigaciones de Historia Económica* 10: 35–68.

———. 2012. Crecimiento económico, redes de comercio y fiscalidad en Castilla a fines de la Edad Media. In *Los negocios del hombre. Comercio y rentas en Castilla. Siglos XV y XVI*, ed. Juan Antonio Bonachía and David Carvajal, 17–35. Valladolid: Castilla Ediciones.

———. 2015. Los negocios de la compañía Pesquera-Silos en Florencia en los inicios del siglo XVI. In *Hacienda, Mercado y Poder al norte de la Corona de Castilla en el transito del Medievo a la Modernidad*, ed. Ernesto García and Juan Antonio Bonachía, 69–97. Valladolid: Castilla Ediciones.

Caunedo, Betsabé. 1985. Los negocios de Diego de Soria: mercader burgalés. In *La ciudad de Burgos: actas del Congreso de Historia de Burgos: MC aniversario de la fundación de la ciudad*, 163–172. Valladolid: Junta de Castilla y León.

———. 1993. Compañías mercantiles castellanas a fines de la Edad Media. *Medievalismo* 3: 39–57.

———. 1998. Factores burgaleses, ¿privilegiados o postergados? *En la España medieval* 21: 97–114.

———. 2012. Mercaderes castellanos: algunos aspectos de su formación teórica. In *Los negocios del hombre. Comercio y rentas en Castilla. Siglos XV y XVI*, ed. Juan Antonio Bonachía and David Carvajal, 37–51. Valladolid: Castilla Ediciones.

De Ruysscher, Dave, Albrecht Cordes, Serge Dauchy, and Heikki Pihlajamäki, eds. 2017. *The Company in Law and Practice: Did Size Matter? (Middle Ages-19th Century)*. Leiden; Boston: Brill.

Herrero, Mauricio, and Mirem Díaz. 2009. *El archivo del mercader Hernando Daza Medina ([1505]–1566)*. Valladolid: Fundación Museo de las Ferias.

Le Goff, Jacques. 2004. *Mercaderes y banqueros de la Edad Media*. Madrid: Alianza.

Medrano, Violeta. 2007. El comercio terrestre castellano-portugués a finales de la Edad Media. *Edad Media. Revista de Historia* 8: 331–356.

Mercado, Tomás de. 1569. *Suma de Tratos y Contratos*. Ed. N. Sánchez-Albornoz, 1977. Madrid: IEF.

Ortega, Ágatha. 2012. Estrategias, dinero y poder. Compañías financieras castellanas a finales de la Edad Media: Una primera propuesta metodológica. In *Los negocios del hombre. Comercio y rentas en Castilla. Siglos XV y XVI*, ed. Juan Antonio Bonachía and David Carvajal, 261–286. Valladolid: Castilla Ediciones.

Ortego, Pablo. 2012. Auge y caída de una gran compañía financiera en Castilla Luis de Alcalá, rabí Mayr y la quiebra de la receptoría y pagaduría general de rentas (1477–1495). In *Tesoreros, "arrendadores" y financieros en los reinos hispánicos: la Corona de Castilla y el Reino de Navarra (siglos XIV–XVII)*, ed. Ernesto García and Imanol Vítores, 101–122. Madrid: IEF-Arca Comunis.

Otte, Enrique. 1996. *Sevilla y sus mercaderes a fines de la Edad Media*. Sevilla: University of Sevilla.

Vítores, Imanol. 2011. Compañías vascas en torno al arrendamiento y recaudación de la renta de los diezmos de la mar de Castilla a fines de la Edad Media. In *Redes sociales y económicas en el mundo bajomedieval*, ed. David Carvajal et al., 234–263. Valladolid: Castilla Ediciones.

CHAPTER 3

# Simón Ruiz: A Great Businessman in Sixteenth-Century Europe

*Hilario Casado Alonso*

## 3.1 Introduction

In 1955, the grand professor Henri Lapeyre stated in his book *Une famille des marchands: les Ruiz* (Lapeyre 1955) that Simón Ruiz was a magnificent example of a sixteenth century businessman, and was representative of many others who, like him, contributed towards European integration and helped it to take its place in the world. His claim remains true to this day, as the research carried out since then has served to confirm. Simón Ruiz, or more correctly his family, came to be the *aristocrats* of trade and finance in the sixteenth century, as did the Germans Függer (Fúcares, in contemporary Spanish), Welser, and Hoechstetter; the Genovese Centurione, Spinola, Di Negro, Doria, Vivaldi, Lomellini, Gentile, Pinello, Grimaldi…; the Florentines Bonsignori, Acciaiuoli, Bardi, Peruzzi, Medici, Frescobaldi…; the Lucchesi Bonvisi, Michaeli and Arnolfini; the

H. Casado Alonso (✉)
University of Valladolid, Valladolid, Spain
e-mail: hilario@emp.uva.es


M. Vázquez-Fariñas et al. (eds.), *Companies and Entrepreneurs in the History of Spain*, Palgrave Studies in Economic History,
https://doi.org/10.1007/978-3-030-61318-1_3

Castilians Bernuy, Salamanca, Gallo, Maluenda, Quintanadueñas, Lerma, Astudillo, Haro, Carrión, Astudillo, and Espinosa (Casado 2003).

The Ruiz Embito family's involvement in the world of trade stretched back to the fifteenth century. They hailed from Belorado, a town located on the Camino de Santiago and a meeting point between the region of La Rioja and the Duero valley. Similar to some other families of traders from Burgos, they were probably converts, very likely since the early fifteenth century, although from that moment on those who lived in Spain as well as abroad behaved as if they were true Christians and removed all trace of their Jewish past. They even obtained several reports stating that they had cleansed their blood during the sixteenth century. This long career, and their kinship with other families of merchants from Burgos, such as the San Román, Santo Domingo, Miranda, La Presa, Embito, and Sanvitores, explains why their behaviour, their mindset and—what is of interest to us here—how they managed their businesses were so similar to those of other Castilian merchants (Casado 2017b; Ruiz Martín 1990; Sánchez del Barrio 2016).

## 3.2 Family and Business

As is well known, Simón Ruiz's business was based on family alliances and economic interests with his brothers, Andrés and Vítores. Whereas Simón settled in Medina del Campo, his elder brother did so in Nantes, while Vítores made his home in Burgos, even though he spent long periods in the town of Medina del Campo. As did the great Castilian merchants of the time, they married women who were involved in trade in those cities, a policy which was to be repeated by their children and grandchildren. The aim was clear: to gain a foothold in local trade networks in order to further their business prospects and climb the social ladder in each of these cities.

This dispersion throughout Spain and Europe had an underlying business logic: the linen trade in France. Whereas in the mid-sixteenth century, the Castilian drapery industry had boomed and penetrated all the different market niches of expensive, high-quality cloth—Courtrai cloth, fine cloth, *velartes*, thirties (3000 threads in the warp), twenty-fours (2400 threads) and twenty-twos (2200 threads) from Segovia, Toledo, and Cuenca—; those of a medium quality—Perpignan cloth from Cataluña, twenties and eighteens from Cuenca, Segovia, Toledo, Ávila, Piedrahita, Ciudad Real, Aragón, and Logroño—; and the inexpensive cloths—the fourteens, *buriel*, twill, saia d'Irlanda, *palmillas*, coarse woollen fabric, brown cloths, *papales*, friezes and small friezes from Ávila, Palencia, Dueñas, La Nava, Tordesillas, Valladolid, Burgos, Logroño, etc.—, the same could not be said of linen, since that which came from Galicia and Portugal was of very poor quality. As a result, there was a need to seek a new market that could offer supplies, particularly if the aim was to provide medium-quality linen, since the very expensive kind was still being imported from the Low Countries. What could be better, therefore, than Breton linen, which had improved in quality and which offered a very competitive price. As a result, for many Castilian companies their base for importing was Rouen and, above all, Nantes. The Ruiz family chose the latter, and from there they were able to trade with the workshops around Brittany and Normandy and to send shipments to Spain from the port (Casado 2000, 2010; Galli 2018).

In addition, from the end of the Middle Ages, the fairs at Medina del Campo provided the main textile redistribution centre for the whole of Spain, Portugal, and, through Seville, Spanish America. In the town's squares and streets could be found all kinds of merchants, ranging from the leading importers who hailed from Burgos, the Basque Country, Italy, and Flanders, to cloth merchant-manufacturers from Cuenca and Segovia, as well as small-scale producers from la Rioja, Andalusia, Ávila, Palencia, and Valladolid, down to the retailers and hawkers, the *regatones*. Together with these, the local shopkeepers traded in streets specially set aside for them. As a result, the town attracted people looking to buy and sell from all parts of Spain and Portugal, with Medina acting as a hub for redistributing all kinds of fabrics throughout the Iberian Peninsula and the Americas. This explains why Vítores Ruiz and, later, his brother Simón settled in the town. The former spent only part of his life there, often travelling to Burgos to attend to private as well as family business with the company he ran with Francisco de La Presa, who was from Burgos (Casado 2001).

In sum, the trade in Breton linen explains the management structure of the Ruiz family business. Andrés, together with his sons and sons-in-law, who had settled in Nantes, purchased the fabrics. These were shipped to Bilbao, from where the *factor* (mercantile agent) had them dispatched to Burgos. There they were controlled by Vítores and Francisco de la Presa, who had them sent to be sold at the fairs at Medina del Campo. This was where Simón came in, wholesaling to other merchants who were attending the fairs or to local sellers. Some of the shipments were sent directly to Seville, Oporto, and Lisbon, where the partners and company mercantile agent had them shipped off to the Americas or sold them in the Portuguese market. The network set up by the Ruiz family was similar to that of many other Castilian families and businesses of the period: the Quintanadueñas, who were based in Rouen and Bruges; the Bernuy in Antwerp, London, Lisbon, and Toulouse; the Gallo in Bruges; the Salamanca in Antwerp, Rouen, and Florence; the Astudillo in Mexico, Seville, Burgos, Antwerp, and Florence, and so on. Differences between them were minimal, except for the fact that some had specialised in certain goods (the Bernuy in pastel cloth, the Astudillo in Italian silks and *rajas* and Mexican cochineal, or the Gallo in wool), although they all tended to diversify so as to spread their risk. Despite being rivals, these companies helped one another, since they all formed part of the same great Castilian mercantile network which had spread throughout Europe, and which was controlled by the Burgos Consulate. This meant that the Ruiz family was just one amongst many and was not necessarily the wealthiest. Their virtue lies in having preserved their great archive, which undoubtedly affords one of the best opportunities for studying sixteenth-century Europe. Thanks to the abundant documentation they provide, it is possible to accurately reconstruct the way in which Simón Ruiz ran his business.

It should be remembered that the May and October fairs at Medina del Campo were the great markets for exchanging money throughout the Iberian Peninsula in the sixteenth century. This meant that credit flowed easily and, as a result, that there were enormous opportunities for engaging in all kinds of business that could provide substantial profit.

## 3.3 From Merchandise Trade to High Finance

The way in which Simón Ruiz's activities evolved may be summed up as follows: from trading goods to high finance, without abandoning trading. As pointed out, in the twenty years after 1551, business revolved around the sale of fabrics, paper, and haberdashery from Brittany, to which were added other goods: gold-threaded cloths from Milan, coarse cloth from Italy, tapestries from Flanders, pepper from Lisbon, steel and iron from the Basque Country, ram hides from Cordoba, woollen sacks from Castile, and so on. The practice was simple: to acquire the goods from France in order to sell them on at the fairs in Castile and Seville in exchange for shipping products back there from Spain, Portugal, and Italy. The different types of goods traded gradually expanded, particularly after 1568 when the markets of Portugal and the Americas began to grow. In order to conduct all of these transactions, Simón Ruiz resorted to the use of bills of exchange between the fairs of Castile, Lyon, and Antwerp. He conducted most of the transactions on his own behalf, although, like certain other Castilian merchants, he did often accept other merchants' money, charging the subsequent commissions and speculating with exchange rates. Hence, there was a link between trade and finance from those early times, although trade remained the primary activity (Lapeyre 1955).

Although Simón Ruiz's business was only small scale in those early days, the skill he showed at the time when handling the most complicated trading techniques was already apparent. First, there was his use of associative practices, setting up various companies at the same time, even though their structure was fairly straightforward. There was one company in which he held a significant share of the capital together with other partners, who were often relatives and close acquaintances, but which also involved others who had deposited a certain amount of capital in exchange for annual interest. At the same time, however, the general company, or indeed he himself, had signed company contracts for a given number of years (3/5 years) and for specific purposes, with other merchants from Castile and Nantes. This was a technique used by many other leading merchants, such as the Pesquera, Astudillo, Salamanca, and Maluenda of Burgos. The system was based on mutual trust amongst all the partners, but was materialised through the signing of various contracts. This legal system, which was meticulously reflected through the mercantile accounting, was flexible and efficient, as it allowed a company to have its own business and at the same time to set up other companies with other people—relatives or otherwise—for different purposes and markets. The responsibilities and sharing of losses or profits were thus established in each case, depending on the amount of capital each partner had individually contributed to the parent company and, in turn, depending on what the company had invested in the subsidiary companies. They were thus able to weave an extensive mercantile network composed of a large number of people, partners, mercantile agents, agents, and so on, who, although they mainly came from Castile, might also be local traders. Yet, what is more important is that it enabled them to be present in many markets throughout Europe at the same time and to span different economic activities. Therein lay their success, by being able to take advantage of scale economies and diversification, and so minimise the risks. These continue to be the objectives of the large multinationals today (Casado 2017a).

In order to control and manage such a multifaceted company, it was necessary to make sure that information flowed smoothly. This was the task of mercantile correspondence. Simón Ruiz's archive is the best example of this sound business management practice, since over 70,000 letters have been preserved, although many more were sent and received. This amount is unique in the world in terms of quantity and quality. Together with these, a vast number of other mercantile documents were also sent: accounts, pricelists, *listini* (lists of exchange rates), shipping bills, receipts, payment slips, settlement slips, bonds, promissory notes, powers of attorney, reports, payment and purchase orders, and so on, totalling over 20,000 documents. These entered Medina del Campo and were sent out to all corners of the Earth, from Chile to Vienna, preferably passing through the major business centres of the time: Antwerp, Lyon, Nantes, Rouen, Lisbon, Oporto, Seville, Burgos, Bilbao, Genoa, Florence, and Venice. For any sixteenth-century businessman who wished to succeed in the world of finance, it was necessary to stay well informed, as it is today, and is something which Simón Ruiz was, to perfection (Sánchez del Barrio 2016; Pulido Serrano 2017).

In order to complete his management, Ruiz made extensive use of bills of exchange, an instrument which originated in Italy but which had been well known in Castile since the early fifteenth century. Over 21,000 original bills have survived, together with numerous sheets and copy books of bills of exchange. A recent study by S. M. Pinto (2012) and A. M. Ribeiro (2015) of one part of the documents shows how Simón Ruiz negotiated with bills of exchange from 45 financial markets throughout Europe, although most prominent in terms of number were those from Antwerp, Lyon, Lisbon, Piacenza, Florence, Rome, and Rouen. In fact, it can be said that most of the money transfers bound for or leaving Spain, Portugal, and the Americas passed through the fairs at Medina del Campo, where one of the main agents and intermediaries was Simón Ruiz himself. To achieve this, he forged a trusting relationship and cooperated with very well-known bankers such as the Függer, Balbani, Spinola, Bonvisi, Affaitadi, Centurione, Grimaldi, Strozzi, Capponi, Jorge, Baz, Gomes de Elvas, Ximenes, and Rodrigues de Evora. He was thus able to make substantial profits by charging the corresponding commissions. Above all, however, this enabled him to speculate with the exchange rates. Having reliable information meant being able to obtain attractive profits. In contrast, Simón Ruiz was scarcely involved in the world of insurance, which was more in the hands of his fellow countrymen from Burgos (Casado 2008, 2017a).

Such a quantity of documents and data would, however, prove useless vis-à-vis securing sound business management if the information were not treated properly. This is why the double-entry book-keeping system was used. The analysis of the 165 accounting books, in addition to the numerous accounts and balances conserved, shows that Simón Ruiz and his cashiers, as has been studied by R. Rodríguez González (1995), were accomplished masters in accounting. Through the different accounting series, the information flowed so as to join up with the Accounts Books or Major Books, before finally ending up in the Books of Positions (not conserved), where the profits and losses were shared amongst the various partners. By analysing the different steps involved in the accounting in the respective entries, it is possible to trace how the business was progressing at each moment. This provides an insight into the business strategy employed throughout each of the years.

Figure 3.1 shows the progression of the trade and financial profits the company obtained from 1569 up until the death of Simón Ruiz in 1597. It can be seen that, despite the sharp yearly changes—which were the result of the outdated accounting techniques employed at the time, where the accounts were not closed at the end of the year, but simply noted down randomly at particular moments—the company returned a profit in most of the years it was in existence (Casado 2017a).

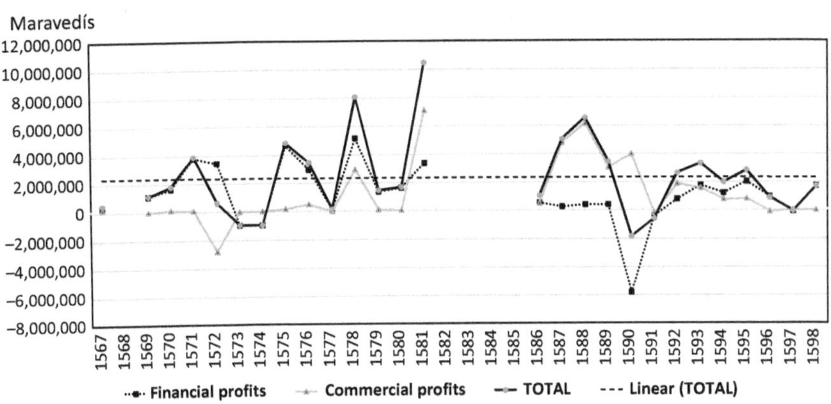


**Fig. 3.1** Profits of Simón Ruiz company (1567–1598). (Source: Author's own elaboration with data from Simón Ruiz's accounting books. Books 51, 52, 53, 54, 55, 62, 63, 74, and 75)

## 3.4 As an Epilogue

It comes as no surprise that after 1576, and particularly after the 1580s, Simón Ruiz opted to give a more financial slant to his business, although this did not mean that he completely gave up the world of trade. As well as dealing in bills of exchange, financial speculation, or private loans, he became involved in the complicated business of extending credit to the monarch, and became one of Philip II's main suppliers of goods. This allowed him to deal with the leading international financial powers on an equal standing, and to gain the respect of the Board of Finances as well as of the monarch himself. He had therefore reached the peak of his career. After 1592, he handed over part of the business to his nephew Cosme Ruiz, and concerned himself more with the construction of his hospital than with trade and business affairs (Ruiz Martín 1990).

Yet, in order to reach the top, Simón Ruiz, as I have described, had to engage in skilful business management, without which he could not have been successful. As pointed out by H. Lapeyre:

> his career shows a steady rise: he begins by importing fabrics from Brittany, later becomes engaged in trading a wide range of goods, makes huge sums of money by speculating with exchange rates and is involved in a large number of transactions, whether by actually providing capital or by simply making do with a commission. Castile can be proud of having produced such a notable businessman who can be compared to his Italian or German rivals. (Lapeyre 1955)

These words, written in 1955, today ring even more true in light of the abundant research carried out since then.

## References

Casado Alonso, Hilario. 2000. Le commerce des "marchandises de Bretagne" avec l'Espagne au XVIe siècle. *Annales de Bretagne et des Pays de l'Ouest* 107 (2): 29–50.

———. 2001. Medina del Campo Fairs and The Integration of Castile into 15th to 16th Century European Economy. In *Fiere e Mercati nella Integrazione delle Economie Europee. Secc. XIII–XVIII*, ed. Simonetta Cavaciocchi, 495–517. Firenze: Le Monnier.

———. 2003. *El triunfo de Mercurio. La presencia castellana en Europa (siglos XV y XVI)*. Burgos Cajacírculo.

———. 2008. Los flujos de información en las redes comerciales castellanas de los siglos XV y XVI. *Investigaciones de Historia Económica* 10: 35–68.

———. 2010. Crédito y comercio en las ferias de Medina del Campo en la primera mitad del siglo XVI. In *Il mercato del credito in età moderna. Reti e operatori finanziari nello spazio europeo*, coordinated by Elena María García Guerra and Alessandro de Luca, 21–47. Milano: Franco Angelli edizioni.

———. 2017a. Comercio y flujos financieros en los negocios de Simón Ruiz. In *Simón Ruiz y el mundo de los negocios en Europa en los siglos XVI y XVII*, ed. Hilario Casado Alonso, 139–163. Valladolid: Ediciones Universidad de Valladolid, Colección Cátedra Simón Ruiz n° 3.

———, ed. 2017b. *Simón Ruiz y el mundo de los negocios en Europa en los siglos XVI y XVII.* Valladolid: Ediciones Universidad de Valladolid, Colección Cátedra Simón Ruiz n° 3.

Galli, Gabriele. 2018. *Mercaderes de lienzos vestidos de seda: los Ruiz. Los tejidos y la indumentaria en la Castilla del siglo XVI.* Valladolid: Ediciones Universidad de Valladolid, Colección Cátedra Simón Ruiz n° 4.

Lapeyre, Henri. 1955. *Une famille des Marchands: les Ruiz. Contribution à l'étude du commerce entre la France et l'Espagne au temps de Philippe II.* Paris: SEVPEN (Spanish Translated, Valladolid, Junta de Castilla y León, 2008).

Pinto Gomez, Sara. 2012. *A Companhia de Simón Ruiz. Análise espacial de uma rede de negócios no século XVI.* PhD diss., University of Oporto.

Pulido Serrano, José Ignacio, ed. 2017. *Más que negocios: Simón Ruiz, un banquero español del siglo XVI entre las penínsulas ibérica e italiana.* Madrid: Iberoamericana.

Ribeiro, Ana Sofia. 2015. *Early Modern Trading Networks in Europe: Co-operation and the Case of Simon Ruiz.* London: Routledge.

Rodríguez González, Ricardo. 1995. *Mercaderes castellanos del siglo de oro.* Valladolid: University of Valladolid.

Ruiz Martín, Felipe. 1990. *Pequeño capitalismo, gran capitalismo: Simón Ruiz y sus negocios en Florencia.* Barcelona: Crítica.

Sánchez del Barrio, Antonio, ed. 2016. *Simón Ruiz. Mercader, banquero y fundador.* Medina del Campo: Fundación Museo de las Ferias.

CHAPTER 4

# A Great Modern Capitalist: Jakob Fugger

*Agustín González Enciso*

## 4.1 Introduction

It has often been said of Jakob Fugger (Augsburg, 1453–1525) that he was the world's first millionaire.[1] But was he really the first millionaire or the first capitalist? Many would regard these two epithets as the same thing; whichever way you look at it, they argue, capitalist and millionaire are synonyms. But such an outlook balks a true understanding of the key word: capitalism. Nicknamed "Jakob Fugger the Rich", he came up with that no-nonsense quote: "I want to earn as much as I can". This implies the intention of becoming rich, but it explains only part of what we call capitalism. Fugger was a millionaire—in all likelihood the first—as many other capitalists are, and there is certainly no question that he was a capitalist. But not all capitalists are millionaires; neither are all millionaire capitalists. Neither is a necessary and sufficient condition of the other.

[1] First published as "Jacobo Fugger, un gran capitalista moderno", *Nuevas Tendencias* (Instituto Empresa y Humanismo, Universidad de Navarra) 96, 2016, pp. 2–10. I Thank Dave Langlois for the translation.

A. González Enciso (✉)
University of Navarra, Pamplona, Spain
e-mail: agenciso@unav.es





M. Vázquez-Fariñas et al. (eds.), *Companies and Entrepreneurs in the History of Spain*, Palgrave Studies in Economic History,
https://doi.org/10.1007/978-3-030-61318-1_4

## 4.2 Interest in Wealthy People

Today, in a time of economic downturn oddly twinned with unbridled spending, there seems to have been a growth of public interest in the wealthy, especially those who have built up their wealth on business: G. Soros, G. Sachs and S. Jobs are only some contemporary examples to be tagged on to the older figures like Rockefeller, Rothschild or, going even further back, the Florentine Medici. The Fuggers, hitherto attracting less attention, have now been taken up by this renewed wave of interest. The recent book by Steinmetz (2015), a fine work of historical popularisation, with all the concomitant virtues and faults, helps us to discover the studies published on this merchant-banker family since 2006. They are only a handful; this is not a subject of mass interest. What strikes the eye, however, is that the last thoroughgoing historical studies of the Fuggers, by Strieder and Schick, were published between 1931 and 1957. A seventy-year hiatus for a family that set up what can safely be called Europe's mightiest bank, without the slightest exaggeration, during the first half of the sixteenth century.

The Fuggers came in for keen attention from German historians up to the mid-twentieth century, interest that then fell away. A notable aspect of the new studies on the family is the lack of much further news about its business. Barring minor details, most of the information on this business had been fleshed out beforehand, in the works of Pölnitz (1949), Ehrenberg (1955, 1985 [1928]) and Schick (1961), to quote only the most important authors. Recent studies, following a long-standing current trend, look at the social and cultural side issues of the Fuggers' business life (Dauser and Ferber 2010; Häberlein 2012).

Oddly enough, Steinmetz's summary changes tack anew, touching only lightly on the social questions and homing in instead on the essence of the business itself, especially of Jakob Fugger, showing how closely this business was tied in with the main political questions of the time. Today's historians, in other words, seem to be more concerned with the social and cultural setting of the phenomena they study, including the major financial business, whereas the journalists—of which Steinmetz is one—seem to realise that what interests the public at large is how the wealthy built up their fortune and the clout that came with it. Their working assumption seems to be that the public has a right and obligation to know this. It is a question, once more, of telling a success story. The author pulls this off, quite starkly, truth to tell, swayed by the zeitgeist mindset, although the historical account is not completely bereft of rigour.

Many regard today's abovementioned clique of wealthy as the key to our prosperity and progress. Others, on the contrary, argue that this abundance cloaks much behind-the-scenes tawdriness: selfishness and overweeningness towards the less powerful. One thing rings out clearly, however: capitalism is not simply a question of amassing wealth. Those who criticise capitalism because of the wealthy few forget that the term also enshrines other meanings such as a rational use of the means of production, business organisation, market development and so on. The downside of capitalism lurks in its margins, the abuses and flouting of fair rules, the excess of power or even what Braudel (1985, p. 65) has dubbed the anti-market, that is, where the fair-and-square rules of the public market we all know no longer hold true.

Those capitalism factors we consider to be public and widely known—rules, fair regulations, accepted quality, established prices—make up what we call the free-market economy, based on private ownership, unshackled business and freedom (John Paul II 1991, n. 42)—which is certainly a form of capitalism no one would quibble—at. Over and beyond this, where this economy's control cannot reach, "emerges", claims Braudel, "the capitalist process" (1985, p. 67), and this occurs especially in long-distance trade. There are three main reasons for this: firstly, consumer ignorance of market conditions, with the consequent impossibility of demanding a fair price; secondly, lack of competition; and, thirdly, the intervention of the various political authorities, with different currencies, allowing capitalists to negotiate in several fields and exploit the differences to be found in all the chinks. From this viewpoint capitalism is what strays beyond the free-market economy, but this would be a more restrictive definition of the term.

## 4.3 Great Historical Changes

What did Jakob Fugger mean in his time? Before looking in more depth at his character we need to bear in mind that he lived in a time of exceptional changes, when the market economy, precisely, was being overhauled, opening up new possibilities for capitalism. Shortly before Fugger was born the Turks had taken Constantinople (1453), bringing down the curtain on the Byzantine empire and upsetting the worldwide power game: the Turks cut off the lifeblood of mercantile capitalism, which had been developed by Venice and Genoa from their trading relations with the East (India and China) through Constantinople and the Black Sea. In other words, the economic unity of the medieval world was smashed. The 1453 fall of Constantinople definitively closed the Old World order based on the Mediterranean; from then on Christians would have to look to the Atlantic.

By the time Jakob died in 1525, barely seventy years later, these changes had gelled. Elcano had just completed the first round-the-world trip (1519–1522), while Cortés had routed the Aztec empire in 1521; in the year of 1525 itself the Holy Roman Emperor Charles V defeated King Francis I of France in the Battle of Pavia, thereby guaranteeing Spain's control of Italy. Meanwhile the Portuguese had completed their explorations of the African coast, forging a new route to India. Everything had changed drastically in a few decades. Now a Christian emperor, Charles, truly dominated the West, as his paternal grandfather Maximilian had desired in vain; what is more, this was an enlarged West, representing a true globalisation.

Such sweeping changes represented a true change of era. And they were equally crucial for Fugger. Not only did they favour his city, Augsburg, which stepped into Venice's breach, but they also exacerbated the money needs of his biggest client, the German Emperor, first Maximilian and then Charles. This new world order also kindled a new economy, even more global in scope, and also a new politics, since domination of this world now called for mightier entities: the modern nation-states. The upshot was a need for greater means of payment, for precious metals but other metals too: the Fuggers' fortune was tied in with both copper and silver.

As well as the economy and politics, religion was undergoing a change too. Renaissance popes were religious chiefs fending off a changing culture, but they were also sovereigns of a state that had to play its political role at a time of modern state-building. The popes therefore had to tread a delicate political path with completely new ground rules, wielding arms, money, art and even new diplomacy, as when Alexander VI sanctioned in 1494 the share-out of the world between Spain and Portugal, leaving all the rest out of this new world scheme, almost as if it was a new testament of Adam, as the King of France would later say tongue firmly in cheek. Luther went much further than such ironic statements; in 1517 he nailed his famous theses to the doors of Wittenberg Cathedral. They had to play with new economic rules too. Not too far off, the Turks, pushing back the boundaries of their empire, now threatened Belgrade.

But politics isn't everything. Nature also has its say. Tyrol is a country of copper and silver. During the fifteenth century rich fields were found. But it was not until halfway through the century, urged on by pressing need, that a procedure was discovered for extracting silver from the copper, kicking off its large-scale mining. Jakob Fugger soon cottoned on to the possibilities this opened up. In 1485 he asked his siblings to allow him to invest in the metal business. A coincidence? The zeitgeist trend chimed in with a lifetime career change in Jakob, switching him from the church to business.

## 4.4 A Risk-taking Entrepreneur

Who exactly was Jakob Fugger? Jakob was the descendant of a family of immigrants who had set themselves up as weavers in Augsburg in the late fourteenth century, at a time when the textile industry of fustians (cotton-linen mixtures) was really taking off in the city. Fustians were traded off in Venice for Eastern spices. The earnings from this family business enabled Jakob's grandfathers to break into trade in a small way, enlarging their business thereafter, moving into banking and money lending, handing on this business to his sons. Jakob Fugger the Elder died in 1469, leaving behind an already hefty fortune. His money and business were shared out between ten siblings, in due accordance with a traditional family strategy in Augsburg.

A distinction should be made here between sons and daughters. Suitable marriages were sought for the daughters; of the sons, Markus and Jakob the Younger, called after his father, went into the church while the five remaining brothers plumped for a business career. The family business continued to grow but death took its toll of Jakob's elder brothers. By 1478 only two remained, Ulrich, the eldest and Georg, who called on Jakob to help them in the family business. Jakob thereupon left the Church and went as an apprentice to Venice, further advanced than Germany in mercantile affairs.

To get from Venice to Augsburg you have to pass through Tyrol. Jakob therefore saw the growing metal business, piquing his curiosity until he decided to take up this business in 1485. His brothers did not seem so keen. Although the company was owned by all the brothers and bore the name of Ulrich Fugger and Brothers, Jakob ploughed his own furrow in mining, which proved to be the quickest-growing activity. Copper took off before silver. These metals then became the bedrock of Jakob Fugger's business, since he also outlived Georg and Ulrich, who died in 1506 and 1510 respectively.

Many people get rich by spotting chances others overlook, by daring to take a risk, by adopting groundbreaking techniques or by outperforming competitors in an established business. Jakob Fugger pulled off all these feats and more, thanks to his acumen and audacity but also his common sense, his orderliness and industriousness as well as his mastery of economic, accounting and personal aspects. According to some eyewitness accounts, neither did he lack selfishness and nor harshness if need be. All these qualities, including a dash of good fortune, which he sought and found, helped him to build up his business grew from just mining to making loans to the emperor and the pope. Since he had a lot to work with, he had a lot to offer and could afford to enforce repayment; his economic clout enabled him to look even an emperor in the eye.

## 4.5 An Emperor's Dreams

By the end of the fifteenth century, business and politics were increasingly interlinked. The Fuggers' fortune, especially Jakob the Rich's, was closely tied in with the Habsburg emperors, who became Jakob's biggest client while he himself became their main banker and financial consultant. The relationship was intense, not always straightforward and often on the point of snapping. But it lasted, and in fact could be called one of the most important public/private relationships in history, spawning the fortune of both parties. This relationship started almost by accident. In 1473 the emperor of that time, Frederick III, struck off on a journey to the Low Countries in search of alliances and power. One of his aims was to marry off his son Maximilian, future emperor, to Mary, daughter of the Duke of Burgundy and heir of the dukedom, one of Europe's richest territories. This was a red-letter event; Mary would become the grandmother of Charles V, who, through her, inherited the Burgundian Netherlands, whereby the territory became part of the Spanish monarchy.

But this would happen later. For the moment, in 1473, Mary's future father-in-law was wrestling with another problem: he lacked enough money for this epoch-making journey. The Holy Roman Emperors sported a fine title but their real power was meagre. His unreliable creditworthiness meant bankers were loath to lend him anything. Only one stepped up, Ulrich Fugger a minor banker at that time, but he saw his chance. This loan won him an important honour, a shield of arms with lilies, thereafter to become the family's distinctive emblem. But the most important result of this initial agreement was that it forged the Fuggers' subsequent relationship with the Habsburgs.

The next occasion, however, was some time coming. It had to do with the territorial disputes within the empire. Tyrol, the mining territory, was under the sway of Archduke Sigismund, a relative of the Habsburgs, although the land belonged to the latter. Sigismund squandered his money on a lavish lifestyle; at a moment of particular need it was Jakob Fugger, back in the world of trade, who came to his aid when no one else wanted to. He now saw his chance of breaking into the mining business. Jakob played it hard; as the counterpoint for his loan he demanded as security a hand in Tyrol's mining business. Sigismund fell down on the repayment, enforcing this security and giving Jakob a certain control over the mining activity.

Shortly afterwards Frederick III sent his son Maximilian to take over Tyrol from his debauched relative. Maximilian obeyed this order but it called for a certain amount of cash and who better to ask for it than Jakob Fugger? Frederick reminded the banker's family who helped him in the important trip of 1473; Fugger, for his part, now had experience in Tyrol affairs and knew how to up the ante. The dealings with Maximilian were easy and the banker's loan-security demands higher, thereby increasing his control over the local mining.

Metal continued to loom large in subsequent business. Maximilian was on the point of being made emperor in 1493, but his dreams didn't stop there. He had other tasks in mind. One of them was to wrest Vienna back from the hands of the King of Hungary, who had seized it from the Habsburgs years earlier. Another was to be crowned emperor in Rome like the previous Holy Roman Emperors. Maximilian got his way in terms of expanding Habsburg territory. By marriage he had won the Netherlands; then he recovered Tyrol from his relative; now Vienna, which proved to be a springboard to control of the kingdom of Hungary too. All this with the aid of Fugger, naturally, who was the first German businessman who arrived on the scene in quest of Tyrol's mining wealth. A key figure in Hungary was János Thurzó, a Hungarian businessman and a necessary right-hand man for insider knowledge of the country's problems.

The emperor did not fare so well in the field of international politics. He ran into problems with Vienna and the Swiss. In the end he couldn't be crowned in Rome due to the opposition of France. Later with Julius II ill (1513), he even toyed with the pipedream of being chosen as pope, softening up the cardinals beforehand with big handouts. All these dealings were done with Fugger's support, who rendered it at times at an enormous financial and political risk. But it all came good in the end, largely because Maximilian was keen to keep his prime banker sweet.

Maximilian has gone down in history as an intelligent dreamer, endowed with good ideas but incapable of bringing them to fruition. Above all, he is known as a woeful financier. All this strengthened Jakob Fugger's hand. Not only did he defray all the emperor's increasingly intense and costly military adventures and daydreams, but he also took full advantage of his financial disorderliness. The fundamental security for all these loans was the silver and copper mines of Tyrol and Hungary. Since the nineties Fugger had been taking over the ownership of more and more of these mines; in Schwaz, site of the biggest mine, he set up a major mining, ore-smelting and cannon-casting factory called Fuggerau. It also proved to be a formidable fortress against Turkish attacks.

## 4.6 The Richest Man of All

Ulrich Fugger died in 1510. Jakob inherited his brothers' commercial and banking business. This was no bagatelle. Since the times of Jakob the Elder the banking business had grown substantially on the strength of the commercial fustian and spice interests. This business, now added to Jakob's silver, copper and cannon-casting concerns, prompted the opening of a flood of firm branches scattered around the main cities of the empire and Europe. This mighty network knitted together Augsburg with Vienna, Krakow, Danzig, Antwerp and Lisbon, plus a fundamental link to Rome. By then Jakob Fugger could safely claim to be the richest man in the world, a veritable millionaire; his fortune was calculated to add up to over one million florins, overshadowing all rivals.

Jakob had inherited the banking business from his father and brothers. Another branch of his family, his cousins, also ran a banking business until going bust in 1504. All this was par for the course. Augsburg, for reasons we have already seen, turned itself into a textile, mercantile and financial hub of worldwide importance even before 1500. And it wasn't only the Fuggers; other important families like the Welsers or the Hoschtetters also lived in Augsburg and featured among Europe's most important bankers. The difference is that Fugger doubled them in wealth, influence and bargaining power, thanks to his business acumen based on judicious risk-taking and a shrewd appraisal of the chances of success. In order to lend,

Fugger had to borrow, receive deposits, but people tended to hand over the money readily enough on the strength of his prestige and responsiveness. Everyone knew he would pay back with interest thanks to the heavy interest he himself charged on the emperor's loans and in the metal business.

Of special interest here are his long-standing relationships with Rome. Fugger progressively ousted Italian bankers in all transfers from Germany to the Holy See, drawing on his wide-ranging contacts and his greater business acumen. He also paid the Swiss mercenaries who protected the pope, germ of today's Swiss Guard, and supported the election of Julius II in 1503. He made inroads too into papal finances; an important part of the papal mint ended up leased to Fugger. He was also a personal financier of many prominent personages of the Roman curia.

Preferred banker of the emperor, banker also of the pope, head of Europe's mightiest trading house, holder of a de facto monopoly of the world copper market on the strength of his many mining properties..., what did Fugger lack? Truth to tell, nothing. But when you climb so high in the commercial world, the political itch sets in. If an emperor needs a banker, a high-calibre banker needs an emperor; that is, Fugger needed to stir up the political waters in his favour. He had already been doing this by supporting Maximilian, although this was really a case of seconding the emperor's own desires. From here on he would not be happy with seconding anyone; he had to take the helm, sail between two reefs and learn how to steer a just course between two high authorities in conflict.

## 4.7 The Hour of Politics

Until 1507, shortly before taking over the whole family business, helping the emperor had posed a financial but not political risk: Jakob was in the rightful camp and the position was clear. No one could raise any qualms. After 1507, however, Maximilian began to take increasing political risks by sending his armies into Italy, showing that things could get stickier. The wars of 1507–1511 were a big commitment for Fugger. The trouble is that the imperial policy forced Maximilian to confront powers outside the empire, such as Venice and the Holy See, who were also Fugger's clients. Could he stay neutral without betraying anyone?

In alliance with the League of Cambrai, but with his coffers almost empty, Maximilian took on Venice in 1508–1509. The problem here, as we have already seen, was that Venice was a Fugger client too. The banker had to administrate his aid to the emperor. First, he agreed to give him only a part of it against the collateral of territorial possessions, turning Fugger into a vassal-owning Count. Maximilian got as far as Trento but could limp no further. When, despite everything, the emperor continued southwards, the Venetians proved to be stronger, beating him and driving him back. A Venetian army entered Tyrol and took Fuggerau. This made it a personal matter for Fugger. He had no other choice than to defend himself and show his mettle. Fugger's subsequent ability to lend Maximilian a heavy sum just a few weeks later and at relatively little risk proved his skill in wielding bills of exchange and arbitration, as well as the importance of his many relations. Thanks to this support Maximilian was able to sue for peace with the Venetians, who withdrew, saving the emperor and the banker both.

## 4.8 Choosing the Emperor

The position now reached by Fugger turned him into someone capable of changing the course of history or at least with enough economic clout to reshape European politics of the time. The chance came with the imperial election of who would become Emperor Charles V. For Fugger the imperial election meant treading a delicate line between his own personal interests and German interests. For Charles himself it posed a difficult financial dilemma: to be made emperor he needed Fugger's express permission—not written permission on paper, of course, but wrought in the conviction that without the great banker's support he could not become emperor, confirming the banker's high—stakes. It goes almost without saying that this support could have swung behind any of the would-be emperors.

As is well known, the Holy Roman Emperor was an electoral post, depending on seven electors, princes or archbishops of as many territories. The emperor was the visible head of a confederate organisation, so his force resided not so much in his own might but rather in the alliances he could strike with other princes of the empire. Winning the title of empire was therefore a difficult political question and, as might only be expected, an economic question: the electors' vote would go to whoever guaranteed their independence and paid them most. The first factor was pretty much set in stone; no emperor could stand against it. The second, on the contrary, was negotiable. In practice, the imperial election had become big business.

The election of Charles was kicked off by his now aging grandfather, Maximilian, in 1517. The first step was to gain election as King of the Romans, a title considered to be heir apparent but without being an obligatory inheritance.[2] The negotiations dragged on; Maximilian died in 1519; only a few months later Charles was elected. The problem of Charles's election resided not so much in the political infighting within the empire; indeed, in 1517, the electors were in agreement about his election. The real problem was raised by King Francis I of France, in view of the changing circumstances.

Francis had just risen to the throne in 1515, and he sought to play a hegemonic role in Europe. He revived France's expansionist policy in Italy, initiated by Charles VIII back in 1494. In 1515 he defeated the hitherto invincible Swiss in the Battle of Marignano and recovered the Dukedom of Milan. Elsewhere, the death of Ferdinand II in 1516 ushered Charles to the Spanish throne, built on the recovered union of Castile and Aragon, now with Granada and Navarre included in the deal. Charles would also inherit the Netherlands on the supposedly imminent death of Maximilian. Charles's total inheritance, therefore, formidable in itself, represented a territorial stranglehold around the France of Francis I, especially if Charles was elected emperor. Faced with the prospects opened up by Maximilian in 1517, therefore, Francis had little choice but to play it hard and throw in his bid for the imperial crown himself to counter the power of his now formidable rival Charles.

The empire itself was now pitched into a huge international cauldron: the new emperor might equally be the king of Spain or France. This heady situation was unprecedented. Everyone knew how to play it: slapping hordes of money on the table. But the problem with such sums was not only raising them at any particular time but also guaranteeing their repayment later. In view of the contenders, the electors upped the asking price and Europe's top bankers swung behind the rival candidates. But the bankers needed some security: the higher the price, the bigger the security. Were the candidates reliable enough?

Another moot point was whether or not the bankers were up to level of the needs and risks at stake. When it came to the crux, only one of these bankers was really capable of playing it alone, Jakob Fugger. Jakob of

[2] Technically the heir apparent was an emperor elected by the seven electors without yet being crowned or accepted by the pope. In practice the King of the Romans was the emperor's heir, but this did not completely guarantee his subsequent election.

course preferred Charles but he also needed sufficient security, so he also left a door open for negotiation with Francis, a chance the Frenchman tried to take. For his part Charles, who had already held negotiations with Fugger in Flanders, was tempted, once back in Spain (1517), by the Italian bankers. This raised misgivings in Fugger, who not only felt tempted to give greater support to the King of France, but also began to doubt Charles' payback capacity.

Fugger held the imperial election in the palm of his hand, because the electors were ready for just about anything. In the end German logic prevailed; Fugger trusted in Charles and the electors chose him. Patriotism? Loyalty? Historians have pondered this question, stressing the loyalty claims of Jakob himself. But many have pointed too to the importance of his own mercantile interests, Jakob finally deciding that Francis I's security was just not up to it.

## 4.9 Fugger Against the Reformation

The relations with Rome also led Jakob Fugger to play a standout role in several matters to do with the Protestant Reformation, such as the sale of indulgences or the defence of Catholicism in Augsburg. The former had a more general scope, although Fugger almost stumbled into the affair. The latter, on the other hand, was of more local importance; nonetheless, Fugger's money and influence were decisive in freeing Augsburg, at a given time, from the grave threat posed by the social revolution of the German Peasants' War.

Renaissance popes were an idiosyncratic lot. Besides their religious function, which they never ceased to perform, they also concerned themselves with other questions perhaps straying outside a pope's rightful remit, although popes too are sons of their time. Julius II was a warrior, Leon X, a businessman; all of them were great patrons of the new Rome. This new papal role scandalised many, Luther included. Luther stood out against the emperor and the pope, and Jakob Fugger was the banker of both. Small wonder, then, that decisive roles should fall to him. Fugger made transfers of religious money from Germany to Rome. One of the payments Rome demanded was the *servitium*, an investiture fee paid by prelates. In the case of Albert of Brandenburg, in 1514, this question became embroiled with the indulgences recently renewed by Leon X for Germany. The sale of indulgences had become a racket; recent popes dipped into them at will to boost their revenue and to defray special expenditure. Such was the case in Germany, where Fugger had gained control of the business.

Albert of Brandenburg needed money to pay his *servitium* for investiture as Archbishop of Mainz, so he asked Fugger for a loan. As security the archbishop managed to get Pope Leon X to concede him the right to farm indulgences within his territory. Given that it was Fugger who had raised the funds, it was only logical for Fugger too to run the business that served as collateral for the loan. Jakob Fugger thus became farmer of indulgences in Mainz. Half of this revenue would now be collected by Fugger's agents. But this threw the banker head first into such a bed of thorns as the Protestant Reformation; it was precisely the sale of indulgences that raised the ire of Luther. This of course brought Luther up against Jakob Fugger. If Fuggers' usury wasn't bad enough, even more contemptuous in Luther's eyes was his indulgence business. Playing in the emperor's camp would also lead Fugger to fight actively against the varied social revolts sparked off by other reformists who opted to go down the road of violence.

## 4.10 Is This Capitalism? Self-interest and Public Interest

One of the problems that have always besieged capitalism is the risk of clashing interests between individuals and the common weal. Capitalism arose from the bosom of society, the estates-based society in which the common good was established as the norm, as well or ill as it may actually be pursued. The particular estate granted specific rights and obligations to each person born therein, each set of rules standing out from the other; for that reason, any social and economic dynamic was overridden by the estates-based legislation. The use of money, as Duby (1997) pointed out with respect to the twelfth century, upset the applecart; the nobles of that time, far from being capitalists themselves, sniffed the beginning of a new way of life in which individual worth outweighed the common weal. Common interests were based on the traditional estates, whereas individuals took their cue from money, bringing in a whole new set of interests and ever-shifting possibilities. As we see, capitalism goes way back.

But the capitalists of that time, trading merchants above all, also brought a lot to the table. Up to the sixteenth century businessmen still hung on to what Sombart has dubbed a love of business but also a love of life and persons, showing concern "for the benefit or harm that might accrue [from his activity] for the real, living man" (1972, p. 164). Does Jakob Fugger fit in with Sombart's idea or was he an "upsetter" of the whole caboodle, as the twelfth-century nobles feared?

Maybe both things at once. Fugger was a man of his times, who also knew how to look to the future, or at least a type of future. He always looked out for his own interests, while also respecting throughout his career non-mercantile mores. He was faithful to his family; if he ran a business his own way it was because he outperformed all the rest. When all his brothers had died he shared the firm with his nephews, while always keeping the hierarchy clear and unchallengeable. And he chose as his heir the worthiest among them, Anton, as from 1525 the Fugger of Charles V, weeding out the weaker. He was faithful to his city, the hub of his business interests where he always lived. He had a positive influence on the municipal government, albeit always indirectly, and did so decisively when it was necessary.

He was faithful to his emperor and his empire. He always supported Maximilian, whom he helped to create the new power of the House of Habsburg, the union of Austria and Hungary, nursed into being by Fugger's money and advice after the Vienna congress of 1515. He apparently dithered about the election of Charles V, but deep down this was nothing more than a business wile to make bigger profits. These profits would also enhance the House of Habsburg within the empire, over and above other princes, so his loyalty also extended to the Habsburgs as territorial princes. His world was thus a world of shared loyalties that he deftly blended with his own interests.

Likewise, he was always faithful to his religion, Catholicism, and the pope, whoever that might be at each time. He would come to know a total of seven popes, though his main business was done with Julius II and Leon X (1503–1521). These popes had a set of needs and interests, some of them personal but most of them economic, true enough, but they also defended a faith to which Fugger held true, even defending it against the rebels as from 1517.

His loyalty on all these scores did not always hold him in good stead. There were times when his support for the emperor or the church drove him to the verge of bankruptcy, won him the opprobrium and hate of rival financiers or full-out flak from his enemies. This was the risk he decided to take in the interests of his long-term loyalty. Other bankers of the time—Welser, Hoschtetter, also from Augsburg—did not reap such huge profits but neither did they stick their necks out as much. Ironically, Fugger's house was to outlast most of them.

Like other businessmen of his time, Fugger's particular idea of "maximising profits" took in not only the possibility of taking risks in the interests of family or political loyalty but also left an ample leeway for other less profitable investments, more proper of his time. Fugger did not turn up his nose at public honours and social recognition; he became a count with the corresponding seigneurial revenues but did not actually use the title. He was a patron of the arts and lived in a lavish mansion. He was sober in his personal life but he also liked to organise parties to hail his guests or celebrate newsworthy events. His mansion was the hub of his business and a lively social life at the same time.

Fugger also chimed in with the zeitgeist idea of helping the poor. His trademark building, the *Fuggerei*, lives on today with a similar charitable purpose, as a residence for the poor, workers who pay a token rent to enjoy a dignified home and services that, elsewhere, only the rich can enjoy.

Yes, Fugger spent time and money on all these things, without, of course, forfeiting the chance of prospering with his business interests.

## 4.11 Time to Work

To wind up, a glance at an aspect that is often overlooked but is nonetheless a key question here: work. The abovementioned *Fuggerei* serves as a tell-tale sign of Fugger's mindset: the value he attributed to work, especially work to earn a living. Luther's writing exalted the idea of "calling," understood in relation to a livelihood. On this bases all exegetists since have tended to argue that Protestantism introduced a new concept of work. I don't wish to downplay Luther's thinking in this regard, but this idea already existed before the Reformation, much as the reformers may have reformulated the idea or introduced new facets.

Witness the attitude of Fugger. When the banker gave preference to worker families for his charitable housing rather than the downright poor, he was not only saying that these destitute poor already have people looking after them but also stressing the dignity of work, often undertaken by those of few resources. Only workers, therefore, were eligible for his charity. Fugger himself, after all, came from a family of immigrants and manual workers. By dint of hard work his grandfather had carved out a business in the lowest levels of the textile industry. Fugger, therefore, always held work in high esteem, not only his own workers but his poorer co-citizens who worked for others.

He himself never stopped working. He always believed that the idea of "earning as much as you can" did not necessarily involve shady wheeling and dealing but honest-to-goodness work. This work should also be rational, well done, vouched for by painstaking accounts and meticulously run, as all his businesses were. Such careful accounting was by no means the norm in other business houses of this time. This did not stop him, at times, from taking risky decisions, even dodgy decisions in the eyes of his rivals, but always based on hard work and dedication. This ethic of hard work, even when undertaken under the most arduous circumstances, has a clear example in Jakob Fugger, a crucial man of his time and, as a worker, a role model for other businessmen.

## References

Braudel, Fernand. 1985. *La dinámica del capitalismo*. Madrid: Alianza.

Dauser, Regina, and Magnus Ferber. 2010. *Die Fugger und Welser*. Augsburg: Verlagsgemeinschaft Augsburg.

Duby, George. 1997. *Guillermo el Mariscal*. Madrid: Alianza.

Ehrenberg, Richard. 1955. *Le siècle des Fugger*. Paris: S.E.V.P.E.N.

———. 1985 [1928]. *Capital and Finance in the Age of the Renaissance. A Study of the Fuggers and Their Connections*. Fairfield, NJ: A. M. Kelly.

Häberlein, Mark. 2012. *The Fuggers of Augsburg (1367–1650)*. Charlottesville, VA: Virginia Press (Original German Edition of 2006).

John Paul II, Saint. 1991. *Encyclical Centesimus annus*. Vatican City: Acta Apostolicae Sedis.

von Pölnitz, Götz. 1949. *Jakob Fugger*. Mohr & Siebeck: Tübingen.

Schick, Leon. 1961 [1957]. *Jakob Fúcar. Un gran hombre de negocios del siglo XVI*. Madrid: Aguilar.

Sombart, Werner. 1972 [1913]. *El burgués*. Madrid: Alianza.

Steinmetz, Greg. 2015. *The Richest Man Who Ever Lived. The Life and Times of Jacob Fugger*. New York: Simon & Schuster.

Strieder, Jakob. 1931. *Jacob Fugger the Rich: Merchant and Banker of Augsburg, 1459–1525*. New York: Adelphi.

CHAPTER 5

# Speculation and Collusion in the North of Castile. 1820–1880

*Rafael Barquín*

## 5.1 Introduction[1]

In the mid-nineteenth century, the former region of *Castilla la Vieja* was enjoying unusual economic prosperity. As a result of the outbreak of the Crimean War, since the winter of 1853 the Russian cereal supply to Western Europe had stopped, a problem that worsened with the bad harvests in 1854. Like other neutral countries, Spain came to fill that gap. In 1854 and 1855 exports grew, and the income of Castilian farmers and merchants boomed. This unexpected situation is the origin of a Spanish saying that remained for a long time: wealth in Castile relied on three things, "Agua, sol, y guerra en Sebastopol" (water, sun, and war in Sevastopol).

But not everyone celebrated the war. During those years, bread in Castile became more expensive; what was a blessing for farmers became

[1] A larger version in Barquín (2019).

R. Barquín (✉)
UNED, Madrid, Spain
e-mail: rbarquin@cee.uned.es





M. Vázquez-Fariñas et al. (eds.), *Companies and Entrepreneurs in the History of Spain*, Palgrave Studies in Economic History,
https://doi.org/10.1007/978-3-030-61318-1_5

ruinous for workers. On June 22 and 23, 1856, several uprisings took place in Valladolid, Palencia and Medina de Rioseco. Despite being quickly suppressed, the riots revealed profound discomfort within a part of the urban population. Taking advantage of the restlessness, and with the timely collaboration of the Queen, General O'Donnell became the new Prime Minister, bringing an end to the Progressivist Biennium.

Such a contradictory situation leads to the question of whether the welfare of peasants implied the suffering of the urban working classes. Strictly speaking, price levels should not say anything about the people's welfare. In the long term, the relation between prices and wages is stable. The cost of acquiring bread accounted for about 20% of the income for the urban working classes, both in Spain and in Europe. It is a high percentage, but it remains enough for other food and consumer goods. In fact, the wealthiest nations in Europe were also those with the most expensive bread, as in England, where farmers and urban workers probably enjoyed the best living conditions in Europe in the middle of the nineteenth century.

The true challenge for the well-being of the urban people occurred during the agrarian crises because the increase in the prices of commodities was not followed by a proportional increase in wages. Even less so in Spain, where the price fluctuations were higher than in other European countries. This differential performance can be explained by the reduced supply of substitute foods (corn, potatoes, legumes, etc.), and by difficulties in accessing the international market.[2] However, the moral responsibility of the authorities has also been pointed out. According to Blas Lopez Morales (a genuine representative of the Valladolid bourgeoisie), the mutineers of 1856 blamed flour manufacturers and grain speculators for the rising cost of bread. In his view, they would have been seduced by "perfidious suggestions" into believing that the greed of these merchants was the cause of the high prices. They would think the rich were building their "colossal fortunes on the hunger of the poor people" (López Morales 1856, pp. 7–8).

Of course, López Morales did not believe such allegations. From his point of view, the real problem only appeared when, after the bad harvest, the Town Hall of Valladolid raised the *impuesto de puertas*, a tax paid on the entry of cities (López Morales 1856, pp. 16–17). But the

[2] Barquín 2001, pp. 123–124. Spanish wheat prices at www.iisg.nl/hpw/data.php#spain, and from my homesite www.uned.es/cee/rbarquin.

interpretation of mutineers, which came from a long tradition, remained for a long time. The 1856 "especuladores" would have been the precursors of other speculators and oligopolists: the "estraperlistas" of the 1940s, the real estate speculators of the 1960s and so on. Behind each shortage, there will always be a greedy businessman. This chapter addresses that issue. Were there collusive structures? Was there speculation, hoarding and cartels? And if there were, were they the cause of the hunger and riots that followed?

## 5.2 Speculation: The Individual's Perspective

First we will provide a brief description of those economic activities. In the middle of the nineteenth century, wheat from the North of Castile was turned into flour in many mills and "wheat factories" scattered along the route that led to the port of Santander, known as the "Reinosa route". In a part of that route, the Canal of Castile, transport was by barge. But after 1857 barges were replaced by trains, and after 1866 the entire route between Valladolid and Santander could be traversed in this way. The bags of flour were shipped to three destinations: Cuba (and Puerto Rico), Catalonia (and other peninsular ports) and Europe. In Cuba, this was possible because a very high custom tariff prevented the entry of flour from North America. In Catalonia, Cantabrian flour benefited from a law that prohibited the entry of foreign flour and wheat. Only to Europe were there significant exports in specific years, such as during the Crimean War.[3]

In all of these operations numerous people participated, such as millers, barrow hauliers, contractors, shipowners and merchants of all kinds. Each of them occupied and defended their small market niche and merchandise was bought and sold among everyone. For this reason, everyone speculated in one way or another.

The word *especulación* (speculation) takes its current meaning from mid-nineteenth century. Previously, it used to be a synonym for "contemplating" or "anticipating." In the 1817 *Diccionario de la Real Academia Española* (DRAE) it is defined as "the action to buy, sell, move, etc. something tradeable to achieve a forecasted profit." Only in the 1869 dictionary, we can find a negative connotation when adding to the previous

[3] A general description of this set of activities can be found in Hoyo (1993, 1999), Moreno (1995, 1996, 2002, 2006), and Barquín (1999, 2011, 2019).

definition "and generally any business that promises profit". But even today the old meaning is still used.[4]

Speculation is a widespread activity. All small traders are speculators of the merchandise with which they deal. They buy and sell as "price-accepters", taking advantage of their variations, and anticipating them to obtain a benefit. That is, they speculate in an economic sense, but also as a forecaster. No one can ensure them that transactions will be successful. No one can tell them by how much the price of a product is going to rise (if it does) and therefore no one can tell them when to sell. This decision becomes more difficult because they must also assess the storage and deterioration costs.[5] Furthermore, the opportunity cost should also be evaluated: if they do not sell the merchandise because the price is low, they will not be able to buy more, since their store is full.

Some of these decisions made no sense in nineteenth-century Castile due to the state of technology. Normally, the economy actors just followed the custom. Whether as a farmer or as a wholesaler, selling wheat a few months after harvest was an operation with low risk (and therefore little benefit). Its storage did not involve significant challenges. In Castile, the usual way to store wheat was to place it inside holes with the walls and ground lined with mortar, clay, straw or any material that would ensure a certain degree of tightness. Yet raising a speculative operation in a period longer than one year was dangerous, since the deterioration of the product increased rapidly. Indeed, it was possible to use more sophisticated storage systems that reduced losses, but they were inefficient and expensive. The lack of suitable storage methods in Castile before the twentieth century shows that long-term speculation was not profitable and that it was better to assume the loss of part of the storage.[6]

[4] On the meaning of the words *especular* and *especulación*, see Barquín 1999, p. 299.

[5] Estimating these costs is not easy. As for the first, the Spanish public granaries (*pósitos*) set the annual interest of loans, called *creces*, at 8% per year. However, it should be noted that these were loans intended for charity purposes; and that, not by chance, the granary were ruinous companies (Anes 1969, pp. 76–94). For medieval England, McCloskey and Nash (1984) estimate the annual storage costs at 30% of the initial investment, which could be an upper limit in Spain, where the climate is not as rainy.

[6] There is a way to store wheat without storing it physically: buying the crop in advance. This was a common practice among flour manufacturers for two reasons: first, it brought benefits as a credit operation, and second, it ensured the supply of raw material for the business (Moreno 2002, pp. 176–177). However, purchase aimed at speculation is still a risky operation. The wholesaler cannot know in advance how much the harvest will be worth

In Castile, as in any place at any time, more risk implies more profit. It is possible to imagine more conservative and more aggressive entrepreneurs, with different strategies of speculation (but not in the long term). In any case, these practices would not oppose the interests of the community but rather protect them. The result of buying goods when they are cheap and selling them when expensive stabilizes the market, that is, raising the price when it is low and reducing it when it is high. As it is almost impossible for a single trader to influence a large market, for this result to be significant the concurrence of many small traders and manufacturers would be necessary. And this is what happened. The economic conditions of the Castile wheat market in the nineteenth century were typical of free competition: atomization, product homogeneity, absence of entry barriers, low information costs and so on.

However, there was one aspect in which the wheat and flour market in Castile was different from Europe: trade legislation (Vallejo 2018; Montañés 2009). Between 1820 and 1868 (although with some interruptions) imports of wheat and flour were prohibited if their prices did not reach a certain level in three adjacent coastal provinces. This commercial policy was called "prohibitionism". Furthermore, the market in Cuba and Puerto Rico was reserved for Spanish flour, since tariffs on foreigners were prohibitive. Consequently, farmers and flour producers on the Reinosa route were sure that, if worst came to worst, they could always sell part of their storage in those markets.

America and Catalonia are two slightly different cases. Although shipping to Cuba was not banned from any Spanish port, vessels mostly departed from Santander. In order to take full advantage the cargo of the vessels on a very long journey, only flour was exported. But since this merchandise was delicate, and much more so in the Caribbean, the freight had to be organized in advance to ensure quick unloading and distribution, bypassing hurricane season. These circumstances did not exist in Barcelona, where Cantabrian flour arrived regularly and competed with flour from Castilla-La Mancha and Aragón.

In the European market, the Spanish merchants competed unevenly with foreign farmers, who took advantage of the tariffs of their governments. Unlike in Cuba and Catalonia, many of these exports were wheat. The Spanish competitiveness in Europe was minimal and decreasing and

when it is delivered. It may be that the value of the wheat that liquidates the loan is even less than what was borrowed.

**Table 5.1** Exports and outputs of wheat and flour from Santander. Annual average. Thousands of quintals (ql.)

| | *America* | *Mainland Spain* | | *Abroad* | |
|---|---|---|---|---|---|
| | *Flour* | *Flour* | *Wheat* | *Flour* | *Wheat* |
| 1825–1847 | 96.3 | | | 73.0 | |
| 1848–1856 | 201.5 | 203.7 | | 192.5 | |
| 1858–1868 | 225.3 | 200.8 | 6.8 | 51.8 | 39.5 |
| 1869–1883 | 278.2 | 213.4 | 29.5 | 58.7 | 84.1 |

Source: Author's own elaboration with data from *Boletín Oficial del Comercio de Santander*, *Gaceta de Madrid*, 15, 16 and 20 May 1847; Torrente 1853, p. 273. See also the homesite: www.uned.es/cee/rbarquin and Barquín 2003

Note: Between 1825 and 1847 there were regular departures to Barcelona and other places in the Mediterranean, but there is not enough data

usually exports were small. But there were also some years with notable exports, and still others, although few, with even more notable imports. From the 1880s onward, with a relatively liberal regime, the latter was the most common. Table 5.1 summarizes these movements until 1883.[7]

To what extent did this market reserve affect the internal prices in Castile? Figure 5.1 should be able to explain this. In a close market, the supply and demand curves would be S and D1. The balance point would be reached with an exchange of the quantity q1 to the price p1. But if that market were to be opened to a foreign market capable of absorbing any production at a price p2, the demand curve would be D2, that is, it would have a first section identical to D1, and a second horizontal section in p2. Moving from the initial point to the latter would increase production from q1 to q2′, but it would reduce national consumption from q1 to q2. And, more interestingly, the domestic market price would also grow from p1 to p2. On the Reinosa route that price would be fixed as the difference between the international price and the transport costs up to that point. That is, wheat (or flour) would be exported as long as the price in Castile did not rise above the level at which it would be preferable to sell it domestically, at an even lower price, but without transportation costs.

[7] The national figures of exits and exports of wheat and flour from 1849 onwards in Grupo de Estudios de Historia Rural (1985, pp. 356–357), and *La crisis agrícola y pecuaria* 1887–89, volume VI, p. 156.

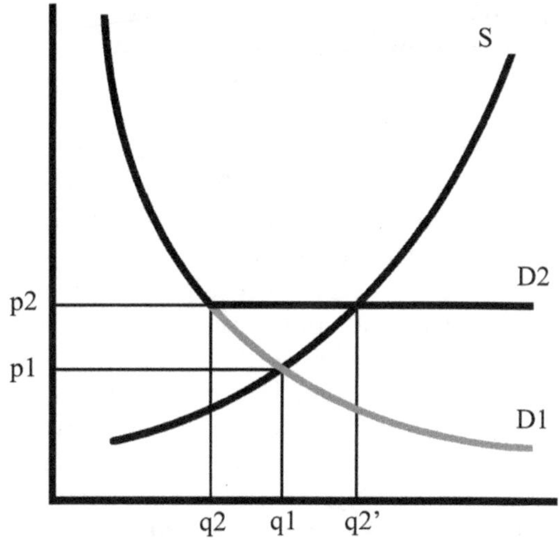


**Fig. 5.1** Castile wheat market model. (Source: Author's own elaboration)

**Table 5.2** Wheat prices in several inland cities. Reales/fanega[a]

| | *Rioseco* | *Segovia* | *Zaragoza* | *León* | *Mérida* |
|---|---|---|---|---|---|
| 1820–1830 | 21.31 | 26.18 | 38.41 | NA | NA |
| 1830–1840 | 28.18 | 32.03 | 38.99 | 36.37 | NA |
| 1840–1850 | 27.23 | 28.44 | 37.05 | 34.76 | 27.31 |
| 1850–1860 | 35.75 | 37.83 | 41.57 | 39.67 | 37.05 |
| 1860–1870 | 43.28 | 43.98 | 42.65 | 45.80 | 46.64 |
| 1870–1880 | 41.60 | 41.36 | 44.43 | 40.68 | 43.93 |

Source: Author's own elaboration with data from mercurials from those cities. See also the homesite: www.uned.es/cee/rbarquin, Barquín 2001, 2011, p. 279

[a]*Real* was a Spanish currency equivalent to a quarter of the peseta (0.0060 euros). *Fanega* was a unit of capacity equivalent to 55.5 litres

Table 5.2 suggests that the difference between p2 and p1 was tiny. Until the 1860s, wheat from Valladolid/Medina de Rioseco was the cheapest in Spain. That is, it was the lowest among inland production areas. After that prices converged in that broad region, as well as with those from the rest of the country, although less so. Nevertheless, Valladolid would remain one of the places with the cheapest wheat in Spain.

Since the Cuban and Catalonian markets were closed abroad, and the former was dominated by flour from Cantabria, it is logical to conclude that the demand at the p2 price could not be unlimited. The fact is that Cuba, Catalonia and even Europe were small markets for Castile. In Cuba, an island with two/three million people, only some of the Spaniards and Creoles ate bread. In Catalonia lived less than two million people, who ate bread made with wheat from Castile, but also from Aragón, Valencia and own inland Catalonia. As for Europe, as mentioned earlier, exports were small, although sometimes significant. Europe was a smaller market than Cuba or the Peninsula in the long term (Table 5.1). With such markets, the effects on Castile's cereal price were modest.

But there is a second reason to explain the reduced external influence on the price of wheat in Valladolid: risk. Foreign sales were complicated. Even with up-to-date information, the agents did not have any guaranty that prices would not slump during the time between the purchase of the flour in Castile and its sale in these three markets. Consequently, their behaviour was highly prudent. Castilian wholesalers did not make long-term forecasts—they simply sold the merchandise when they deemed it possible and profitable—. And they did so with preference towards Castile or Santander, retailers, bakers or any other agent who would want to take that risk. The construction of the railway changed things slightly because flour and wheat exits became less expensive and, above all, easy.[8] And not only due to the speed of the train but also due to the telegraph. These allowed for information to be transmitted much faster, reducing transaction costs. With their help, prices rose in Valladolid, and more so than in the rest of inland Spain. Even so, Valladolid remained a place with cheap wheat, probably due to the productivity and specialization of *Tierra de Campos* (Table 5.2).

The external markets of Cuba and Catalonia promoted the agricultural and industrial development of Castile, but surely not as much as its inhabitants would have hoped. The Cuban market reservation did not encourage the development of any "perverse" practices in the Castilian flour businessmen. They adopted a passive and cautious attitude keeping their sights on possible demand changes. There is nothing to suggest that speculative movements had important consequences for the regional market. Moreover, there is no evidence that wheat in Castile became more expensive due to detractions towards the coast or overseas, except at exceptional times, such as the Crimean War. And this was precisely the problem. There

[8] Which caused the brokerage revenues on the route to fall compared to the previous period. See Barquín (2011, pp. 272–276).

was not a problem regarding speculation in Castile, but rather a lack of speculation, and a lack of trade ambition. Perhaps Castilian grain traders would have regularly carried out more operations if they had had a broader view of their position in Europe and the world. In that sense, the safety of a controlled market could have been a discouraging factor for agricultural modernization, although this is difficult to determine.

Regarding the welfare of the population, the costs that resulted from prohibitionism are not negligible. Sometimes harvests were poor, and hence prices rose dangerously and exports stopped, and yet imports did not arrive because they were prohibited. Note that from the moment the ban was lifted until wheat reached Spanish ports, several weeks had usually passed in negotiation and transportation. In other words, prohibitionism prevented a faster resolution of the subsistence crises (Barquín 2003, pp. 133–140). It was precisely on one of these occasions that bread riots broke out.

## 5.3 Cartels and Lobbies: The Group's Perspective

So far we have assumed that wholesalers were price-accepters, and therefore had no control over the supply curve. Indeed, given a large number of agents participating in the Cantabrian-Castilian market, imagining that any of them had actual market power seems to be unrealistic (there is a late and irrelevant exception, the railway, which we will comment on later). But that would not prevent the establishment of a cartel or pact between several agents to monopolize the merchandise and control the price. Incidentally, we can also imagine situations in which wholesalers would unite to defend their shared interests, but without forming a cartel: what is known as a lobby. All these possibilities will be analysed in this section.

The word *oligopolio* (oligopoly) is a neologism in Spanish that did not appear until the DRAE 1984. The word *cártel* (cartel), with its modern meaning, only appears in the DRAE 1956: "an agreement between similar companies in order to avoid mutual competition and regulate production and prices in an industry". In contrast, *monopolio* (monopoly) is an ancient word. It appears for the first time in the DRAE 1737 as "an agreement made between merchants to sell goods at a specific price, which is prohibited and is called *monopolio*". It is important to note that what is immoral, and illegal, is not the institution itself, but the usurpation by individuals of a state privilege called *estanco*. Only in the nineteenth century did the word *monopolio* acquire a separate immoral meaning. Thus, the Núñez Dictionary of 1825 defines it as the "abusive and hateful trading by which a company or private individual sells merchandise that should have free trade."[9]

Hoarding to raise the product's price is a theoretically viable operation with durable goods, such as real estate, strategic minerals or Public Debt. But it is too risky with perishable goods. Let us imagine a cartel which dominates the market for one of these goods, for example bananas. If supply is reduced, the price rises. But in this way, the supplier will be not richer; this would only be the case if they were to sell the merchandise. The problem is that, in doing so, the value of the product will depreciate. Thus, the only way to avoid a substantial loss of the product's storage value is to reduce sales enough that the price does not fall below the purchase price. But this is not possible because bananas are perishable items, and they have to be sold. No one is going to eat a vast quantity of bananas simply because they are perishable. The wealthiest person in a community will not eat more than the poorest one. No one will eat twice as many bananas because they have not been able to do so in the previous months. Thus, if the cartel doesn't sell the bananas when they can, they will probably never be able to sell them. In short, hoarding perishable goods is a sure way to go bankrupt.

This section could end here, which would lead directly to the lobby problem. But let us force the example. Let us imagine that merchandise is not a perishable good, or not to a great extent. This requires that we contemplate only wheat because flour is very similar to bananas: a delicate commodity that deteriorates quickly. Its only advantage is that it occupies less space, which explains why it was exported to Cuba. But Castile was spacious and there was no lack of land, so no one stored or speculated with flour, but rather with wheat. This is why mills stored sacks of wheat that were then ground upon request.[10]

[9] The word *acaparar* (hoarding) with a pejorative connotation appears for the first time in the Domínguez Dictionary from 1853, defined as "to seize or acquire anything that can produce some utility by selling it with profit".

[10] Here it can be seen how the issue of speculation mixes with the issue of hoarding. Millers need to store wheat to work, but in doing so, were they speculating? This question was answered with the Law of Promotion of Industry and Commerce from May 8, 1822, which tacitly allowed hoarding and speculation. The Commerce Code of 1829 and the *Real Decreto de Libertad de Comercio* of January 20, 1834, again sanctioned freedom. Finally, the *Real Decreto* of November 19, 1835, established the "the power to build flour mills freely",

Let us suppose now that a hypothetical cartel of businesspeople bought wheat from farmers and stored it in a place where it could be kept for some time. Who exactly would do this? At what stage of the production and distribution of the Reinosa route would that cartel be located? The logical course of action would be to place it among flour manufacturers rather than among Santander merchants, because of the proximity to the raw material which is subject to hoarding. But whoever they might be, what could be done to guarantee their cooperation?

Many circumstances boost the establishment of oligopolies, but the main one is the existence of entry barriers. There are several kinds, but the two most important are the need for a substantial initial investment and the control of technology. In nineteenth-century Castile, the storage of wheat should not be a capitalized industry. There is no evidence that its store-men used any sophisticated technology. High-rise granaries only appeared in the twentieth century. Until then, any investor could enter the wheat hoarding business by doing little more than digging a grain silo. The same can be said about the rest of the activities carried out on the Reinosa route, except the railroad. For example, flour manufacturing experienced improvements from 1830 onwards with the introduction of new milling methods, but they were not particularly complicated. Only in that way it is possible to explain the presence of scattered milling that coexisted with modern techniques (Moreno 1995, pp. 237–242). Something similar can be said about road transport and the merchant marine. By the way, the latter was open abroad industry, since only the introduction of flour was forbidden, but not the trade from Santander to any port; which, on the other hand, was appealing given the shortage of means.

Along the Reinosa route, there were a large number of companies in every activity of production, transport and distribution. This was the case among Castilian flour mills. Surely the most detailed list of flour factories (but not complete) is the one that Luis M.ª Sierra collected for Cantabria in 1845, which Luis Ratier would expand to other provinces in 1848. Sierra only collected the name of an owner in two factories, and thus there are 61 factories and 60 owners. According to Ratier, there were 26 flour factories in Cantabria (with 124 milling stones), 21 in the Canal de Castilla (123 stones) and 14 outside both of these areas (64 stones) (Sierra 1845,

another fundamental milestone in the fight against obscurantism (Maluquer 1983, pp. 85–86).

p. 84; Ratier 1848, pp. 24–31). He also states that each stone could grind up to 60 fanegas of wheat in 24 hours, which Sierra confirms (Ratier 1848, p. 25; Sierra 1845, p. 84). Therefore, a single ten-stone mill, operating at full capacity, could generate approximately 600 tonnes of flour a month, of which 40% was exported to Cuba in 1848, which was a good year for exports, and 100% was exported in a regular year. A hypothetical cartel would be unsustainable with three, two or even a single mill not being part of it (Barquín 2011, p. 269). Of course, from a local or regional viewpoint, we could find some business concentration. But even in these small areas, the property was distributed among families. For example, in Grijota, a flour district in the province of Palencia, there were several owner families: Pombo, Lecanda, Illera, Bustamante and others.

The same can be said about Santander merchants. Throughout the middle of the nineteenth century, the flour business was controlled by approximately 55 families (Hoyo 1993, pp. 108–126; 1999, p. 278), which is slightly less than the number of flour factories in 1848, according to Sierra and Ratier. Nor was there an entrepreneur or group of entrepreneurs with a significant market power. Thus, in 1874 the largest commercial house, the López-Dóriga, only had 13.2% of the total commercial investment. In 1845 the Spanish ships enrolled in Santander were 66, according to Ratier, which were only a fraction of total. The main shipowner had seven with 8.2% of the overall tonnage; the next four had four to five ships, with 4.6–7.2% of the overall tonnage, and so on. This is the typical structure of a non-collusive industry, similar to the Castilian flour sector, another non-collusive industry.[11]

Because of the absence of collusive practices, the information was broad and public, even overwhelming.[12] We do just have data on prices, but also all sorts of news, opinions and gossip about freights, insurance, carriage transport, interest, market forecasts and even the prices of the reams of paper used to line the sacks. All this information was displayed in newspapers such as *Boletín Oficial del Comercio de Santander* and *Norte de Castilla*, in which there are separate sections, and journalists specialized in those areas. The pages of these newspapers are definitive evidence that we are looking at a broad, deep and transparent market, not a closed market controlled by unknown cartels (Barquín 2011, pp. 269–272). All this is

[11] Ratier 1848, pp. 120–124. Quoted by Moreno (2018, p. 14). Similar figures in Sierra (1845, pp. 94–98).

[12] See my website, www.uned.es/cee/rbarquin.

also in line with the development of a futures market in Valladolid, where the risk, not the wheat, was bought and sold. The existence of such a market is further proof of the non-existence of cartels. A collusive market does not need to negotiate anything because everything has been agreed in a private and clandestine way (Moreno 2018, p. 15).

But if the cited arguments are not sufficient, here is the last one: we do not have any proof of the existence of formal associations to promote collusive practices. It is a relevant argument because, in this arena, appearance is important, even more important than materiality. For any cartel, breaking the collusion agreements and selling undercover is a strong temptation. That is why there must be sanctions. We saw that, until 1825, there was not even a pejorative definition of the word *monopolio*, except as *estanco*. Even when its existence was recognized, the problem must not have attracted attention, since no anti-monopoly legislation was passed throughout the nineteenth century. In sum, nothing prevented the existence of formal cartels. If we do not have any news from them, it must be because they did not exist. In recent decades, Spanish scholars have carried out a great deal of research on economic and social control institutions, such as chambers of commerce, casinos and, above all, families. For example, there have been several studies that have outlined the marital relationships between members of different commercial houses of flour companies. These studies are undoubtedly of interest to Social History, but they do not depict the existence of collusive structures. And, in addition, we all know that families are complicated, and large families are even more complicated.[13]

There is only one exception, a late industrial sector in which there were high technological and investment barriers, and that, undoubtedly, was a monopoly: the railroad. In Spain, its construction was fuelled by high expectations. It was assumed that wherever they were built, they would promptly oust other means of transportation. Hence, the Legislator imposed the obligation to establish maximum transport prices to avoid

[13] According to Hoyo (1999, p. 278), the Santander cartel of merchants would have maintained the cohesion through "careful marriage strategies". Moreno (1991, p. 187; 1995, p. 245; 2006, p. 317) also points out the importance of these ties in the flour companies of Palencia, but he believes that such a structure was a "burden" since it was "marked by schisms and family tensions". Interestingly, the vast majority of these companies were created in the 1830s and 1840s, and they started to go into decline within 30 or 40 years. Therefore, there would have been little more than one generation to consolidate the family relationships, and all in a very competitive environment with an evident excess of productive capacity.

abusive practices. These were useless. It turned out that the railroad was not profitable at all due to lack of income. The railway companies had to approve lower fares called "specials"; these were equivalent to half or one-third of the first fares, but traffic did not increase in that proportion. Almost all the railroad companies went bankrupt between 1865 and 1866. The railway from Venta de Baños to Santander was no exception. Its first stretch opened in 1857, and the last in 1866. It was managed by the *Compañía del Ferrocarril de Isabel II*, which was later absorbed by the *Compañía de Caminos de Hierros del Norte de España*, one of largest in Spain. Before 1865 the Company fixed the majority of "special fares", and there no were significant modifications over the following decades. Fares rewarded large freights but penalized extended storage in the stations. Therefore, railroad companies did not organize or promote hoarding operations.

Finally, let us take a look at the possibility of the existence of lobbies. They usually receive less moral censorship than cartels. The lobby does not impose prices or set fees. Moreover, it supposedly protects the interests of consumers by guaranteeing some quality standards. This is the reason why it is not only public but also often tries to sway public opinion. The lobby is a political institution before it is an economic one.

Prohibitionism took its full shape with the Real Decreto January 29, 1834, published on January 30, which banned imports if they did not reach a price of 70 reales/fanega for wheat and 110 reales/quintal for flour in three adjoining provinces.[14] This act was simply the update of another Real Decreto on September 6, 1820, published on September 26. This norm, like the rest of the "triennial" legislation, was abolished on October 10, 1823, with the restoration of Absolutism. However, the suspension lasted only a few months. After the foreign occupation, the import ban was restored by the Circular February 17, 1824, published on February 26 (Montañés 2009, pp. 58–63 and 79–87; Vallejo 2018, pp. 66–69). The unique difference between the legislation of 1820/1824 and 1834 was the intervention prices, which were a little higher during the reign of Ferdinand VII: 80 Spanish reales/fanega and 120 Spanish reales/quintal.[15] Note that the trade policy was the only one on which absolutists

[14] *Quintal* was a unit of weight equivalent to 46 kilograms. For *real* and *fanega* supra.

[15] In fact, the 1820 legislation was not original either. It was only the update of the Pragmatic Sanction of July 11, 1765, in which a much lower level was set, 22 Spanish reales/fanega, and therefore useless given the price levels in the following decades.

and liberals agreed. Regarding the Cuban market, the first protective tariff for Spanish flour was also approved in the Trienio, the Real Decreto February 7, 1822, published on February 22. Later, tariff changes in Absolutism and Liberalism reinforced or relaxed that protection slightly.

The crucial fact is that in the approval of these policies there was no role for an alleged lobby of Cantabrian and Castilian entrepreneurs. When the tariffs of 1820 and 1822 were approved, business activity on the Reinosa route was irrelevant. In 1834, when the absolutist decree of 1824 was modified (downward), the flour business was growing but remained small. Hence, three years before, exports to Europe and America reached a peak of 38,000 Tm of wheat and "equivalent flour", a remarkable figure but still far from the export (and import) levels of the mid-nineteenth century.

Until the 1869 Figuerola Tariff Law, the essential lines of the prohibitionist legislation did not change. The political representatives of Cantabria, Palencia and the other provinces of *Castilla la Vieja* did not have any significant role in the discussions on trade policy. There are several reasons for the lack of an organized group that defended the demands of the milling industry. The first is their size, smaller than the banking and industrial groups in Madrid, Barcelona and Vizcaya. But the primary reason is that there was no need for an organized group. Deputies of inland provinces effectively defended the reserve of the national market (including Cuba). Medium and large landowners were the best represented social group in Parliament. They had identical interests to the Palencia flour companies and Santander merchants likewise many small business owners and, by reciprocity, the cotton industrialists of Barcelona. The only serious resistance against prohibitionism came from the governors of provinces with chronic shortages (such as Malaga and the Balearic Islands), the representatives of the island of Cuba (for obvious reasons) and some active exporting groups, such as the producers of refined wines from Western Andalusia (Montañés 2009, pp. 79–87, 114–126, 202–206, 224–232 and 271–273).

## 5.4 Conclusions

This chapter tries to fight against a common prejudice, that Spain has been a country of mercenary businessmen whose only goal was (and is) to extort money from the consumer. This supposition is ridiculous, not only for obvious psychological reasons but also because the alleged collusive practices were often not possible. At least, they were not in the set of industrial and commercial activities developed on the Reinosa route in the nineteenth century. A conservative and not very aggressive business attitude was dominant there. These manufacturers and merchants only made modest and beneficial speculations as wholesale price-accepters. There was no hoarding or cartelization since this would have involved too many risks. Lobbies did not exist because they were not necessary.

To conclude, two observations. First, I believe that semantic misunderstandings are at the base of most of the charges against the entrepreneurs. Monopoly, cartel and lobby are well-defined concepts that are still misused. The simple fact that there were great businessmen, or that they were rich, does not make them monopolists. As for speculation, defined as any dictionary does, what is wrong with it? Let us be compassionate with ourselves.

Second, anti-competitive practices are well known in the history of Spain. The insufficient development of capitalism and the putting in place of patriotic economic policies led to the rise of such techniques. But this took place in the twentieth century, and especially during early Francoism. Outside that dire period, the norm was something more or less like free competition (Serrano et al. 1978).

## References

Anes, Gonzalo. 1969. *Economía e Ilustración en la España del siglo XVIII*. Barcelona: Ariel.

Barquín, Rafael. 1999. El comercio de la harina entre Castilla y Santander y la crisis de subsistencia de 1856/57. In *Consumo, condiciones de vida y comercialización*, ed. Bartolomé Yun and Jaume Torras, 293–309. Valladolid: Junta de Castilla y León.

———. 2001. *Precios de trigo e índices de consumo en España. 1765–1883*. Burgos: University of Burgos.

———. 2003. El comercio exterior de trigo y harina y las crisis de subsistencias en España. *TST: Transportes, Servicios y telecomunicaciones* 5: 127–148.

———. 2011. El comercio de harina entre Castilla, Santander, Barcelona y Cuba: ¿Cártel o libre comercio? *Revista de Historia de la Economía y la Empresa* 5: 265–288.

———. 2019. Teoría, mito y realidad del acopio y la especulación. El comercio de trigo y harina en el norte de Castilla. In *Empresas y empresarios en España. De mercaderes a industriales*, coordinated by Juan Manuel Matés-Barco, 99–117. Madrid: Pirámide.

GEHR (Grupo de Estudios de Historia Rural). 1985. Los precios del trigo y la cebada en España 1874–1906. In *Historia agraria de la España Contemporánea. Tome II*, ed. Ramón Garrabou and Jesús Sanz, 321–368. Barcelona: Crítica.

Hoyo, Andrés. 1993. *Todo mudó de repente*. Santander: University of Cantabria.

———. 1999. Gestión comercial, precios y crisis de subsistencias en Castilla, 1820–1874. In *Consumo, condiciones de vida y comercialización*, ed. Bartolomé Yun and Jaume Torras, 275–292. Valladolid: Junta de Castilla y León.

*La Crisis Agrícola y Pecuaria*, 1887–89. Madrid: Sucesores de Rivadeneyra.

López Morales, Blas. 1856. *La cuestión de subsistencias*. Valladolid.

Maluquer, Jordi. 1983. La despatrimonialización del agua: movilización de un recurso natural fundamental. *Revista de Historia Económica* I (2): 79–96.

McCloskey, Donald N., and John Nash. 1984. Corn at Interest: The Extent and Cost of Grain Storage in Medieval England. *American Economic Review* 74 (1): 174–192.

Montañés, Enrique. 2009. *Grupos de presión y reformas arancelarias en el régimen liberal, 1820–1870*. Cádiz: University of Cádiz.

Moreno, Javier. 1991. La fiebre harinera castellana. La historia de un sueño industrial (1841–1864). In *Estudios sobre capitalismo agrario, crédito e industria en Castilla (siglos XIX y XX)*, coordinated by Bartolomé Yun, 161–202. Valladolid: Junta de Castilla y León.

———. 1995. Protección arancelaria, distorsiones de mercado y beneficios extraordinarios: La producción de harinas en Castilla la Vieja. 1820–1841. *Revista de Historia Económica* XIII (2): 227–250.

———. 1996. Empresas y empresarios castellanos en el negocio de la harina, 1778–1913. In *La empresa en la Historia de España*, ed. Francisco Comín and Pablo Martín Aceña, 187–202. Madrid: Civitas.

———. 2002. La harinería castellana y el capitalismo agrario en el tránsito a la industrialización. *Historia Agraria* 27: 165–189.

———. 2006. Factor empresarial y atraso económico en Castilla y León (siglos XIX y XX). In *Historia Empresarial de España. Un enfoque regional en profundidad*, directed by José Luis García and Carles Manera, 315–336. Madrid: LID.

———. 2018. Los harinócratas. Organizaciones, mercado e inquietudes inversoras de los empresarios de Castilla la Vieja y León, 1820–1868. *Investigaciones de Historia Económica* 14: 11–22.

Ratier, Luis. 1848. *Anuario Estadístico de la Administración y el Comercio de la Provincia de Santander*. Valladolid.

Serrano, Ángel, Santiago Roldán, and Juan Muñoz. 1978. La involución nacionalista y la vertebración del capitalismo español. *Cuadernos económicos de ICE* 5: 13–221.

Sierra, Luis María. 1845. *Cuestión de harinas. Contestación al Sr. D. Mariano Torrente*. Santander: Imprenta de Martínez.

Torrente, Mariano. 1853. *Bosquejo económico político de la Isla de Cuba. Tomo II*. La Habana: Barcina.

Vallejo, Rafael. 2018. La política comercial liberal desde 1820 a 1869. Entre la apertura exterior y las resistencias prohibicionistas. *Áreas* 37: 61–77.

CHAPTER 6

# Wine Entrepreneurs in Nineteenth-Century Cádiz: Pedro Lacave Miramont

*María Vázquez-Fariñas*

## 6.1 Introduction

The city of Cádiz has a long tradition of trade, in which sherry wines have always played a prominent role. Around the middle of the eighteenth century, the traditional viticulture in the area began the process of transformation into a modern wine agribusiness. The notable expansion entailed numerous advances involving the ageing of the wines, storage, the vertical integration of the business and the construction of large wineries (Maldonado Rosso 1996, pp. 17–21). Many great wineries were founded in Cádiz during that time, such as *Manuel Moreno de Mora*, *Lacoste & Company*, *J. Díaz Tezanos & Company*, *Guillermo Shaw & Company* and *Aranda & Cesteros*, among others (Ravina Martín 2011, pp. 132–283). Especially significant players in the Cádiz wine business were the Lacave family, the Gómez family and the Abarzuza family. All three enjoyed a leading position in the national and international markets, and had a wide

M. Vázquez-Fariñas (✉)
University of Jaén, Jaén, Spain
e-mail: mfarinas@ujaen.es



M. Vázquez-Fariñas et al. (eds.), *Companies and Entrepreneurs in the History of Spain*, Palgrave Studies in Economic History,
https://doi.org/10.1007/978-3-030-61318-1_6

variety of wines in their products portfolio (Vázquez-Fariñas and Maldonado Rosso 2017).

This chapter is focused on the Lacave family; more specifically, on Pedro Lacave Miramont and the commercial activity of his company, *Lacave & Echecopar*. To that end, the company's internal information, stored in the Lacave Archive, which the family donated to the Historical Wine Studies Unit of the University of Cádiz in 1996 has been used. By studying the company accounts, direct knowledge of the structure of the company and the actions and strategies developed has been gained. Nevertheless, there are long time gaps in the series of data preserved in this archive; thus, this issue has been attempted to address using external information, such as the documentary records in the Provincial Historical Archive of Cádiz (the deeds for the foundation, renewal and dissolution of companies), or the registers and censuses of foreigners in the Municipal Historical Archive. Print documentation, such as newspapers, official reports and export lists have been especially interesting for gaining an understanding of the historical context of Pedro Lacave's company and the individuals related to it. In addition, publications such as the *Partes de Vigía*[1] have proven to be an invaluable source of information on the trade figures for the Port of Cádiz. Lastly, an issue of the Spanish magazine *El Álbum Nacional* dedicated to *Lacave & Company* is conserved, detailing its activity and the volume of production and sale of wines. Drawing on these sources, the very interesting case of Pedro Lacave Miramont's business in the first half of the nineteenth century has been studied, as well as the strategies implemented to maintain the company's position in a constantly changing market. Furthermore, given the lack of studies on this businessman and his wine company, this chapter adds to the knowledge on the business and economic life of the city of Cádiz in the nineteenth century.

## 6.2 The Beginning of the Business (1804–1830)

Pedro Lacave Miramont was born in 1776 in the French town of Navarrenx in the Department of Basses-Pyrénées (now Pyrénées-Atlantiques). He was the sixth of the eleven children of Juan Lacave and Catalina Miramont,

[1] This source provides us with detailed information about the state of trade in the Port of Cádiz, as these reports include complete information on the entry and exit of ships, as well as imports and exports (Gullón Abao and Fortela Miguélez 1994).

both farmers in Navarrenx (Lacave Ravina 2009). Little is known of his childhood, only that around 1787, at the age of eleven, he came to Cádiz to work in the trade with his uncle Juan Miramont and his cousin Lucas Miramont (Ruiz Rivera 1988, p. 185). His arrival in Cádiz coincides with the issuance of two decrees to expel French citizens, the first in 1791 and the second in 1793, in response to the revolutionary movement that had begun in France a few years earlier (Bustos Rodríguez 2005, pp. 108 and 147). From 1791 on, Pedro Lacave appears in the register as a resident of Cádiz,[2] under the protection of his relatives, thus fulfilling the conditions stipulated by the government for the French to be allowed to stay in the city.[3]

He started his business at a critical time in Cádiz. The first difficulties affecting trade began in the 1790s, as a result of the war against Great Britain. The blockade of the Port of Cádiz by the British starting in 1796 caused many businesses to suffer a noticeable contraction and many merchants left the city (García-Baquero González 1972, pp. 133–134), leading to a stage of economic stagnation.

After the signing of the Peace Treaty of Amiens in 1802, trade in Cádiz returned to normal with an increase in exports and the resumption of overseas trade relations. But there was a return to conflict in 1805, fighting against France in the Battle of Trafalgar. As a result, business stagnated once again, a situation that would last until the middle of 1808, thus overlapping with the outbreak of the Spanish War of Independence. The shift in alliance, however, allowed the Cádiz merchants to develop their businesses under a degree of security provided by the British Navy (Cózar Navarro 2012), thus boosting port activity in the city. In spite of this, Cádiz remained in a critical stage in terms of commerce, as business and trade were strongly affected by all the political events of the time.

Notwithstanding the difficulties, Pedro Lacave managed to gain entry into the business world. In August 1804, he joined with Hugo and Juan Macdermot under the corporate name of *Hugo Macdermot & Company* for a period of three years.[4] Hugo and Juan Macdermot were capitalist partners who took on Pedro Lacave as an industrial partner in recognition

[2] Municipal Historical Archive of Cádiz (hereinafter MHAC). *Register Section L1000*, 1791.

[3] The decrees to expel the French were aimed at preventing revolutionary propaganda and ensuring the loyalty of foreigners. The government decreed that those who wished to remain in Spain must prove their residence.

[4] Provincial Historical Archive of Cádiz (hereinafter PHAC), Notary 1, 1804, file 49, 632–639.

of his previous years of work as an employee in Hugo Macdermot's business, as well as his experience in commercial practice (Vázquez-Fariñas 2017).

In 1810, in the midst of the French siege, Pedro Lacave opened his own business, partnering again with Hugo Macdermot under the name of *Lacave & Company*. Their business was dedicated to the trade of colonial products and shipping agency services, especially for British ships, which allowed them to establish commercial relations with the rest of Europe and expand their network of contacts (Vázquez-Fariñas 2018, p. 75). By this time, Pedro Lacave was already involved in the wine business; he exported 35 hectolitres (hereinafter, hl) of wine in 1811, and 7155 hl in 1820, which represents an increase in annual exports of 7120 hl in just nine years (Greiner Gindroz 1897, pp. 18 and 78).

Moreover, his marriage in 1821 to Ana María Lacoste Salazar, a member of a prominent winemaking family from Jerez de la Frontera (Cádiz), helped improve his business and socio-economic standing (Vázquez-Fariñas 2017). His father-in-law, Bernardo-Luis Lacoste, was one of the merchants who drove the development of the wine business in the province of Cádiz in the late eighteenth century, by establishing large wineries and increasing the volume of exports to Great Britain, expanding the market for sherry wines (Maldonado Rosso 1999, p. 261). Matrimonial alliances had assumed an important role in mercantile Cádiz, since marriage was a fundamental way of securing financing, reinforcing the power of companies and preventing the dispersion of the family fortune (Cózar Navarro 2007, pp. 42–43). As such, this union was an indication of the social prestige and economic level achieved by Pedro Lacave, who not only strengthened his relationships and interests, but also linked himself to a family with a history and a prominent position in mercantile Cádiz.

During all those years, he gradually accumulated social prestige and ever-greater wealth, due to the expansion and growth of his business activities. After the death of his partner Hugo Macdermot in 1824, Pedro Lacave continued his business alone until, in 1830, he decided to go into business with Juan-Pablo Echecopar Jaureguiberry, who was his countryman and nephew-in-law (Vázquez-Fariñas 2020, p. 31).

## 6.3 The Family Business: *Lacave & Echecopar* (1830–1851)

This new stage began in 1830, when Pedro Lacave Miramont and Juan-Pablo Echecopar Jaureguiberry formed a partnership. The latter was born on 31 March 1791 in Libarrenx, a French town in the Department of Basses-Pyrénées. He was the son of Lorenzo Echecopar and Mariana Jaureguiberry, both of whom were French. He arrived in Cádiz around 1830[5] and in 1831, in Jerez de la Frontera, he married Margarita Josefa Capdepon Lacoste,[6] daughter of Juan-Bautista Capdepon and María Josefa Lacoste Salazar, once again creating a union between members of prominent families in the business world to protect their wealth and family heritage. Seven children[7] were born of this marriage, and the first-born, Eduardo, would also be part of the family business in the second half of the century.

In terms of the business, the two partners set up the companies *Lacave & Echecopar* and *J. P. Echecopar & Company* in Cádiz and Gibraltar, respectively, dedicated to general trade.[8] The choice of Gibraltar was not made at random; this British colony had become a major trade hub of great strategic value due to its geographical location between the Atlantic Ocean and the Mediterranean Sea (Sánchez Mantero 1989, p. 20). Moreover, it provided the perfect platform for introducing goods into Spain, as protectionism was an obstacle to British exports to Spain, giving rise to the smuggling of British goods (García León 1991, p. 205). In short, the volume of trade registered and the strategic position of its port made Gibraltar an ideal place from which to export products and try to expand commercial activities.

On 13 March 1830, the general partnership[9] *Lacave & Echecopar* was formed, in which the two partners were also responsible for the

[5] MHAC, *Register Section L2016*, 1875.

[6] Margarita Josefa Capdepon Lacoste was the niece of Ana María Lacoste, the wife of Pedro Lacave Miramont.

[7] PHAC, Notary 2, 1877, file 650, 5210–5215.

[8] PHAC, Notary 14, 1830, file 3206, 452–453.

[9] The Commercial Code of 1829 does not provide an exact definition of a general partnership, but it does point out that it had to operate under the name of all or one of the partners, and that all those who formed the company would be jointly and severally liable for the results of the operations carried out under the company signature, regardless of whether or not they were administrators of the capital (Arts. 266 and 267).

administration. The deeds do not record the amount of the share capital, merely stating that Pedro Lacave contributed wines stored in Jerez de la Frontera, wood, iron, pending expeditions to America, *vales reales* (government bonds) and some real estate, but the company's general ledger indicates that this capital amounted to 1,620,408.1 *reales de vellón* (hereinafter rv).[10] In both the company in Cádiz and the one in Gibraltar, two-thirds (66.67%) of profits and losses corresponded to Pedro Lacave, and one-third (33.33%) to Juan-Pablo Echecopar. In addition, 15,000 rv were allocated annually to Pedro and 10,000 to Juan-Pablo for their respective personal expenses. Moreover, neither of them could undertake other business on their own account, meaning that they both assumed an exclusive commitment to the business. With these characteristics, the duration of the company was set at three years.

At this point, it is worth introducing Pedro Lacave Mulé, the nephew of Pedro Lacave Miramont, who had come over from France to begin learning the trade. At that time, the person selected to succeed a business-owner was prepared for the role by sending him to university, abroad, to a company outside the family, or introducing him to the family business from a young age (Díaz Morlán 2013, p. 27). This last practice was the one most commonly used by the Lacave family, with the relationship between the partners constituting an element of trust, security, loyalty and allegiance, which guaranteed the future of the business.

During the first three years, the company built up substantial business in Cádiz, a city undergoing major economic and entrepreneurial growth; this growth was reflected in the arrival of businessmen, new investments and the emergence of many companies, most of which were dedicated to trade (Cózar Navarro 2003, pp. 142–147). In March 1833, the partners renewed the company for a further four years under the same terms and conditions, except for each partner's stake in the profits and losses, which was changed to 60% for Pedro Lacave and 40% for Juan-Pablo Echecopar.[11] According to the general ledgers, the share capital now amounted to 3,050,179.32 rv, a considerable increase that reflects the good performance of the company as it benefitted from the economic expansion that the city was undergoing, with an upward trend in trade, especially wine (Cózar Navarro 1998, p. 27).

[10] *Lacave & Echecopar General Ledger*, 1830–1835.

[11] PHAC, Notary 14, 1833, file 3212, 298–301.

Indeed, there was continuing growth in the wine business in those years, with a notable increase in the exports of sherry wines. This trend was fostered by the rise in British demand and the reduction in extraction rights in Spain, but above all by the production of wines that were popular with consumers (Maldonado Rosso 1999, pp. 301–318). *Lacave & Echecopar* also took part in that expansion. Pedro Lacave's experience as a shipping agent in the Port of Cádiz gave him an important competitive edge, as he used his extensive network of contacts to export his wine products on advantageous terms and without having to rely on shipping agents outside the company. He also drew on these relationships to secure orders for his company (Vázquez-Fariñas and Maldonado Rosso 2017, pp. 101–103). The volume of overseas sales of *Lacave & Echecopar* wine reflects the fact that the company had swiftly gained a foothold in an emerging market (Fig. 6.1). In 1831, there was a slight decline in exports, dropping from 9180 hl in 1830 to 7605 hl the following year, which is not surprising given that they were starting up the business. However, they soon recovered: in 1833, their exports had grown to 11,330 hl per year. After another decline in 1835, the volume of sales rapidly rebounded to 13,840 hl in 1838, the year registering the highest growth in the entire period analysed. The figures in the 1840s show relative stability, with the exception of 1847 and 1849, when there were slight decreases, although

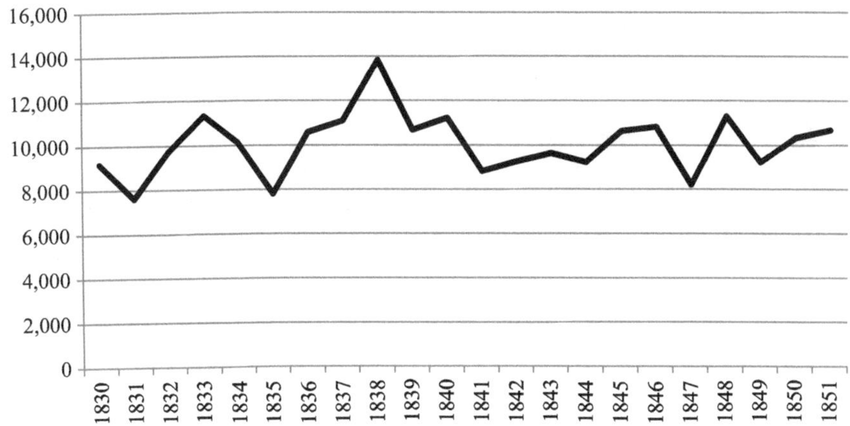


**Fig. 6.1** Wine exports by *Lacave & Echecopar*, 1830–1851 (hectolitres). (*Source*: Authors, based on Greiner Gindroz 1897, p. 78)

in those years the volume never fell below 8000 hl per year. Between 1830 and 1851, the total exports of *Lacave & Echecopar* amounted to 221,307 hl, a fairly substantial figure for a company that had only been in business for a few years.

In this context of business growth, in March 1837, a deed of renewal[12] was granted, incorporating Pedro Lacave Mulé as an industrial partner, thus continuing his process of learning the family business. He was given the use of the company signature[13] and awarded 500 *pesos* a year in recognition of the work he had been doing. The company was thus renewed for two more years.

In the early 1840s, Cádiz remained at the forefront of Spanish commercial activity; the structure of trade had changed and the predominant products in the Cádiz economy were now wine and salt. Exports of wine products became especially important due to the land liberalization policy, the increase in prices and the rise in demand from Northern Europe, particularly from England (Cózar Navarro 2007, p. 37). In addition, this growth in foreign demand for wines, coupled with the modernization of maritime and land transport, greatly facilitated the trade of these products in the Bay of Cádiz (Maldonado Rosso 1992, pp. 25–26).

In the midst of this economic boom that the city was witnessing, the partners decided to focus on the wine business. In 1843, they formalized a new deed to continue their activities under the corporate name of *Lacave & Echecopar* in Cádiz, *Juan Pablo Echecopar & Company* in Gibraltar and *Echecopar & Company* in El Puerto de Santa María.[14] The main objective of the seat in Cádiz was general trade, in El Puerto de Santa María it was dedicated to the extraction and trade of wines, and in Gibraltar to general commissions. In recognition of the work that Pedro Lacave Mulé had been doing in the company, he was promoted to a capitalist partner,[15] and the three partners became equally responsible for the administration of the company and the use of the company signature. The amount of the share capital is unknown, but in all three establishments Pedro Lacave Miramont

[12] PHAC, Notary 14, 1837, file 3224, 414–417.

[13] Unlike the capitalist partner, the industrial partner did not contribute capital to the company, only his work. However, Pedro Lacave Mulé was jointly and severally liable for the results of the operations he did on behalf of the company, under its signature, as he was authorized to use it (Commercial Code 1829, Art. 267).

[14] PHAC, Notary 14, 1843, file 3243, 1622–1625.

[15] From then on, Pedro Lacave Mulé had a stake in the share capital and was therefore entitled to the distribution of dividends.

had a 45% share of profits and losses, Juan-Pablo Echecopar had 35%, and Pedro Lacave Mulé had 20%. In addition, the company would pay 15,000 rv annually to the founding members, and 10,000 rv to Pedro Lacave Mulé for personal expenses, and none of the members could undertake any business or liability outside of the company.

During those years, the main export houses were formed, as the mercantile boom attracted numerous businessmen who settled in the province of Cádiz, such as Julián Pemartín, the Abarzuza brothers, Benito Picardo y Picardo, Miguel Martínez de Pinillos and Juan-Pablo Lasanta Herreros, among others (Cózar Navarro 2007, pp. 40–42). *Lacave & Echecopar* also benefited from this expansion, as it had managed to position itself among the main producers of sherry, along with other prominent extractors, such as Duff and Gordon, Domecq or Hauries Bourdon (Siegrist de Gentile 1992, p. 56).

It is worth noting the opening of *Echecopar & Company* in El Puerto de Santa María, an exceptional wine region where large wineries had been established in the preceding decade. These wineries prompted a rise in wine production and made this activity the driving force behind the commercial development of the city from then on (Borrego Plá 1986, pp. 460–461). In those years, *Echecopar & Company* sold their wines to London and Liverpool (England), Dublin (Ireland), Montevideo (Uruguay), Gothenburg (Sweden), Elsinore (Denmark) and Valparaiso (Chile). Their production and sales figures varied widely in the mid-1840s (Table 6.1). In 1844, they sold 23,544.18 hl of wines abroad, an amount that rose to 77,263.27 hl in 1845, before dropping again in the following years. Between 1844 and 1854, the company exported a total of 207,330.62 hl from their wineries in El Puerto de Santa María. This figure is relatively low if we compare it with some of the most prominent houses of the era, such as that of Juan Guillermo Burdon, which shipped 12,773,852.67 hl overseas in the same period; *Duff Gordon & Company*, with 9,370,319.85 hl; or *Díaz Merello & Company*, with 6,448,111.90 hl.

In parallel with the development of its wine business, the company had become extremely dynamic by the late 1840s; the partners were involved in different businesses, such as banking, shipping agency services, textiles and mining, among others, implementing a clear strategy of business diversification, spreading the risk of their investments (Vázquez-Fariñas 2020, pp. 42–43). This practice was fairly standard among the Cádiz merchants, who diversified their businesses primarily in order to secure their capital and generate more income (Ramos Santana 1992, pp. 97–100).

**Table 6.1** *Echecopar & Company* wine exports, 1844–1854[a]

| *Year* | *Exports (arrobas)* | *Exports (hectolitres)* |
|---|---|---|
| 1844 | 1486.00 | 23,544.18 |
| 1845 | 4876.50 | 77,263.27 |
| 1846 | 605.50 | 9593.54 |
| 1847 | 2197.00 | 34,809.27 |
| 1848 | 1182.75 | 18,739.49 |
| 1849 | 579.75 | 9185.56 |
| 1850 | 545.75 | 8646.86 |
| 1851 | 452.00 | 7161.49 |
| 1852 | – | – |
| 1853 | 367.50 | 5822.67 |
| 1854 | 793.00 | 12,564.29 |
| Total | 13,085.75 | 207,330.62 |

*Source*: Authors, based on Lists of exports from El Puerto de Santa María, 1844–1854

[a]The figures are expressed in arrobas (@), but we have converted them to hectolitres according to the equivalent value in the mid-nineteenth century: 1 @ = 15,844 litres (Lepore 2010, p. 21)

As we know, one of the main activities of *Lacave & Echecopar* was providing shipping agency services in the Port of Cádiz. The company worked primarily with American frigates and brigantines, and brought in—from North America and England, respectively—the wooden staves and the iron strips needed to make the barrels for its wineries.[16] This activity not only formed part of the diversification strategy, but also the vertical integration of the business, as it allowed them to access supplies of the goods they needed, in addition to placing their products and securing orders in the foreign market without relying on outside shipping agents (Maldonado Rosso 1999, p. 335). We do not know the percentage commission they charged for this business, but it provided them with an extra income in addition to that earned through the sale of wines. Furthermore, it enabled them to reduce distribution costs in the Port of Cádiz.

The partners had started this move towards diversification some years earlier. In March 1841, they teamed up with Charles Pickman, a London merchant based in Seville, to set up a pottery factory in the Andalusian capital (Maestre de León 1993, p. 26). Similarly, in July 1844, they took

[16] *Partes Oficiales de Vigía*, 1845–1852.

joint ownership, together with other entrepreneurs, of the mining company *La Gaditana*, to operate a mineral smelting plant in the province of Almería.[17]

In addition, during that time they created the limited partnership[18] *Juan Pedro Lacave & Company* in Seville, specializing first in the commission business, and a few years later in the production of cereals, olive oil, olives and corks. To do so, they called on the collaboration of Juan-Pedro Lacave Soulé, another of Pedro Lacave Miramont's nephews, who had come over from France to settle in the Andalusian capital and develop his business career from there (Álvarez Pantoja 1989, p. 206). This company was a pioneer in its sector, as it was one of the first companies in the region's cork industry, achieving a prominent role in international trade through the manufacture and sale of cork stoppers and other manufactured products, such as sawdust and panels (Arenas Posadas 1995, p. 154). The emergence of companies like this is due to the development of the cork-stopper industry in the south and south-west of Spain in the middle of the century, driven by the lack of cork in Girona. Up to that point, Girona had enjoyed absolute hegemony in the sector, although it gradually lost its dominance to the benefit of other regions (Zapata Blanco 1996, p. 45).

In 1847, they became involved in the textile sector, establishing together with other merchants a woollen mill called *Los Amigos*, also in Seville (Madoz 1849, p. 406).

Thus, the city of Seville constituted one of the basic pillars for the development of the strategy of business diversification, as it offered multiple business opportunities. Indeed, it was considered an emerging city, and would go on to bolster its industrial role in the mid-nineteenth century (Rueda et al. 2008).

In addition to the above, the company ledgers show that *Lacave & Echecopar* held an ownership stake in a number of other companies: *Empresa Gaditana del Trocadero*, *Empresa Fabril Gaditana*, *Empresa del camino de hierro de Jerez al Puerto, Rota y Sanlúcar* and *Tabacos Ygueravide*.[19]

[17] PHAC, Notary 3, 1844, file 822, 882–894.

[18] Unlike collective partnerships, in limited partnerships, the partners who managed and directed the company, or those who were included in the company's corporate name, were jointly and severally liable for the results of all operations (Commercial Code 1829, Art. 270).

[19] *Lacave & Echecopar General Ledger*, 1845–1849.

It can be seen that, by the 1840s, the company had grown to include Pedro-Luis Lacave Soulé—another of the nephews of the main partner who had come over from France—with a minority stake in the company. Since the late eighteenth century, individual and family businesses had dominated the business landscape, as the family had become the main source of physical and human capital, providing both financing and trusted employees as needed (Valdaliso Gago and López García 2000, pp. 198–199). The human resources were thus crucial in order to consolidate the business in family companies (Fernández Pérez 2005, p. 455). In this sense, Pedro Lacave's nephews were a determining factor in the smooth running of the company, as they provided it with valuable human capital, occupying positions of responsibility at different key times for the expansion of its business.

In 1848, Pedro Lacave Miramont, Juan-Pablo Echecopar, Pedro Lacave Mulé and Pedro-Luis Lacave Soulé signed a new company deed to conduct their businesses solely out of the seat in Cádiz, under the same corporate name of *Lacave & Echecopar*, dedicated to general trade and the commission business.[20] As with the previous deeds, this one does not provide the figure for the share capital. Pedro Lacave Miramont had a 38% share in profit and loss, Juan-Pablo Echecopar had 30%, Pedro Lacave Mulé had 18% and Pedro-Luis Lacave Soulé, 14%. In addition, Pedro Lacave Miramont and Juan-Pablo Echecopar were given 20,000 rv a year for their personal expenses, while Pedro Lacave Mulé and Pedro-Luis Lacave Soulé were assigned 10,000 rv. Another new development was that the company seat in Gibraltar ceased to be part of the firm. It was stipulated that Juan-Pablo Echecopar could continue on his own account and in his own name, the commission business of this establishment under the corporate name of *Juan Pablo Echecopar & Company*. The duration of the company was again set at four years, until 31 December 1852.

Following the signing of this deed, there was a major shift in the company, as the partners decided to centralize their wine business in Cádiz (Vázquez-Fariñas 2018, p. 79). They came up with the idea of creating a winery in the capital to integrate the entire process of production, marketing and sale of their products, thus saving production costs. To that end, they began to purchase properties in the area known as Segunda Aguada, in the Extramuros neighbourhood in Cádiz. This process of centralizing business management in one place was notably innovative for its time.

[20] PHAC, Notary 14, 1848, file 3258, 1236–1240.

They purchased a number of farms and plots of land, where they built several wineries, warehouses and even their own iron quay with a crane, which was to be used exclusively at the service of their warehouses and wineries (Greiner Gindroz 1897, p. 34). Moreover, a few years later, they sold some of their properties to carry out works on the State railways, which, together with the construction of their own quay, would give them a huge competitive advantage. Their strategic location, by the sea and with the railway running past its facilities, enabled them to easily send out their products and acquire raw materials and other goods (Vázquez-Fariñas and Maldonado Rosso 2017, pp. 103–104).

All these investments show the trend towards the vertical integration of the company, in an attempt to control the entire wine production process, from the sourcing of raw materials, through the production and preparation of wines, to the transport, distribution and sale of the end product in different markets. By situating the warehouses and externalities in one place, they saved costs, making the production process more efficient and increasing business profits. Thus, over the following years they gradually managed to integrate all the stages of the wine production process into a single business.

As such, these were years of growth and business prosperity, but it was during this golden age that Pedro Lacave Miramont died, in September 1850. However, his death did not lead to the dissolution of the company, as the partners continued on in the company for the rest of the duration established in the deeds. His widow, Ana María Lacoste, then came into the entity to represent him, highlighting the role that women had started to play in business by that time. In the following years, the partners continued to develop their diversification strategy, notably their banking activity, the commission business, the shipping agency services in the Port of Cádiz, and investments in real estate aimed at expanding their facilities (Vázquez-Fariñas 2020, pp. 54–70).

As a result of all this, the Lacave and Echecopar families formed part of Cádiz's elite merchant class throughout the nineteenth century, managing to position their company among the main ones of the time, and enjoying great national and international importance.

## 6.4 Conclusions

Over the course of this chapter, we have seen that Pedro Lacave Miramont developed a remarkable business in the wine sector in the first half of the nineteenth century, through his company *Lacave & Echecopar*. The role of the founder was fundamental to the success of this company, a family business model that, thanks to the management of human capital and the strategies developed, was able to hold its place in a constantly changing market.

It has been shown that, around the mid-nineteenth century, the company considered the wine business its main activity. However, like many contemporary businessmen, the partners adopted a clear strategy of diversifying their businesses in order to secure their capital and achieve higher income (the cork and oil factory in Seville, *Juan Pedro Lacave & Company*; the Sevillian pottery manufacturing company *Pickman & Company*; the mining company *La Gaditana*, and the woollen mill in Seville, *Los Amigos*, among others), which endowed the company with great dynamism.

At the same time, they strove to integrate the wine business, controlling the extraction, production, transport and distribution in the market. Thanks to these strategies, *Lacave & Echecopar* managed to cope with the changes in the market, and thus was able to deal with both the competition and the situation in the sector. It adapted to the circumstances and characteristics of each era and moulded the organization over time, an indication of great flexibility and adaptability to the market.

Despite the death of the main partner, which in other cases could be a major setback for the business, the other partners managed to continue the business and diversification strategy, dedicating themselves to the commission business and speculation in staves, iron, wines and spirits, while developing the banking business and shipping agency services. They also continued their acquisition of warehouses and wineries that had begun before the founder's death, aimed at creating their large business complex in Cádiz. Therefore, human capital—more specifically, the founder's nephews—constituted a fundamental factor in the consolidation of a hugely successful project, which became one of the most important wine-exporting companies nationally and internationally, and created a weighty historical tradition.

## Sources

### Manuscripts

#### Lacave Archive

*Lacave & Echecopar General Ledger*, 1830–1835 and 1845–1849.

#### Municipal Historical Archive of Cádiz

L1000 (1791). Register of foreign residents, Barrio de la Cruz Verde.
L2016 (1875). General register of residents, Barrio de San Francisco y San Carlos.

#### Provincial Historical Archive of Cádiz

Notary No. 1: File No. 49.
Notary No. 2: File No. 650.
Notary No. 3: File No. 822.
Notary No. 14: File No. 3206, 3212, 3224, 3243, 3258.

#### Regulatory Council of the Denominations of Origin "Jerez-Xérès-Sherry", "Manzanilla-Sanlúcar de Barrameda" and "Vinagre de Jerez"

Lists of exports from El Puerto de Santa María, 1844–1855.

#### Biblioteca Unicaja de Temas Gaditanos "Juvencio Maeztu"

Partes Oficiales de Vigía, 1845–1852.

### Print Documents

Commercial Code, 1829.

## References


Álvarez Pantoja, María José. 1989. Banqueros privados en la Sevilla del siglo XIX: Juan Pedro Lacave. *Archivo hispalense: Revista histórica, literaria y artística* 219: 199–218.

Arenas Posadas, Carlos. 1995. *Sevilla y el Estado (1892–1923). Una perspectiva local de la formación del capitalismo en España*. Seville: Publicaciones de la Universidad de Sevilla and Fundación Fondo de Cultura de Sevilla.

Borrego Plá, María del Carmen. 1986. El comercio del vino y el Puerto de Santa María en la crisis del noventa y ocho. In *Andalucía y América en el siglo XIX: Actas de las V Jornadas de Andalucía y América, vol. 1*, coordinated by Bibiano Torres Ramírez and José J. Hernández Palomo, 455–478. Seville: Consejo Superior de Investigaciones Científicas (CSIC) and Escuela de Estudios Hispano-Americanos (EEHA).

Bustos Rodríguez, Manuel. 2005. *Cádiz en el sistema atlántico. La ciudad, sus comerciantes y la actividad mercantil (1650–1830)*. Madrid: Sílex.

Cózar Navarro, María del Carmen. 1998. *Ignacio Fernández de Castro y Cía. Una empresa naviera gaditana*. Cádiz: Servicio de publicaciones de la Universidad de Cádiz.

———. 2003. El tejido empresarial en la ciudad de Cádiz. *Revista de Estudios Regionales* 67: 139–166.

———. 2007. La actividad comercial en la bahía de Cádiz durante el reinado de Isabel II. *TST: Transportes, Servicios y Telecomunicaciones* 13: 34–60.

———. 2012. Comerciantes y empresarios en el Cádiz sitiado por Napoleón. *Revista Parques Empresariales, Industriales y Tecnológicos* 33: 16–17.

Díaz Morlán, Pablo. 2013. La sucesión de las empresas familiares británicas y españolas en los siglos XIX y XX. El papel del mérito, la formación y el aprendizaje. In *La profesionalización de las empresas familiares*, coordinated by Paloma Fernández Pérez, 17–33. Madrid: LID.

Fernández Pérez, Paloma. 2005. Redes familiares e innovación tecnológica en la España de fines del siglo XIX: los casos de José María Quijano y François Rivière. *Revista Historia Contemporánea* 31: 439–456.

García León, José María. 1991. Consideraciones económicas sobre Cádiz durante el Trienio Constitucional. *Trocadero: Revista de Historia Moderna y Contemporánea* 3: 199–210.

García-Baquero González, Antonio. 1972. *Comercio colonial y guerras revolucionarias. La decadencia económica de Cádiz a raíz de la emancipación americana*. Seville: Publicaciones de la Escuela de Estudios Hispano-Americanos.

Greiner Gindroz, Edmundo. 1897. Los vinos finos de España y la Casa Lacave y Compañía, Cádiz. *El Álbum Nacional, revista ilustrada. Serie de números dedicados a la industria y al fomento de la producción española*.

Gullón Abao, Alberto José, and María José Fortela Miguélez. 1994. Los partes oficiales de la Vigía de Cádiz: análisis y posibilidades de una fuente (1890). *Baluarte: Estudios gaditano-cubanos* 1: 63–78.

Lacave Ravina, Javier. 2009. Pedro Lacave Miramón. *Revista Hades* 7: 18–19.

Lepore, Amedeo. 2010. *Mercado y empresa en Europa. La empresa González de la Sierra en el comercio gaditano entre los siglos XVIII y XIX*. Cádiz: Servicio de Publicaciones de la Universidad de Cádiz.

Madoz, Pascual. 1849. *Diccionario geográfico-estadístico-histórico de España y sus posesiones de Ultramar, volumen XIV*. Madrid.

Maestre de León, Beatriz. 1993. *La Cartuja de Sevilla: Fábrica de Cerámica*. Seville: Pickman.

Maldonado Rosso, Javier. 1992. Consideraciones sobre la participación del vino en la economía del Marco del Jerez y de la Bahía de Cádiz. In *Solera: Exposición sobre los Vinos de Nuestra Tierra. Catálogo*, directed by Javier Maldonado Rosso and Alberto Ramos Santana, 18–28. Seville: Consejería de Cultura de la Junta de Andalucía.

———. 1996. Génesis de las vinaterías jerezana y sanluqueña contemporáneas. In *El jerez-xérès-sherry en los tres últimos siglos*, coordinated by Alberto Ramos Santana and Javier Maldonado Rosso, 11–28. Cádiz: Ayuntamiento de El Puerto de Santa María,

———. 1999. *La formación del capitalismo en el marco del Jerez: de la vitivinicultura tradicional a la agroindustria vinatera moderna (siglos XVIII y XIX)*. Madrid: Huerga y Fierro Editores.

Ramos Santana, Alberto. 1992. *Historia de Cádiz, vol. III. Cádiz en el siglo XIX. De ciudad soberana a capital de provincia*. Madrid: Sílex.

Ravina Martín, Manuel. 2011. *Catálogo de las compañías mercantiles de Cádiz (siglo XIX)*. Cádiz: Consejería de Cultura de la Junta de Andalucía.

Rueda, Germán, Luis Sazatornil, and Carmen Delgado. 2008. *Las principales ciudades portuarias en la España del siglo XIX*. Paper presented at the *IX Congreso Internacional de la Asociación Española de Historia Económica*, Murcia, Spain, September 9–12.

Ruiz Rivera, Julián Bautista. 1988. *El Consulado de Cádiz: Matrícula de comerciantes (1730–1823)*. Cádiz: Diputación Provincial de Cádiz.

Sánchez Mantero, Rafael. 1989. *Estudios sobre Gibraltar: política, diplomacia y contrabando en el siglo XIX*. Cádiz: Diputación Provincial de Cádiz.

Siegrist de Gentile, Nora L. 1992. *José Joaquín de Mora y su manuscrito sobre la industria y el comercio de España hacia 1850*. Cádiz: Servicio de Publicaciones de la Universidad de Cádiz.

Valdaliso Gago, Jesús María, and Santiago López García. 2000. *Historia económica de la empresa*. Barcelona: Crítica.

Vázquez-Fariñas, María. 2017. *El negocio del vino en el Cádiz del siglo XIX: Las Bodegas Lacave*. PhD diss., University of Cádiz.

———. 2018. La industria vinícola en el Cádiz decimonónico. Lacave y Echecopar: bodegueros y consignatarios marítimos. *TST: Transportes, Servicios y telecomunicaciones* 37: 70–90.

———. 2020. El negocio del vino en la ciudad de Cádiz. Historia empresarial de Lacave y Compañía, 1810–1927. Madrid: Marcial Pons.

Vázquez-Fariñas, María, and Javier Maldonado Rosso. 2017. Cádiz, ciudad vinatera entre mediados de los siglos XIX y XX. *Revista de Estudios Regionales* 109: 43–78.

Zapata Blanco, Santiago. 1996. Corcho extremeño y andaluz: tapones gerundenses. *Revista de Historia Industrial, Economía y Empresa* 10: 37–68.

CHAPTER 7

# The Sociedad Azucarera Antequerana and the Commercialization of Its Products (1890–1906)

*Mercedes Fernández-Paradas and Francisco José García Ariza*

## 7.1 Introduction

The beet sugar industry in Spain began its journey in 1883, when production got under way in two beet sugar factories, López-Rubio in Granada and Martel Fernández de Córdoba in Córdoba.

A few years later, in 1890, the Sociedad Azucarera Antequerana (Antequera Sugar Company) was established. Based in the Andalusian municipality of Antequera, in the northern part of the province of Málaga, it was founded in response to the growing demand for this product and to the fin-de-siècle crisis. From the beginning of the 1800s up until 1875, Antequera had been a major centre for woollen textiles, before entering a period of stagnation that culminated in a crisis (Parejo Barranco 1987).

M. Fernández-Paradas (✉) • F. J. García Ariza
University of Málaga, Málaga, Spain
e-mail: paradas@uma.es





M. Vázquez-Fariñas et al. (eds.), *Companies and Entrepreneurs in the History of Spain*, Palgrave Studies in Economic History,
https://doi.org/10.1007/978-3-030-61318-1_7

Overseas competition with countries that benefited from lower labour costs and cheaper raw materials than in Europe complicated the situation for the most important agricultural products, primarily cereal, olive* and vine production. Furthermore, domestic competition intensified, also in textiles, due to the development of the railways (Jiménez Blanco 1986, pp. 32–34; 2012, pp. 38–39). There thus arose a need to seek out alternatives offered by the second industrial revolution and new industrial sectors, among them agro-industry. Of these new sectors, our focus in this research is on the sugar industry.

This study covers the key period between 1890, the year the company was founded, and 1906, the year of the death of the principal driving force behind the company, Francisco Romero. His death marked the start of a different stage, as founding partner José García Sarmiento took absolute control of the company.

Following this introduction, which sets out the reasons behind the foundation of the Sociedad Azucarera Antequerana, the study then explains the importance of the company and analyses the strategy it deployed to ensure a commercialization network for its products that would guarantee their sale.

## 7.2 Sociedad Azucarera Antequerana, a Noteworthy Company

The Sociedad Azucarera Antequerana was formed in 1890 by ten men, most of whom formed part of Antequera's high society. The principal driving force behind the company was Francisco Romero Robledo (1838–1906), one of the great conservative politicians of the Restoration. He served as minister on several occasions and was President of the Congress of Deputies (Parejo Barranco 2006).

There are three reasons that can explain his interest in the sugar business. First, he was married to María Josefa Zulueta y Samá,[1] who was part-owner of a sugar mill in Cuba. Second, as a large owner of rural properties in Antequera, he was affected by the fin-de-siècle crisis. Third, he knew about the reported economic rewards of beet farming in Vega de Granada in the province of Granada.

[1] In honour of his wife, he named the sugar mill Ingenio San José (*ingenio* was a term used in Cuba for a sugar mill).

The share capital totalled 1,250,000 *pesetas* (pts); in 1891, the founding partners accounted for more than 43% of that total, with Romero Robledo holding 12.19%. However, if we add in the share capital held by his relatives, this percentage reached 20.49%.[2]

In the first season (1891–1892), the company's San José sugar factory produced just over 387,000 kilograms (kg) of sugar. In the 1900–1901 season, it registered the highest figure in the entire period studied here: almost 3.3 million kg, which represented 5.8% of the national production, 13.75% of total production in Andalusia and 93.8% of that in the province of Málaga (Rural History Study Group 1991, pp. 784–786; Casado Bellagarza 2018).[3] The fact that a market could be found for this production was thanks to a sales network that distributed sugar to a large part of the Spanish territory.

## 7.3 The Commercialization of Sugar

The ultimate aim of the Sociedad Azucarera Antequerana was to sell the beet sugar that it manufactured in the national market. It could not break into the international market due to its lack of competitiveness with international sugar production, whether with the sugar cane of the colonies or the beet sugar of the industrialized European nations, where the beet had a higher sucrose concentration and the factories achieved higher productivity with lower costs.

Thus, the beet sugar by-products, including molasses—the residue left after the crystallization of cane or beet sugar—were sold on the Spanish market. It was therefore necessary to develop a network of distributors to convey these products across the Spanish peninsular. We also examine the means of transport the company used to distribute its products: coastal shipping through the Port of Málaga, rail and road. Regarding rail transport, the railways and sidings, built at the same time as the factory which began operations in October 1891 (García Ariza 2016–2017), not only served as a way of receiving the supply of production inputs but was also an essential means of distributing the sugar.

In the first season, 1891–1892, the Sociedad Azucarera Antequerana produced 387,308.50 kg of sugar, which it sold for 0.71 pts/kg; as such,

[2] Municipal Historical Archive of Antequera (MHAA), Company Archives (CA), Sociedad Azucarera Antequerana Archive (SAAA), file 339, folder 32, *Shareholders in December 1891*.

[3] MHAA, CA, SAAA, files 336–338 and 341.

**Table 7.1** Sociedad Azucarera Antequerana's selling expenses as a percentage of total expenses (1891–1906)

| *Season* | % |
|---|---|
| 1891–1892 | 2.48 |
| 1892–1893 | 2.56 |
| 1893–1894 | 2.28 |
| 1894–1895 | 1.87 |
| 1895–1896 | 4.07 |
| 1896–1897 | 2.71 |
| 1897–1898 | 3.57 |
| 1898–1899 | 3.53 |
| 1899–1900 | 4.20 |
| 1900–1901 | 2.25 |
| 1901–1902 | 2.58 |
| 1902–1903 | 2.55 |
| 1903–1904 | 2.24 |
| 1904–1905 | 2.35 |
| 1905–1906 | 2.16 |

Source: MHAA, CA, SAAA, files 336–341. Compiled by the authors

it generated revenues of 273,976.59 pts. For 150,000 kg of molasses, sold at 0.10 pts/kg, the company received 15,000 pts. Thus, total revenue amounted to 288,976.59 pts. The sugar was distributed to Antequera, Lucena, Montilla (Córdoba), Málaga, Cádiz, Madrid, Murcia, Valencia and Barcelona, meaning that it reached the regions of Andalusia, Madrid, Murcia, Valencia and Catalonia. Two bags were even sent to Cuba as a sample.[4]

Selling expenses in this season amounted to 5507.32 pts, which included costs for discounts, commissions, freight, shipments and so on. It is worth noting that these expenses represented 2.48% of total expenses (Table 7.1), with this percentage ranging between 1.87% and 4.07% over the period under study. It was the least significant expenses line item; conversely, the largest outlay was on the supply of beets, which represented between 38.14% and 68.45% of expenses, depending on the year, followed by manufacturing costs, accounting for between 18.70% and 47.2% (Fernández-Paradas and García Ariza 2019, 175).

[4] MHAA, CA, SAAA, file 337, folder 7: *Expenses paid by the Caja de Antequera, 1891–1892 Season*; and *Commissions paid and distribution locations, 1891–1892 Season.*

**Table 7.2** Representatives, sales total, % commission and other selling expenses incurred by the Sociedad Azucarera Antequerana as at February 1892[a]

| *Representative* | *Municipality* | *Amount of sugar sold (pts)* | *Commission (%)* | *Other expenses (pts)* |
|---|---|---|---|---|
| Francisco Serrano Rivera | Lucena | 363.83 | 1.00 | |
| Juan B. Pérez | Montilla | 2317.72 | 1.00 | |
| Pedro Barón | Antequera | 3950.65 | 2.00 | |
| Diego Rus | Murcia | 3639.48 | 1.00 | |
| Federico Herrera | Barcelona | 7033.35 | 1.00 | |
| Joseph Ramell | Madrid | 11,882.50 | 1.00 | |
| Emilio Marzán | Cádiz | 21,181.48 | 1.00 | |
| Joaquín Almagro | Valencia | 22,118.60 | 1.00 | |
| Francisco Castilla | Antequera | 44,575.30 | 1.00 | |
| Grille y Gracián | Málaga | 87,068.11 | 2.00 | |
| Eduardo Guerrero Luque | Málaga | n/a | | 221.20 |
| Roura y Cía. | Barcelona | 7748.76 | | 33.04 |
| Shipment of consignments. | | | | 1753.57 |
| Post and telegrams | | | | 6.19 |
| Cancellations for low weight | | | | 539.98 |
| Total | | 211,879.78 | | 2555.48 |

Source: MHAA, CA, SAAA, file 337, folders 11 and 42, *Commissions paid 1891–1892 season. February 1892*. Compiled by the authors

[a]We know that this refers to the sugar sold up to that date but we do not from when it was sold

As Table 7.2 shows, in February 1892 most of the representatives selling the product received a commission of 1% of sales. Moreover, it can be seen that the bulk of the sales were registered in the province of Málaga, specifically in Antequera and the capital, which accounted for 135,594.06 pts in sugar sales, almost 64% of the total. On the other hand, it is worth highlighting Grille y Gracián in Antequera and Francisco Castilla in Málaga for the large amount of sugar they sold, representing 41.1% and 21.04% of the total, respectively. The company inventories included a section for accounts receivable *for sugar and other items*, which included debts owing to the company for sugar, molasses, coal, wood and so on. According to the 1892 inventory, the debtors listed under this item owed 79,453.68 pts.[5]

[5] MHAA CA, ledger 134, *Inventory Ledger 1, 1892 Inventory.*

In 1892–1893, the factory produced 678,585.50 kg of sugar. The company sold it at an average of 0.88 pts/kg, yielding a total of 595,856 pts. In addition, it sold 500,000 kg of molasses at 0.098 pts/kg, that is, for 49,000 pts. The two products together generated a total of 644,856 pts.[6]

Selling expenses amounted to 13,527.64 pts, 2.56% of total expenses, slightly higher than in the previous season.[7] As of 30 April 1893, commissions on sugar sales cost the company 5001.17 pts; as this figure represents 1% of sales, it can be inferred that sales amounted to 500,117 pts. At 0.088 pts/kg, we can estimate that the representatives placed a total of 568,315 kg of sugar in the market.

The distribution by means of domestic coastal shipping was carried out via the ports of Cádiz, Huelva, Galicia, Asturias and Bilbao on the Atlantic coast, and the ports of Cartagena-Murcia, Alicante, Valencia and Barcelona on the Mediterranean. By rail, the product reached Linares, Lucena, Montilla, Seville, Madrid, Murcia, Valladolid and Zaragoza, among other locations.[8] It can thus be seen that there was a rise in the number of municipalities and regions receiving the sugar from Antequera, with new locations including Castile and Leon and Aragon.

The company's *Annual Report* for 1892–1893 recorded that the Board of Directors were worried about the difficulty of selling molasses, due to the excessive duties imposed on industrially produced alcohols which would prevent their production. Furthermore, the Board communicated with Finance Minister Germán Gamazo y Calvo "via important people" and proposed a change to this tax that would foster sales of molasses and ensure a better price for it.[9]

In 1893–1894, the sugar reached all the same cities mentioned for the previous season, as well as some new cities, such as Gijón (Asturias) and Santander (Cantabria).[10] Selling expenses amounted to 28,036.85 pts, 2.28% of total expenses. The 1% sales commissions paid by the Sociedad Azucarera Antequerana totalled 11,296.49 pts. The company estimated the value of the sugar that remained unsold at the end of the season at

[6] MHAA, CA, SAAA, file 346, folder 48.

[7] MHAA, CA, SAAA, file 337, folder 18, *Statement of Expenditure and Products 1892–1893.*

[8] MHAA, CA, SAAA, file 337, folder 24, *Commissions paid and distribution locations in 1892–1893.*

[9] MHAA, CA, SAAA, file 337, folder 2, *Report of the Sociedad Azucarera Antequerana. Year 1892–1893.*

[10] MHAA, CA, SAAA, file 337, folder 24, *Commissions paid and distribution locations in 1893–1894.*

73,795 pts, out of a total of 1,363,274.40 pts. In the 1894 inventory, receivables for *sugar and other items* accounted for a total of 78,057.23 pts.[11]

At the Board of Directors meeting on 17 December 1893, in light of the difficulties affecting the sale of molasses and the lack of molasses tanks, it was agreed that a new honey tank should be built to achieve the required capacity for two seasons of 20,000 tonnes each.[12]

In the 1894–1895 season, the Sociedad Azucarera Antequerana produced 1,642,327.50 kg of sugar and 120,000 kg of molasses. At 0.81 pts/kg for sugar and 0.75 pts/kg for molasses, sales prices were lower than in the previous season, generating revenues of 1,342,156.36 pts. Selling expenses totalled 20,931.39 pts, representing 1.87% of the season's expenses,[13] less than in the previous year. The receivables for *sugar and other items* amounted to 128,476.53 pts.[14]

In the fifth season, 1895–1896, the sugar company produced 839,199.50 kg of sugar, which was sold at 0.82 pts/kg, yielding 684,410.49 pts. In addition to this, 150,000 kg of molasses was sold at 0.073 pts/kg. The amount received for the two products totalled 695,435.07 pts.

The distribution locations were as follows: Antequera, Cádiz, Granada, Almería, Huelva, Montilla and Seville, in Andalusia; and Madrid and Valladolid in the interior. In addition, sugar was sent to San Vicente de Alcantara (Badajoz, Extremadura), Santander, Cartagena (Murcia), and Tarragona and Barcelona (Catalonia) (Table 7.3).[15] It should be noted that Antequera and Málaga were no longer the municipalities responsible for the highest totals; Barcelona particularly stood out in this regard, accounting for more than 41% of sales, followed by Seville, Valencia, Granada and Huelva.

The debt owed to the company for amounts owing on *sugar and other items* reached 113,317.06 pts.[16]

In 1896–1897, the San José sugar factory manufactured 1,398,630 kg of sugar and 150,000 kg of molasses. Revenues from these products

[11] MHAA, CA, SAAA, Ledger 134, *Inventory Ledger 1, Inventory of 1894.*

[12] MHAA, CA, SAAA, Ledger 141, *Minutes of the Meeting of the Board of Directors of the S.A.A.*, 17 December 1893.

[13] MHAA, CA, SAAA, file 339, folder 17, *Statement of accounts for the 1894–1895 season.*

[14] MHAA, CA, SAAA, Ledger 134, *Inventory Ledger 1, Inventory of 1895.*

[15] MHAA, CA, SAAA, file 338, folder 18, *Commissions paid and distribution locations in 1895–1896.*

[16] MHAA, CA, SAAA, Ledger 134, *Inventory Ledger 1, Inventory of 1896.*

**Table 7.3** Representatives, sales total and % commission, and other selling expenses incurred by the Sociedad Azucarera Antequerana in the 1895–1896, as at 31 April 1896[a]

| *Representative* | *Municipality* | *Amount of sugar sold (pts)* | *Commission (%)* | *Other expenses (pts)* |
|---|---|---|---|---|
| Joseph Ramell | Madrid | 1041.25 | 1.00 | |
| Eduardo Marqués | San Vicente de Alcántara | 1499.10 | 1.00 | |
| Alzurena y Pequeño | Valladolid | 2327.50 | 1.00 | |
| José Megías | Almería | 2695.00 | 1.00 | |
| Juan Bautista Pérez | Montilla | 3006.17 | 1.00 | |
| Luis Pagán y Hermano | Cartagena | 3215.63 | 1.00 | |
| Antonio Ramírez | Santander | 8605.63 | 1.00 | |
| José Martínez Vidal | Tarragona | 17,897.26 | 1.00 | |
| Emilio Marzán | Cádiz | 34,636.89 | 1.00 | |
| Manuel García Ceballos | Antequera | 41,508.78 | 1.00 | |
| Emilio Sánchez Hernández | Huelva | 47,801.96 | 1.00 | |
| Manuel Vilaseca | Granada | 64,522.91 | 1.00 | |
| Joaquín de Almagro | Valencia | 78,414.35 | 1.00 | |
| Rafael Valencia | Seville | 99,824.77 | 1.00 | |
| Manuel Giralt | Barcelona | 310,694.30 | 1.00 | |
| Damages in negotiation of bills | Montilla | | | 1530.04 |
| Damages in negotiation of bills | Málaga | | | 335,947.45 |
| José de Sandoval brokerage | | | | 1013.06 |
| Total | | 717,691.50 | | 338,490.55 |

Source: MHAA, CA, SAAA, file 338, folder 56, *Expenses for reshipments, commissions paid, damages in negotiation of bills.* Compiled by the authors

[a]We know that this refers to the sugar sold up to that date; we do not know from when

amounted to 1,216,393.83 pts. Sugar reached the consumer at 0.86 pts/kg—yielding a total of 1.202.893,83 pts—and molasses at 0.090 pts/kg—generating 13,500 pts. Sugar was distributed to the same destinations as in previous seasons, reflecting the increasing consolidation of the clientele.[17]

[17]MHAA, CA, SAAA, file 336, folder 11, *Commissions paid and distribution locations in 1896–1897.*

The selling expenses in this season dropped by 486.24 pts, a 1.36% decrease, and accounted for 2.71% of total expenses.[18] Outstanding debts for the sale of sugar reached 113,696.70 pts.[19]

In the 1897–1898 season, the company produced 1,594,140 kg of sugar and 280,000 kg of molasses. The sugar was sold more cheaply than in the previous season, at 0.79 pts/kg, generating revenues of 1,262,265.61 pts. Molasses was sold at 0.10 pts/kg, yielding 28,000 pts. The two products together generated 1,290,265.61 pts of revenue.[20] The sugar reached new cities such as Lérida and Reus, in addition to the various locations from previous seasons, reflecting the ongoing search for new markets.[21]

Selling expenses increased in absolute numbers, rising from 21,883.98 pts in the 1896–1897 season to 32,289.25 pts in the 1897–1898 season. Relative to total expenditure, these expenses accounted for 3.57% of the total in the latter season.[22] With regard to the amounts owed for *sugar and other items*, there was a notable rise relative to 1896–1897, reaching a total of 211,788.27 pts.

In 1898–1899, the Sociedad Azucarera Antequerana produced 1,883,710.00 kg of sugar, which was sold at an average of 0.99 pts/kg, the highest price thus far in its history, generating revenues of 1,855,503.30 pts. In addition, 200,000 kg of molasses was sold to consumers at 0.090 pts/kg, totalling 18,000 pts. Revenues from the two products amounted to 1,873,503.30 pts.[23]

Selling expenses amounted to 38,591.83 pts, equivalent to 3.57% of total expenses.[24] As for the amount owed by debtors, corresponding to *sugar and other items*, it rose dramatically to 655,436.69 pts.[25]

In the ninth season (1899–1900) the San José sugar factory produced 3,055,637.40 kg of sugar and 300,000 kg of molasses. The molasses was sold at 0.08 pts/kg, generating revenues of 24,000 pts. The price of sugar was 1.11 pts/kg, giving a total of 3,427,281.39 pts, the highest figure in all the seasons analysed in this study.

[18] MHAA, CA, SAAA, file 336, folder 3, *Statement of accounts for the 1896–1897 season.*
[19] MHAA, CA, SAAA, Ledger 134, *Inventory Ledger 1, Inventory of 1896 and 1897.*
[20] MHAA, CA, SAAA, file 339, folder 3.
[21] MHAA, CA, SAAA, file 339, folder 54, *Commissions paid and distribution locations in the 1896–1897 season.*
[22] MHAA, CA, SAAA, file 339, folder 46, *Statement of accounts for the 1897–1898 season.*
[23] MHAA, CA, SAAA, file 339, folder 13.
[24] MHAA, CA, SAAA, file 339, folder 3, *Statement of accounts for the 1898–1899 season.*
[25] MHAA, CA, SAAA, Ledger 134, *Inventory Ledger 1, Inventory of 1898 and 1899.*

Selling expenses rose considerably. In 1898–1899, they reached 38,591.83 pts and 3.53% of total expenses; in 1899–1900, the corresponding figures were 87,725.24 pts and 4.20% of expenses, that is, an increase of 0.67%.[26] The amount owing for *sugar and other items* once again grew relative to the previous year, almost doubling to 1,212,406.50 pts.[27]

In the tenth year, 1900–1901, the company produced 3,262,908.50 kg of sugar and 552,000 kg of molasses; it was not able to sell the latter due to the tax on non-wine alcohols. The Budget Law of 5 August 1893 replaced the 25 *céntimo* tax on alcohols distilled from grapes with another on production depending on the quality and capacity of the equipment. Similarly, it brought in a change in the tax regime for alcohols manufactured with Spanish or foreign honeys, setting a tax of 37.50 pts per hectolitre, regardless of their alcohol content; it made no changes to tariffs on foreign industrially produced alcohols. It was not a favourable regulatory framework for the development of industrially produced alcohol. It sold the sugar at 0.93 pts/kg, generating revenues of 3,040,794.89 pts. This product was distributed to the locations listed for previous seasons (Martín Rodríguez 1982, pp. 182–196, 247–251).[28]

Selling expenses amounted to 58,247.98 pts or 2.25% of total expenses. The total listed under accounts receivable for *sugar and other items* fell to 1,084,994.05 pts, that is, a decrease of 184,460.24 pts relative to the preceding season.[29]

In 1901–1902, the Sociedad Azucarera Antequerana produced 2,048,067.50 kg of sugar, which was sold to consumers at a price of 0.88 pts/kg. It also produced 327,000 kg of molasses, which it was again unable to sell that season. The company registered 1,795,471.25 pts in revenues from sugar, lower than the previous year's figure of 1,245,323.64 pts. The sugar was sent to consumers in Andalusia in Antequera, Montilla, Puente Genil (Córdoba), Málaga, Huelva and Seville. In Galicia, it reached La Coruña and Vigo for the first time. And on the Mediterranean coast it went to Cartagena, Valencia and Barcelona. In the city of Barcelona, Manuel Giralt sold sugar worth a total of 738,982,48 pts; he was the

[26] MHAA, CA, SAAA, file 339, folder 13, *Statement of accounts for the 1899–1900 season.*

[27] MHAA, CA, SAAA, Ledger 134, *Inventory Ledger 1, Inventory of 1899 and 1900.*

[28] MHAA, CA, SAAA, file 340, folder 7, *Commissions paid and distribution locations in the 1900–1901 season.*

[29] MHAA, CA, SAAA, Ledger 134, *Inventory Ledger 1, Inventory of 1900 and 1901.*

representative reporting the highest sales figures, accounting for one-third of the total. In order of importance, he was followed by Rafael Valencia in Seville (342,006.53 pts), José González Lorenzo in La Coruña and Vigo (284,111.43 pts) and Juan Paché in Antequera (155,569.70 pts) (see Table 7.4).

The *Annual Report* noted that the excess sugar production of the 1900–1901 season had triggered a huge collapse in sugar prices; in response, the company halved its purchases of sugar beet. Similarly, almost all factories in the Spanish peninsula cut production, but as there was so much stock left over from the previous season, prices continued to decline from August through to January before beginning to rise again.

Selling expenses amounted to 37,358.87 pts, 2.58% of total expenses; this percentage was a little higher than that of the previous season.[30] With all the difficulties affecting the sale of sugar in this season, it is worth noting that one of the sales representatives, Manuel Giralt of Barcelona, sold 80,153 pts in 1900–1901 and 738.982,48 pts in 1901–1902. The latter figure is indicative of remarkably strong commercial activity.[31]

Amounts receivable for *sugar and other items* rose to 1,093,482.35 pts, a rise of 3094.24 pts over the previous season. This is a substantial increase given the contraction in sugar production that had occurred.[32]

In 1902–1903, the Sociedad Azucarera Antequerana produced 2,133,215.50 kg of sugar, which it managed to sell at a better price than in the previous season, specifically, at 1.02 pts/kg, in other words, 0.14 pts/kg more than in the previous season. It was also able to sell 215,450 kg of molasses, at 0.095 pts/kg. The two products together generated 2,197,110.96 pts of revenue, 401,639.71 pts more than in 1901–1902.[33] The sugar was distributed to the same locations.[34]

There was a small rise in selling expenses, with the company paying out 39,746.80 pts in commissions, accounting for 2.55% of expenses,

[30] MHAA, CA, SAAA, file 340, folder 14, *Statement of accounts for the 1899–1900 season.*

[31] MHAA, CA, SAAA, file 340, folder 19, *Commissions paid and distribution locations in the 1901–1902 season.*

[32] MHAA, CA, SAAA, *Ledger 134, Inventory Ledger 1, Inventory of 1901 and 1902.*

[33] MHAA, CA, SAAA, file 340, folder 26, *Statement of accounts for the 1902–1903 season.*

[34] MHAA, CA, SAAA, file 340, folder 32, *Commissions paid and distribution locations in the 1902–1903 season.*

**Table 7.4** Representatives, sales total and % commission, and other selling expenses incurred by the Sociedad Azucarera Antequerana in the 1901–1902 season, as at 31 May 1902[a]

| *Representative* | *Municipality* | *Amount of sugar sold (pts)* | *Commission (%)* | *Other expenses (pts)* |
|---|---|---|---|---|
| Luis Pagán y Hermano | Cartagena | 7947.20 | 1.00 | 6.30 |
| Juan Bautista Pérez | Montilla | 11,502.75 | 1.00 | |
| Francisco Uclés | Puente Genil | 14,805.00 | 1.00 | |
| Emilio Sánchez Hernández | Huelva | 26,963.48 | 1.00 | |
| Manuel García Ceballos | Málaga | 77,164.75 | 1.00 | |
| Joaquín de Almagro | Valencia | 77,395.90 | 1.00 | |
| Cándido Corrales | Various municipalities | 127,303.25 | 1.00 | |
| Juan Paché | Antequera | 155,569.70 | 1.00 | |
| José González Lorenzo | La Coruña and Vigo | 284,111.43 | 1.00 | 56.55 |
| Rafael Valencia | Seville | 342,006.53 | 1.00 | 88.54 |
| Manuel Giralt | Barcelona | 738,982.48 | 1.00 | |
| Transport costs to Málaga and loading at the port | To Diego Grille in Cartagena, La Coruña, Vigo and "miscellaneous" | | | 22,951.75 |
| Transport costs to Málaga and loading at the port | A B. Marina in La Coruña | | | 25.99 |
| Total | | 1,863,752.47 | | 22,977.76 |

Source: MHAA, CA, SAAA, file 340, folder 19, *Commissions paid and payable, expenses for transport and loading of sugars in the 1901–1902 season, 31 May 1902.* Compiled by the authors

[a]We know that this refers to the sugar sold up to that date; we do not know from when

compared with 37,358.87 pts and 2.58% in the previous season.[35] Accounts receivable for *sugar and other items* amounted to 1,275,211.01 pts.[36]

In the 1903–1904 season, the factory produced 1,947,467.50 kg of sugar, with a price to the consumer of 1.03 pts/kg—almost the same

[35] MHAA, CA, SAAA, file 340, folder 26, *Statement of accounts for the 1902–1903 season.*
[36] MHAA, CA, SAAA, Ledger 134, *Inventory Ledger 1, Inventory of 1902 and 1903.*

price as in the previous season—for which it earned revenues of 2,001,881.75 pts. In addition, it sold 250,000 kg of molasses at 0.060 pts/kg, yielding revenues of 15,000 pts. The total for both items was 2,016,881.75 pts. The distribution of sugar now reached Gijón and Avilés, in addition to the previously mentioned locations.[37]

In 1903–1904, selling expenses amounted to 33,500.22 pts, representing 2.24% of total expenses. These figures were lower than those of 1902–1903: 39,746.80 pts and 2.55%.[38] The debt incurred by buyers for *sugar and other items* increased to 1,588,100.04 pts, an increase of 296,294.54 pts over the previous year.[39]

In 1904–1905 the company made 3,027,467.00 kg of sugar. Its price rose to 1.09 pts/kg, very close to the highest price of 1.11 pts/kg registered in 1899–1900. Sales of this product generated 3,294,299.72 pts. The 300,000 kg of molasses produced was sold at 0.055 pts/kg, for a total of 16,335 pts. Thus, for the two products together it earned revenues of 3,310,634.72 pts—one of the company's best ever results—. As the company saw it, this justified the decision not to sell out to the Sociedad General Azucarera, which had started operations in 1903. On several occasions, producers had tried unsuccessfully to cut production of sugar to control prices, until, in the 1902–1903 season, a group of financiers and sugar cane and beet growers decided to form the Sociedad General Azucarera. By June 1903, it had managed to incorporate 55 sugar factory owners; the only ones not to join were the Larios Group and six other factories, among them the San José mill (Martín Rodríguez 1982, pp. 280–286).

Sugar distribution continued in the Mediterranean—in Catalonia and the Spanish Levant—as well as on the Atlantic coast—in Galicia, Asturias and the Basque Country—. We also know that it was distributed by rail to Seville, the province of Granada, Madrid and "other places" that are not specified in the documents consulted.[40]

Selling expenses amounted to 53,034.77 pts, corresponding to 2.35% of total expenses: the former figure is higher than that of the 1903–1904

[37] MHAA, CA, SAAA, file 338, folder 10, *Commissions paid and distribution locations in the 1903–1904 season.*

[38] MHAA, CA, SAAA, file 338, folder 3, *Statement of accounts for the 1903–1904 season.*

[39] MHAA, CA, SAAA, Ledger 134, *Inventory Ledger 1, Inventory of 1902 and 1903.*

[40] MHAA, CA, SAAA, file 340, folder 57, *Commissions paid and distribution locations in the 1904–1905 season.*

season, in which a figure of 33,500,22 pts was registered.[41] Accounts receivable for *sugar and other items* continued to increase: in 1904–1905 this figure reached 1,996,711.26 pts, compared to 1,588,100.04 pts in the previous season.[42]

In the 1905–1906 season, the Sociedad Azucarera Antequerana produced 1,230,730 kg of sugar. The price fell to 0.91 pts/kg due to competition with the new beet sugar factories, yielding revenues of 1,121,004.06 pts. It sold 150,000 kg molasses at 0.030 pts/kg, generating 4500 pts. The two products together totalled 1,125,504.06 pts, much less than in previous seasons (Table 7.5). The sugar was distributed by means of coastal shipping, rail and road, to the abovementioned locations.[43]

Comparing the information as at 31 May 1902 (Table 7.4) to that of 31 May 1906 (Table 7.5), which is less complete as it does not list the names of all the municipalities to which the sugar was distributed, we note that Cartagena does not appear in the latter and that the relative importance of the Barcelona representative, Manuel Giralt, decreased considerably. The representative who sold the most sugar was Manuel García Ceballos, with a total of 478,163.78 pts; the documentation does not provide information about the locations in which he operated, although in other seasons he supplied Antequera and Málaga. He was followed by Juan Paché in Antequera with 194,295 pts and Jose Gonzalez Lorenzo in Vigo and La Coruña with 190,368.69 pts.

Selling expenses dropped in line with the amount of the products sold. Thus, these expenses dropped to 21,545.75 pts, 2.16% of total expenses, below the corresponding figures for 1904–1905, which stood at 51,034.77 pts and 2.35%, respectively. Expenditure was thus stabilizing, as the percentage remained at just over 2% in most seasons.[44] In this season, amounts owed by buyers for *sugar and other items* totalled 2,103,393.18 pts—slightly higher than that of 1904–1905.[45]

[41] MHAA, CA, SAAA, file 340, folder 53, *Statement of accounts for the season 1904–1905.*

[42] MHAA, CA, SAAA, Ledger 134, *Inventory Ledger 1, Inventory of 1904 and 1905.*

[43] MHAA, CA, SAAA, file 341, folder 7, *Commissions paid and distribution locations in the 1905–1906 season.*

[44] MHAA, CA, SAAA, file 341, folder 3, *Statement of accounts and distribution locations in 1905–1906.*

[45] MHAA, CA, SAAA, Ledger 134, *Inventory Ledger 1, Inventory of 1905 and 1906.*

**Table 7.5** Representatives, sales total and % commission, and other selling expenses incurred by the Sociedad Azucarera Antequerana in the 1905–1906 season, as at 31 May 1906[a]

| *Representative* | *Municipality* | *Amount of sugar sold (pts)* | *Commission (%)* | *Other expenses (pts)* |
|---|---|---|---|---|
| Francisco Uclés Morales | Puente Genil | 436.10 | 1.00 | |
| Juan Bautista Pérez | Montilla | 9640.75 | 1.00 | |
| Manuel Vilaseca | Granada | 23,598.40 | 1.00 | |
| Cándido Corrales | Various | 40,409.08 | 1.00 | |
| Joaquín de Almagro | Valencia | 46,893.00 | 1.00 | |
| Manuel Giralt | Barcelona | 70,714.36 | | |
| Widow and brother of R. Valencia | Seville | 172,497.15 | 1.00 | 25.00 |
| José González Lorenzo | Vigo and La Coruña | 190,368.69 | 1.00 | 27.34 |
| Juan Paché | Antequera | 194,295.00 | 1.00 | |
| Manuel García Ceballos | Various | 478,163.78 | 1.00 | |
| Transport costs to Málaga and loading at the port | | | | 10,717.90 |
| Total | | 1,227,016.31 | | 13,245.24 |

Source: MHAA, CA, SAAA, file 341, folder 7, *Commissions paid and payable, expenses for transport and loading of sugars in the 1905–1906 season, 31 May 1906*. Compiled by the authors

[a]We know that this refers to the sugar sold up to that date; we do not know from when

## 7.4 Conclusions

In summary, over these 15 seasons the San José sugar factory produced more than 26 million kg of sugar, with an average amount of 1.7 million kg of sugar per season. The company sold the sugar at an average price of 0.96 pts/kg, generating more than 25 million pts. If we add to this figure the revenue from almost 5 million kg of molasses, which was sold at an average price of 0.071 pts/kg, yielding more than 344,000 pts, we can see that in total the company received more than 25 million pts for the sale of these products.

Sugar was distributed to consumers via coastal shipping, rail and road. The Sociedad Azucarera Antequerana managed to sell its products throughout a large part of the national territory, even in places where competition was strongest, such as in the province of Granada, or in

Zaragoza, Valladolid and Asturias, all sugar-producing areas. In short, it managed to deploy a commercialization network that enabled it to find a market for its products.

The selling expenses in the 15 seasons under study amounted to 512,298.11 pts, representing an annual average of 2.72% of the total expenses, a percentage that varied very little over the period analysed here. The amounts receivable for the sale of *sugar and other items* grew in almost all the seasons, rising from 79,453.68 pts in 1893–1894 to 2,103,393.18 pts in 1905–1906, the season recording the highest figure for this line item.

## References

Casado Bellagarza, José Luis. 2018. *El azúcar como origen: la colonia agrícola de San Pedro de Alcántara (Málaga) 1860–1910*. Málaga: Universidad de Málaga.

Fernández-Paradas, Mercedes, and Francisco José García Ariza. 2019. La Sociedad Azucarera Antequerana: una respuesta a la crisis finisecular (1890–1906). In *Empresas y empresarios en España. De mercaderes a industriales*, coordinated by Juan Manuel Matés-Barco, 153–179. Madrid: Pirámide.

García Ariza, Francisco José. 2016–2017. La construcción del ingenio San José. *Revista de Estudios Antequeranos* 19–20: 39–63.

Grupo de Estudios de Historia Rural. 1991. *Estadísticas Históricas de la Producción agraria española, 1859–1935*. Madrid: Universidad Complutense de Madrid.

Jiménez Blanco, José Ignacio. 1986. *La producción agraria en Andalucía Oriental, 1874–1914*. PhD diss., Universidad Complutense de Madrid.

———. 2012. Las raíces agrarias del crecimiento económico andaluz y el grupo Larios. *Documentos de Trabajo de la Asociación Española de Historia Económica* 3: 1–37.

Martín Rodríguez, Manuel. 1982. *Azúcar y descolonización. Origen y desenlace de una crisis agraria en la Vega de Granada. El Ingenio de San Juan, 1882–1904*. Granada: Universidad de Granada.

Parejo Barranco, Antonio. 1987. *Historia de Antequera*. Antequera: Biblioteca Antequerana de la Caja de Ahorros.

———. 2006. *Francisco Romero Robledo. Último político romántico. Ingenio de la Restauración (Antequera, 1838–Madrid, 1906)*. Antequera: Ayuntamiento de Antequera.

CHAPTER 8

# Merchant Bankers, Banking Houses and Large National Banks. The Case of Jaen Province (1800–1936)

*María José Vargas-Machuca*

## 8.1 Introduction

Loaning and funds saving have existed since ancient times, but it is in the Modern Period that this activity experienced an expansion unknown until then. Even though lending between individuals has always been a common activity, in the Modern Age agents began to emerge that are formally dedicated to granting loans and accepting deposits.

During the nineteenth century, the lending activity began to be carried out by businessmen who, parallel to commercial operations, started to develop this other financial activity. As the century went by, the futures of many of these small merchant bankers are similar. The commercial activity starts to give ground to the financial activity, they turn into companies and, in the twentieth century, the next generations turn the business into

M. J. Vargas-Machuca (✉)
University of Jaén, Jaén, Spain
e-mail: mjvargas@ujaen.es



M. Vázquez-Fariñas et al. (eds.), *Companies and Entrepreneurs in the History of Spain*, Palgrave Studies in Economic History,
https://doi.org/10.1007/978-3-030-61318-1_8

a limited company and end up selling it to a great bank that uses it as an expansion strategy (Titos-Martínez 2003, p. 109).

In addition to these merchant bankers, in the nineteenth century the private banking activity in Spain was carried out by other types of agents: investment banking and the credit unions. In addition, the first savings banks started to operate, in several cases linked to pawnshops that had already been working in some Spanish towns.

The aim of this work is to study how the private banking sector structure in Spain was expressed in Jaen province in the nineteenth century and the first third of the twentieth century. For that purpose, a detailed review of the academic literature in this area will be carried out, to attempt to develop a comprehensive list of agents that worked as bankers in this territory until the beginning of the Spanish Civil War.

This list shall be completed, for the 1979–1900 period, with the pieces of information included in the *Anuario-Almanaque del Comercio, de la Industria, de la Magistratura y de la Administración* (Annual Directory of Commerce, Industry, Magistracy and Administration, hereinafter referred to as the Bailly-Baillière Annual Directory), a source that has never been used before in any of the works published for Jaen province. This Annual Directory, first printed in 1879, was a guide that included hundreds of thousands of pieces of information about the people forming the state and provincial institutions in every sector (political, educational, military, religious, judicial, etc.) and about the professionals and professions, shops, businesses, factories and industries in Spain, as well as in the overseas countries and Latin America (and since 1881 also in Portugal).

First, the private banking sector structure in the twentieth century is analysed, during which new banking companies appeared, and the private banker's activity was established. Second, the presence of bankers and banking houses in Jaen province in the nineteenth century is considered, through a review of the published biography related to this area as well as the information gathered in the Bailly-Baillière Annual Directory. Finally, the private banking activity in this territory during the first third of the twentieth century is studied with regard to the entrance of the national bank in Jaen territory and the behaviour of local bankers.

## 8.2 The Private Banking Sector in Spain in the Nineteenth Century: The Task of the Merchant Bankers

The nineteenth century was a period of intense transformations in the Spanish financial system due to the appearance of several regulations that affect banking activity, essentially through the regulation of the banks that were able to carry it out. Thus, activities were beginning to be regulated that, until then, did not have any regulations and depended on sometimes arbitrary concessions of the administration.

The Investment Banking and Credit Unions Law (Spanish law) of 1856 was of high importance, as thanks to this there was a certain specialisation in the Spanish financial system. On the one hand, some "investment banks" were created, closely linked to the government and which, in addition to issuing money, worked granting credits and discounts. On the other hand, the so-called credit unions appeared, which started to develop a wide range of activities, mainly oriented to the industrial promotion linked to the railway sector, but with no investment privileges (Pons 1999, p. 84). Then began a phase of strong bank expansion linked to two circumstances: a permissive legislation and a favourable economic situation, driven by the State and closely linked to the construction of the railway network. In that way, the number of credit institutions in the whole of Spain grew significantly, reaching a total of 60 at the end of 1864 (Titos-Martínez 2003, p. 97). Nevertheless, between 1864 and 1868, some railway companies began to suspend payments, and numerous credit banks found their inversions obliged, which led them to go bankrupt and disappear.

After the credit unions, difficulties arrived for investment banking. The Law of 1874 (known as the Echegaray Decree Spanish law) gave the Banco de España (Bank of Spain) the unique right of investment and obliged the rest of the investment banks to annex to this bank as branch offices or to modify their by-laws to become loan and discount banks. For several of these banks, the chance to join the Banco de España (Bank of Spain) was a great opportunity, given the difficulties that they had experienced since the 1866 crisis.

Therefore, the 1866 crisis and the Law of 1874 brought a final change to the Spanish financial system: there was an important restructuring that brought about a reduction in the total number of private banks and the setting of an investment monopoly from the *Banco de España* (*Bank of Spain*).

On the other hand, in the financial system, besides these unions, the individual bankers continued to provide their services (Tedde de Lorca 1974, p. 253). It is likely that the absence of banks and credit unions in many provinces and their disappearance between 1866 and 1864 contributed to the creation of an emptiness that was filled by the private bankers, the savings banks and other moneylenders of less importance (Titos-Martínez 2003, p. 108).

In the case of the bankers, their activity was first regulated by the First Commerce Code of Spain (1829), included in a wider concept, such as merchants. To be allowed to practise such activity, they were required to enrol as businessmen to be able to carry out the so-called trade activity. The enrolment in the businessmen registry forced them into a certain type of taxation (business subsidy, industrial and business subsidy or industrial property tax, depending on the era) (Titos-Martínez 1999, p. 108). However, throughout the nineteenth century, many agents continued working as bankers without registering themselves in any official registry.

The Spanish legislation provided great freedom of action for the private bankers from the promulgation of the Commerce Code of 1829 to the Banking Organization Law of 1921 (both in Spain). This provided those intermediaries a ruling stability that contrasted with the continuous regulating reforms that affected the banking companies.

For the first years of the century, several such bankers, in addition to working as moneylenders, making discounts, acting as guarantors, transferring short-term drafts and trading in different currencies. But, at the same time, many of them sold textil products or imported goods (Tedde de Lorca 1983, p. 303). In such a way, many such individuals could actually be considered "merchant bankers", that is to say, agents that started their activity as retail traders and that, then, started to carry out on a small scale the main banking operations (transfers, negotiation, loans, etc.). First, this was to fulfil their own needs and, gradually, for a higher number of clients, until ending up specialising and even leaving their original business occupations (García-López 1989, p. 115). Such transformations were, generally, a slow process and, on some occasions, imperceptible. The only recognisable fact in such a process was most likely the registration of the tax enrolment, which was the exterior official appreciation.

In some cases such private banks were set up as partnerships, but they were mainly individual businessmen with a similar historical development.

They began with the bank activity linked to some other commercial type and they worked on it personally. In the second generation, these were turned into companies and the commercial activity was displaced by financial activity. Lastly, a third or fourth generation, well into the twentieth century, turned the business into a limited company and sold the banking business to a large national bank that took advantage of the situation to establish itself in new places, given the difficulties in expansion and access to the banking occupation that existed for a long time (Titos-Martínez 2003, p. 109).

## 8.3 Private Bankers in Jaen Province in the Nineteenth Century

Jaen province did not manage to incorporate at the same rate as others in the expansion process wherein the financial sector experimented nationally in the nineteenth century and that led to the emergence of the modern banking.

The concurrence of two factors prevented the appearance of local financial banks of specific importance and of larger geographical dimensions (Duro-Cobo 1985, p. 3). On the one hand, there was a lack of a booming economic sector requiring capital, for example from the colonial trade in Cadiz or the wine market in Jerez and Cordoba. The province had an important agricultural sector, but its archaic structure made it static and resistant to innovation. Another important sector was mining, even though its expansion was linked to the European capital that, together with the technical means, also provided the financial means. The second factor is the weakness of the internal savings, as a consequence of the low level of income per capita in the province.

Under such conditions, the expectations for establishing a local bank were low. Therefore, in the nineteenth century there was not even one investment bank or credit union in Jaen. As in the rest of the Spanish provinces, in Jaen there were some initiatives to set up savings banks or similar institutions, but these were consistently unsuccessful. This leads to the possible conclusion that some other agents were working in the financial business in this territory.

In many cases, credit requests were satisfied by the agricultural owners or even by members of the aristocracy in the province (Garrido-González 1995a, p. 327), as well as private bankers. Their activity was based, in many cases, on a direct semi-formalised personal relationship with the borrowers, based on the trust derived from knowing each other and the social link between the parties (Garcia-Orallo 2016, p. 23).

The bankers in Jaen developed a similar career path to that of the rest of the country. In addition, in this case, their banking activity began to be linked to other commercial activities that they worked on personally. Over time, the commercial activity was displaced by financial activity, and in some cases leading to the establishment of companies. Finally, in the twentieth century, banks turned into limited companies and sold the banking businesses to large national banks that took advantage of the situation to expand.

From the academic literature research on the bankers in Jaen in the nineteenth century we obtained a list of 16 agents that developed this activity at various times throughout the century, which are analysed chronologically below.

At the beginning of the nineteenth century, banking in Jaen was composed of bankers or small family credit and savings unions, rather than by large banks, some of which would achieve importance. Among them, the most representative are those owned by Juan Esponera and Nephews, Anselmo García Rubio and the *Matínez Pinillos House*, the latter with its main office in Baeza city. All of them continued to work during the Spanish War of Independence, but they were grievously affected during the years of the French occupation of Jaen (1810–1813) (López-Pérez 1977, p. 9).

It is also worth mentioning the *Sáenz, Sáenz, Rivas y Compañía* bank that was founded in Jaen in 1821 by the banker Mr León García Rubio. However, this was not its original denomination. In fact, in the Bailly-Baillière Annual Directory, this house appears under this title between 1902 and 1906, probably as the one continuing with the activity of *Matías Saénz y Cía* (*Matias Saenz and Company*) (1881–1888) and of his successors (1894–1901). According to Garrido-González (1995a, p. 328), this house worked as commissioner of the Spanish Mortgage Bank from 1873. Furthermore, according to the Bailly-Baillière Annual Directory, at least between 1883 and 1900, the representation of the Mortgage Bank of Spain was done by the banking firm *Sixto Santamaría*, and its consecutive denominations, whereas *Matías Sáenz y Cía* (*Matias Saenz and Company*) was the commissioner of the *Banco de España* (*Bank of Spain*) between 1881 and 1883.

Félix García García, the founder's nephew, would be trained at this bank, and would become one of the most well-known local personalities.

He was born in Ortigosa de Camero (Logroño) and settled in Jaen when he was thirteen years old, co-operating, until he was almost 80 years old, the banking house founded by his uncle. Many of the cultural and economic achievements in Jaen were thanks to him, as he devoted a significant portion of his profits from his banking business (Rodríguez 1922).

The Antonio Ortega García banking house was somewhat more modern, and it is there that Sixto Santamaría Sologuren, a man from Malaga who settled in Jaen in the mid-nineteenth century, started to work. Together, they founded a banking company in this city, but the project did not come to fruition (López-Pérez 1977, p. 9).

Sixto Santamaría became independent in 1864, creating his own financial business that, like that of Antonio Ortega, would prosper for many years. Santamaría became the main shareholder of the Bank of Spain in Jaen, holding 100 shares in 1900 (Titos-Martínez 2003, p. 235). The house of Sixto Santamaría would be inherited by his children, Sixto and Eugenio Santamaría Mitjana. The former was not only a renowned banker, but also held important economic and political positions, such as the president of the Agriculture Department in Jaen province. In addition, he also played an influential role in the Spanish Economic Friends Society (Garrido-González 1995a, p. 329). According to the Bailly-Baillière Annual Directory, the denomination of this banking firm developed as follows: *Sixto Santamaría* (1881–1882), *Sixto Santamaría y Sobrino* (*Sixto Santamaria and Nephew*) (1883–1888), *Santamaría y Mediano* (1894–1897), *Santamaría Hermanos* (*Santamaria Brothers*) (1898–1902), and *Sixto Santamaría Mitjana* (1899–1909). The latter coincides with the previous during the last years of the nineteenth century. The Annual Directory includes the fact that this banking house, under its several denominations, worked as commissioner of the Mortgage Bank of Spain between 1883 and 1900.

In the Jaen of that era, other financial family companies were those of the Jontoya brothers, of Mr. Bernardo Jose Jaen, of the widow of Ángel Fernandez, of Rodríguez y Rodríguez and of García y García (López-Cordero 1992, p. 175; Garrido-González 1995a, p. 329).

Outside of the capital, in addition to the previously mentioned *Casa Martínez Pinillos* (*Martinez Pinillos house*), it is worth noting the leading figure of the banker Mr Ignacio Sabater de Arauco, whose family settled in Ubeda in 1815 from Tortella (Gerona). This same year, the family man Mr José Sabater y Camó, together with his brother Salvador, started his commercial operations in Ubeda under the denomination of *Casa comercial Sabater Hermanos* (*Commercial House Sabater Hermanos*), which would become bankrupt in 1828. His son, Ignacio Sabater de Arauco, who proved to have strong business skills since he was very young, constituted in the city the company *Sabater Hermanos* (Sabater Brothers) with his brother, also called Salvador. As time passed, he managed to widen and diversify his operations until he was considered the most important banker in Jaen and to have one of the greatest fortunes in the province (Tarifa-Fernández 2011, p. 21).

The *Sabater Hermanos* (*Sabater Brothers*) company was dissolved in 1864 and Ignacio moved to Madrid, where he founded a banking house with strong moneylending activity linked, on some occasions, with high personages of the state, even Queen Elizabeth II herself (Arroyo 2006).

Unfortunately, the operation of these banking houses is unknown, and thus it is difficult to quantify how many agents worked in this activity at any given time in Jaen.

As mentioned earlier, the First Commerce Code of Spain of 1829 required bankers to register the merchants' enrolment. After this, those agents, to be able to develop their activities, needed to be registered and to pay the corresponding enrolment fee. According to the information provided by García-López (1989, p. 122), the number of enrolled merchant bankers in the Industry Contribution in Jaen province between 1879 and 1900 did not reach ten. However, it must be kept in mind that only those that developed their business legally and paid the enrolment fee to the industry and made a commercial contribution as merchant bankers were included, and not those developing lending activity illegally.

The information in the Bailly-Baillère Annual Directory show numbers that are significantly higher. After consulting this source, we obtained a list of a total of 70 bankers that worked on their business in Jaen province between 1879 and 1900. This number increases up to 96 in the 1900–1911 period. Even so, the distribution per year is further adjusted. The number of registered bankers is three according to this source in 1879, and it increases to 28 in 1900.

The differences between the information gathered by the Annual Directory and the Spanish Industry Contribution most likely arises from the fact that many small merchant bankers did not register in the fiscal enrolment as bankers and thus did not pay additional tax. This was quite common among the smallest agents in the smallest towns, for whom the new request was excessively burdensome in comparison with the benefits they received from the banking operations. However, and more importantly, due to their business volume, it was not possible to hide from the Spanish Tax Office, and it is likely that the rest of the sector was enrolled. Moreover, the lack of bankers' activity delimitation led agents with broader activities than banking to be registered in the Annual Directory. For example, among others, this is the case of Eduardo Carvajal, a banker from Bailen, who, in the Annual Directory of 1894, appears also as a pomace oil maker and in the category of "oil mills". Despite all this, many of the agents registered as bankers in the Annual Directory would continue with the banking business in the following years, and would even register in the Banking Directory.

According to the Bailly-Baillière Annual Directory, at the end of the nineteenth century there existed a total of 28 agents in Jaen province that worked in banking activity, of which three did so in the capital: the *Successors of Matías Saenz y Cía.* (*Matias Saenz and Company*) (in Maestra Baja Street), *Sixto Santamaría Mitjana* (in Colón Street) and *Santamaría Hermanos* (*Santamaria Brothers*) (in Cerón Street, also working as commissioner of the Mortgage Bank of Spain).

Among them, some stand out for the long duration of their activity, which makes them a model in the province's banking system of the end of the nineteenth century, and this has not been mentioned as there is no reference to them in the literature on this matter:

1. *Miñón Hermanos* (*Miñon Brothers*) (Andujar) is included in the Annual Directory constantly under the same denomination, from 1881 to 1991, this last year as correspondent of the Banco de España (Bank of Spain). As we will see further in this chapter, his activity would continue under the same business name until it was absorbed by the Banco de Bilbao (Bank of Bilbao) in 1952.
2. *Puche Hermanos* (*Puche Brothers*) (Baeza) and their successors are included in the Annual Directory between 1897 and 1911, assuming the correspondent's office of the Banco de España (Bank of Spain) in this locality from 1906. This house would also continue its activity until well into the twentieth century, working under the commercial name Banca Puche (Puche Banking).
3. Isidoro Gil de Muro (Andujar) practised his activity between 1881 and 1909, and his widow continued his work until 1911, the last four years as a correspondent of the Banco de España (Bank of Spain).

4. Others: Santos Sánchez (Bailén), Benito de Torres (Porcuna) and Ildefonso Valenzuela (Porcuna) appear in the Annual Directory between 1897 and 1911.

Other credit banks that existed in the capital were the lending houses, which did not practise banking operations strictly, but were mainly focused on loan concession, in many cases with pledge guarantee. This was the case of the houses of *José Francés y Compañía* (*Jose Frances and Company*), in Cañuelo Street, of *Manuel Palomo y Compañía* (*Manuel Palomo and Company*), in Salido Street, of *Manuel Molina y Compañía* (*Manuel Molina and Company*), in the Avenue, and of Antonio Cobo, in Bernardo Lopez Street (López-Cordero 1992, p. 176; Bailly-Baillière Annual Directory).

Therefore, at the end of the nineteenth century, there were no great bankers or banking companies in Jaen province, nor were there any savings banks. Thus, it can be concluded that the provincial banking system was limited to mainly small agents and family houses that, even though they did not cater to individuals, were sufficient to meet the financial needs of the population. However, this is not to say that private banking had a significant presence in the capital or in the rest of Jaen province at the end of the century. In fact, this would not be the case until well into the twentieth century.

## 8.4 Private Banking in Jaen in the First Third of the Twentieth Century

The evolution of private banking in Jaen province in the first years of the twentieth century is characterised by two main features: the beginning of national banking by means of opening branch offices and the consolidation of the activity of some local banking houses.

### *8.4.1 The Beginning of National Banking in Jaen in the First Decades of the Twentieth Century*

At the end of the nineteenth century the presence of banks constituted as companies with headquarters in Jaen province was non-existent. Likewise, the presence of branch offices or agencies of foreign banks was reduced, limited to two offices of the Bank of Spain (in Jaen and Linares) and a commissioner of the Mortgage Bank. These entities existed together with a series of private bankers in charge of covering the financial needs of the population.

In the second decade of the new century, the consolidation of the main Spanish banking institutions took place as well as their structuring as truly national banks. A large geographical expansion was then set in motion with the creation of a significant network of branch offices in the main city centres, with three objectives: to increase their foreign sources, to expand their activity and to mine the primacy that the *Banco de España* (*Bank of Spain*) had at that time (Martín-Aceña 2011, p.123).

The banks in Madrid and Bilbao with the largest operations initiated a strong expansion from 1918, becoming true national banks (Muñoz 1978, p. 98). In Jaen province, this transformation was mainly started by the large banks from Madrid.

The aim of these banks was to be able to transfer and drain the savings generated in some areas, and this remained "unproductive" for the industrial areas where it was "required" (Muñoz 1978, p. 103).

In this way, without counting the *Banco de España* (*Bank of Spain*) and the Mortgage Bank (that eventually had 44 branch offices in 1936) (Garrido-González 1995b, p. 373) between 1909 and 1930, four national banks opened in Jaen province, for a total of 25 offices (Bailly-Baillière Annual Directory, 1909 y 1911; Arroyo-Martín 2000, pp. 11–40; Titos-Martínez 2003, pp. 120–121):

1. The *Banco Español de Crédito* (*Spanish Credit Bank*): opening a total of 11 offices in Jaen province between 1909 and 1928;
2. The *Banco Hispano Americano* (*American Hispanic Bank*): initially opening one office in Jaen (1916) and one in Linares (1921).
3. The *Banco Central* (*Central Bank*) arrived in the province, absorbing the *Banco de Albacete* (*Bank of Albacete*) in November 1921 and obtaining its entire network of offices, among which was the one in Andujar, which had been opened in February of that year (Titos-Martínez 2003, p. 120). Between 1921 and 1928, it opened nine branch offices in Jaen.
4. The *Banco Matritense* (*Bank of Madrid*), founded in Madrid in 1911, expended itself throughout the whole territory of Andalusia. Its presence in Jaen province was organised around the opened branch office in the capital on which depended others, as agencies, that would not last long because of the bank liquidation in 1922.

Creating a continuous list of the number and location of the bank's offices in the province is a difficult task due to the lack of information, especially for the years prior to 1922 (Titos-Martínez 2003, p. 123).

The information available leads one to consider that the number of branch offices significantly increased in the whole of Spain in the 1920s until the beginning of the Spanish Civil War. In Jaen province as well, it reached 20 in 1926 and 44 in 1936.[1]

Unfortunately, there is no information about the activity of these private entities in the province. It can be assumed that they experienced a similar evolution to that in the Andalusia region in which these branch offices' business increased in the years prior to the Spanish Civil War, partially thanks to the cessation of the savings banks and the separation of the *Banco de España* (*Bank of Spain*) (Titos-Martínez 2003, p. 123).

### 8.4.2 Local Bankers' Behaviour

Local private banking was not composed of companies, but only of individual agents and small firms that, in some cases, would end up becoming stock companies in the last third of the twentieth century.

The local banking houses and bankers do not disappear with the geographic expansion of the large national banks. In some cases, large banks transformed the small local agents into correspondents to be able to gain access to certain markets. In some others, the bankers were the beginning of other institutions' activity in a particular area because of the business transfer when the banking *status quo* limited the banks' territorial expansion.

Until the entry into force of the Cambo Law[2] (Spanish law), in 1922, the number of bankers operating in Andalusia, and therefore in Jaen, was as extensive as it was imprecise. This was due to two factors. On the one hand, a not very specialized conception of the business that led to consider as bankers, agents with broader activities than strictly banking. And, on the other hand, the legislation itself, as it also did not help in business delimitation.

[1] Information from the *Anuarios Financieros y de Sociedades Anónimas* (Financial and Limited Companies Annual Directories) gathered in Muñoz (1978, pp. 124–130) and from the *Situación* magazine 1980/1982 used by Titos-Martínez (2003).

[2] Banking Organization Law (Spanish law) of 19 December 1921.

When the Cambo Law was approved, a new voluntary registration mechanism was introduced in the bank and the bankers' registry of the Private Banking Ordering Commission (Spanish organisation). This registration included some privileges: bonus for the operations with the *Banco de España* (*Bank of Spain*), special conditions for the activity with the State and the possibility to agree on some taxes. This contributed to the clarification of the activity of these agents and allowed those with a real banking vocation to regularise their situation by registering themselves with the aforementioned Commission (Titos-Martínez 2003, p. 123).

From the 62 bankers that, according to the Spanish Banking Directory, worked in Jaen province in 1922, only two were registered in the official banks and bankers' registry: *Hijo de Dionisio Puche* (*Son of Dionisio Puche*) (Baeza) and *Miñón Hermanos* (*Miñon Brothers*) (Andujar).

### 8.4.3 Hijo de Dionisio Puche (Son of Dionisio Puche)

This banking house has its origin in the one constituted by the main banker in 1873 in Baeza (Arroyo-Martín 2000, p. 98). Mr Gabino Puche Garre was in charge of the firm. It was included for the first time in the Bailly-Baillière Annual Directory in 1879 under the denomination of *Puche Hermanos* (*Puche Brothers*) and, between 1906 and 1911, Dionisio Puche. In the same source, Dionisio Puche Leal also appears as commissioner of the *Banco de España* (*Bank of Spain*) between 1909 and 1911 this was probably the same agent listed as a banker.

It is registered in the merchants and bankers' registry of 1924. This banking house retained its activity during the Spanish Civil War, and hence, at the beginning of 1940, it was operational (Titos-Martínez 2003, p. 133).

We can deduct from the analysis of its main balance reports[3] that it was a modest bank with few credit vocations and that, in the previous years to the battle, it lost business volume as the other banks and bankers did in relation to the rest of the region's financial system (Titos-Martínez 2003, p. 126).

[3] Information from the Boletin del Consejo Superior Bancario (Spanish Banking Superior Council Gazzete) (1922–1929) and from the three-month balances of the banking registry in the Council (1930–1936) and gathered by Titos-Martínez (2003, pp. 173–179) and Arroyo-Martín (2000, pp. 55–108).

It maintained its headquarters in Baeza until 1975 under the business title *Banco Puche* (*Puche Bank*), although it changed its corporation type and business name. That year it moved to Madrid the name of *Banco Meridional* (*Southern Bank*) after being acquired by the Rumasa Group. Several years later, it would change its headquarters to Seville, where it stayed until it was absorbed by the *Banco Bilbao Vizcaya* (*Bilbao Vizcaya Bank*) in 1994 (Patxot 1999, pp. 89–121).

#### *8.4.3.1 Miñón Brothers*

This is a firm constituted in 1872 of businessmen bankers from Andujar working in activities related to olive oil extraction and ceramics manufacturing (Arroyo-Martín 2000, p. 101). It was included for the first time in the Bailly-Baillière Annual Directory in 1881 and it retained the same denomination until 1911.

This banking house was registered in the register of banks and bankers in 1926. After this, they functioned normally until the beginning of the Spanish Civil War.

It was a bank with much larger dimensions than those of *Hijo de Dionisio Puche* (*Son of Dionisio Puche*) and was more commercially oriented to credit. However, as well as the bank in Baeza, it experimented with an important contraction of its activity in the years prior to the Spanish Civil War.

Once the battle was over, the house of *Miñón Hermanos* (*Miñon Brothers*) continued to be registered in the Spanish Banking Ordering Commission but, apparently, it did not have any activity, or it was at least not known to the Spanish Banking Ordering Commission. Nevertheless, its activity resumed in 1940 after it acquired the pertinent authorisation from the Central Committee of Spanish Banking. And it remained until it was absorbed by the *Banco de Bilbao* (*Bank of Bilbao*) in 1952 (Titos-Martínez 2003, p. 125).

## 8.5 Conclusions

In the nineteenth century, banking activity, in the private sector, was developed in Spain by two types of agents. On the one hand, the banks constituted individually, on some occasions as partnerships or limited partnerships, as is the case of the bankers, merchant bankers and banking houses. On the other hand, others organised as limited companies, such as banks and credit unions.

However, the financial sector in Jaen province did not follow the same consolidation model as other areas in the country, probably due to the lack of a booming economic sector and the weakness of internal savings. Therefore, during the nineteenth century, in this territory there was no bank constituted as a company and the financial needs of the population were covered by individual bankers and small family banking houses.

From the academic research literature on the bankers in Jaen in the nineteenth century, we obtained a list of 16 agents that developed this activity throughout that century. This number is consistent with the one provided by the available statistics from that time related to the enrolments in the industrial contribution that gathered a total of six bankers at the end of the century.

This list was completed, for the 1879–1911 period, with the information gathered in the Bailly-Baillière Annual Directory, a source that had not been used in any of these publications. This Annual Directory is a guide that includes an enormous number of pieces of information at the State level as well as the provincial one, including all the business and administrative sectors. After consulting this source, we compiled a list of a total of 70 bankers that worked in Jaen province between 1879 and 1900. This number increases up to 96 in the 1900–1911 period. Some of them, as can be deduced from the information included in the Annual Directory, did not exclusively work in banking activity, and at the same time were involved in other types of business, fitting more into the category of merchant bankers than that of bankers.

The difference between the numbers is due to two potential key factors. On the one hand, there is the lack of the bankers' activity delimitation that led agents with wider activities than banking to be registered in these Annual Directories. On the other hand, there is the fact that enrolment in the industrial contribution meant a payment of a fee based on the activity carried out. Given that some of these agents were actually more like businessmen-bankers, the recognition of their double activity meant a higher payment to the contribution, and this is why many of them (especially the smallest ones) decided not to register their financial activity, and even continued to work illegally in terms of paying taxes.

In spite of the inaccuracies, this annual directory proved very useful in completing, at least for the years that it was published, information on an age in which the number of bankers in the Spanish provinces was as extensive as it was imprecise.

Regarding the twentieth century, until the entry into force of the Cambo Law (Spanish law) in 1922, the number of bankers working in Jaen was quite uncertain. In fact, there is little reference to them in the consulted literature.

As the years went by, the business delimitation became more specific and bankers were regularising their activity by registering in official registries. In 1922 the Banking Directory included the presence of 62 bankers in Jaen province.

At the same time, in the second decade of the new century, an important consolidation process of the large Spanish banks was implemented that established a broad expansion over the whole national territory. In Jaen province, the leading banks were those in Madrid that, between 1909 and 1903, opened up 25 branch offices in this territory.

The compulsory registration in the Spanish Banks and Bankers' Registry, established by the Spanish Cambo Law (1921) was the key factor in the final configuration of the private banking sector in Jaen province. Of all those working in the banking activity in this territory, only two agents were registered: *Hijo de Dionisio Puche* (*Son of Dionisio Puche*) (Baeza) and *Miñón Hermanos* (*Miñon Brothers*) (Andujar).

Thus, when the 1930s started, the private banking sector recognised officially in the province was composed of two local firms (none of them in the capital) and approximately 20 foreign banking offices in 14 towns (including the capital). Years later, well into the twentieth century, two banking houses disappeared from the provincial banking scene as they were absorbed by large national banks.

## References

Anuario del comercio, de la industria, de la magistratura y de la administración (Bailly-Baillière Annual Directory) (1881–1888, 1894, 1897–1906, 1908–1909 y 1911). Biblioteca Nacional de España, Hemeroteca Digital.

Anuario-almanaque del comercio, de la industria, de la magistratura y de la administración (Bailly-Baillière Annual Directory) (1879–1880). Biblioteca Nacional de España, Hemeroteca Digital.

Arroyo, Mercedes. 2006. "Actitudes empresariales y estructura industrial. El gas de Málaga, 1854–1929." *Scripta Nova. Revista Electrónica de Geografía y Ciencias Sociales* X (215). http://www.ub.edu/geocrit/sn/sn-215.htm. Accessed on March 25, 2020.

Arroyo-Martín, José Víctor. 2000. *La banca privada en Andalucía entre 1920 y 1935*. Bilbao: Archivo Histórico del Banco Bilbao Vizcaya Argentaria.
Duro-Cobo, José Juan. 1985. La actividad financiera y crediticia en la provincia de Jaén. Una reseña histórica. *Boletín de la Cámara Oficial de Comercio e Industria de Jaén* 36: 3–18.
García-López, José Ramón. 1989. El sistema bancario español del siglo XIX. ¿Una estructura dual? Nuevos planteamientos y nuevas propuestas. *Revista de Historia Económica* VII (1): 116–119.
Garcia-Orallo, Ricardo. 2016. Mercados de crédito, crisis económica y estructura social en la Cataluña del Nordeste (1875–1905). *Investigaciones de Historia Económica* 12 (1): 22–33.
Garrido-González, Luis. 1995a. Economía liberal y sociedad jiennense en el siglo XIX. In *Nueva historia contemporánea de la provincia de Jaén (1808–1950)*, ed. coordinated by Luis Garrido-González, 255–349. Jaén: Instituto de Estudios Giennenses.
———. 1995b. Economía liberal y sociedad en el Jaén del siglo XX. In *Nueva historia contemporánea de la provincia de Jaén (1808–1950)*, ed. coordinated by Luis Garrido-González, 353–392. Jaén: Instituto de Estudios Giennenses.
López-Cordero, Juan Antonio. 1992. *El Jaén isabelino: economía y sociedad*. Granada: Universidad de Granada.
López-Pérez, Manuel. 1977. La Caja de Ahorros de Jaén: una frustración histórica. *Boletín de la Cámara Oficial de Comercio e Industria de Jaén* 30: 3–17.
Martín-Aceña, Pablo. 2011. La banca en España entre 1900 y 1975. In *Un siglo de historia del sistema financiero español*, ed. José Luis Malo de Molina and Pablo Martín-Aceña, 117–161. Alianza: Madrid.
Muñoz, Juan. 1978. La expansión bancaria entre 1919 y 1926: la formación de una banca nacional. *Cuadernos Económicos de ICE* 6: 98–162.
Patxot, Victoria. 1999. Medio siglo del Registro de Bancos y Banqueros 1947–1997. Madrid: Banco de España.
Pons, María Ángeles. 1999. "Las grandes sociedades anónimas bancarias 1860–1960." In El sistema financiero en España. Una síntesis histórica, coordinated by Pablo Martín Aceña and Manuel Titos-Martínez. 83–103. Granada: Universidad de Granada.
Rodríguez, Cristino M. 1922. "Muertos Ilustres: Don Félix García." Don Lope de Sosa. Crónica Mensual de la Provincia de Jaén 1922: 131–133.
Tarifa-Fernández, Adela. 2011. El humanista ubetense Juan Pasquau Guerrero. Jaén: Instituto de Estudios Giennenses.
Tedde de Lorca, Pedro. 1974. "La banca privada española durante la Restauración 1874–1914." In La banca española en la Restauración. Tomo I Política y Finanzas, edited by Gabriel Anes Álvarez, et al. 217–455. Madrid: Servicio de Estudios del Banco de España.

Tedde de Lorca, Pedro. 1983. "Comerciantes y banqueros madrileños al final del Antiguo Régimen." In Historia económica y pensamiento social, edited by Gabriel Anes et al. 301–334. Madrid: Alianza Editorial.

Titos-Martínez, Manuel. 1999. "Banca y banqueros privados." In El sistema financiero en España. Una síntesis histórica, coordinated by Pablo Martín-Aceña and Manuel Titos-Martínez. 105–133. Granada: Universidad de Granada.

———. 2003. El sistema financiero en Andalucía: tres siglos de historia (1740–2000). Sevilla: Instituto de Estadística de Andalucía.

CHAPTER 9

# Public Services in Spain: The Role of Water Supply Companies

*Juan Manuel Matés-Barco*

## 9.1 Introduction[1]

This chapter studies the drinking water supply companies in Spain during the second industrial revolution. The period studied spans from 1840 to the early decades of the twentieth century. A long-term approach allows us to analyse the changes that the management of this public service has undergone. The strong growth in the demand for drinking water, prompted by the increase in population that took place in small- and medium-sized cities over this period, led to an organisational model characterised by *regulation* and in which the technique of *administrative concession* has prevailed.

[1]This work is part of the results of the R&D Excellence Project HAR2017-82112-P (2018–2020): "The Gas Industry in Spain: Regional Development and Trajectories (1842–2008)", financed by the Spanish Ministry of Economy and Competitiveness. A more extensive study of the subject, with detailed footnotes, can be found at Matés-Barco (2018a, 2019b).

J. M. Matés-Barco (✉)
University of Jaén, Jaén, Spain
e-mail: jmmates@ujaen.es





M. Vázquez-Fariñas et al. (eds.), *Companies and Entrepreneurs in the History of Spain*, Palgrave Studies in Economic History,
https://doi.org/10.1007/978-3-030-61318-1_9

The historical analysis of drinking water supply companies is of particular interest for several reasons: firstly, because of the leading role that this group of companies acquired throughout the nineteenth century; secondly, because this business phenomenon generated a unique and characteristic typology, and exhibits features that allow us to examine the various forms that the sector took; and finally, it is worth noting the novelty that these companies represented from the technological point of view and the significant concentration of investment—both national and foreign—that their creation brought with it. The academic literature has focused on the study of these elements, especially with the works of Falkus (1977), Goubert (1988), Guillerme (1988), Hassan (1998), Millward (2007) and Tomory (2015, 2017), among others.

In Spain these companies operated within a legislative framework characterised by the emergence of techniques such as the natural monopoly and the administrative concession, which have played a predominant role in the development of public services and in the improvement of health and hygiene. The study of these companies provides an insight into certain forms of market organisation, as well as explains their national and international expansion (Lorrain 2002; Fernández 2014; Matés-Barco 2016). However, until a few years ago, despite the importance of the sector, it was one of the most forgotten by historiography.

In 1840, the first company dedicated to the supply of drinking water—*Mina Pública Aguas de Tarrasa*—was established, and throughout this decade, incipient initiatives to implement a modern supply service are observed. This stage ended in 1936 due to the change in course that occurred with the outbreak of the Spanish civil war. From that date onwards, private companies began to languish, which culminated in the progressive municipalisation of the water supply service by town councils.

The information gathered makes it possible to describe these companies as a whole, their role in the business context and the basic factors that have governed their organisational development in the medium and long term. The sources used have been abundant and varied. Firstly, there are the yearbooks and official censuses from the first half of the twentieth century; for example, the *Anuario Financiero y de Sociedades Anónimas de España* (Financial and Public Company Yearbook of Spain), the *Anuario Financiero de Bilbao* (Financial Yearbook of Bilbao), the *Anuario Técnico Industrial de España* (Technical Industrial Yearbook of Spain) and the *Estadística de la Contribución de utilidades de la Riqueza Mobiliaria* (Statistics on the Contribution of Earnings from Movable Wealth).

Secondly, the reports and existing documentation in the archives of the Ministries of Finance and Public Works, as well as the municipal ones—especially in Madrid and Barcelona—have provided very complete information on companies and supply projects. Thirdly, the *Revista de Obras Públicas* (Journal of Public Works), founded in 1853, together with the official reports and statistics of the time, has furnished relevant data.[2] Likewise, the annual reports of the companies and the commemorative books published at different times have been useful. Finally, it is worth mentioning the *Catálogo de Sociedades de abastecimiento de agua potable* (Catalogue of Drinking Water Supply Companies), which presents an exhaustive study of the existing bibliography and detailed information on each of the 273 water companies that operated in Spain between 1840 and 1990. This set of sources provides an interesting panorama and offers a very complete list of private companies dedicated to the supply of water (Matés-Barco 2014, 2018a).

After this brief introduction, the second section deals with the role of the supply companies within the business context. The third section analyses the different types of companies according to the size of their investments. Section four describes some of the essential characteristics of these companies and of the supply sector: the duration of the concessions, as well as their stability and survival over time. The fifth and sixth sections deal with the nature of this business, as well as business strategy and the struggle for market control. Finally, some brief conclusions are drawn.

## 9.2 The Business Context of Water Supply Companies

Between 1840 and 1936, Spain experienced a period of continuous growth in the number of private companies dedicated to the supply of water. These companies were primarily based in the large cities and in the areas with the greatest urban development and characterised by economic dynamism (Villar-Chamorro et al. 2019). After this period of expansion, private companies began to decline between 1940 and 1980 and progressively disappeared from the business panorama. Only a few companies were able to resist the onslaught of interventionism.

[2] *Estadística de Obras Públicas*, 1895–1900; *Reseña Geográfica y Estadística de España*, 1888; *Revista de Obras Públicas*, 1851–1990; *Dirección General de Contribuciones*, 1901–1933.

The spread of water companies in Spain occurred slowly, to the point that during the second half of the nineteenth century they were only operating in 47 towns, when at this time there were more than 8000 municipalities. These companies sought out the main cities, but they were also found in small towns that already had an entity in charge of the supply. However, there were many companies that could not withstand the difficulties of a sector that was just starting up, and folded soon afterwards. To date, we know of the incorporation of 83 companies before 1900, most of which were centred in the big cities.

The global numbers point to some interesting aspects of the sector. The first shows that the sector was beginning to develop in Spain despite the limited business fabric in the country and the reluctance of private capital to invest in this type of economic activity. The second aspect is that the attraction of large cities is evident; of the 47 cities that had a company before the end of the nineteenth century, 18 had more than 20,000 inhabitants in 1860, and as many again were close to that figure. Within this group, it is worth mentioning that some important centres—Almeria, Bilbao, Malaga, Zaragoza, Las Palmas, Palma de Mallorca and San Sebastian—did not have private initiatives before 1900, and it was the city council that was directly responsible for the management of the service. The long conflict that took place in Malaga starting in 1870, between the city council and the various concession companies, is an example of the vicissitudes that many Spanish cities went through to obtain a modern supply of drinking water (Heredia-Flores 2013). The third and final aspect is the appearance of companies that, at a fairly early stage, were responsible for supplying small municipalities. This presence denoted, in an incipient way, a trend that became more pronounced in the first decades of the twentieth century.

Table 9.1 shows the role that water supply companies played in the business context. The classification of business sectors in 1922, when water companies were at their peak, indicates a similar trend in the following years. The group of water supply companies was in 15th place, on a par with groups such as insurance, public works, tobacco or electrical equipment companies. Logically, the first positions were occupied by banks, electricity and gas companies, railways and mining corporations. Compared to the more than 1.4 billion pesetas of paid-up capital that the banking or electricity companies had established, the 166 million pesetas of the water companies may seem an insignificant figure. But these great differences can be put into perspective if one observes, for example, that the textile

**Table 9.1** Water supply companies (1922–1934). Number of companies and amount of capital and outstanding bonds. Both percentages are in relation to the rest of the business sectors

| *Year* | *Companies* | | *Authorised capital* | | *Paid-up capital* | *Outstanding bonds* |
|---|---|---|---|---|---|---|
| | *Number* | *Percentage* | *Millions of pesetas* | *Percentage* | *Millions of pesetas* | *Millions of pesetas* |
| *(1)* | *(2)* | *(3)* | *(4)* | *(5)* | *(6)* | *(7)* |
| 1922 | 101 | 2.66 | 166 | 1.67 | 151 | 103 |
| 1926 | 110 | 2.53 | 192 | 1.69 | 171 | 156 |
| 1927 | 116 | 2.48 | 204 | 1.57 | 175 | 187 |
| 1930 | 122 | 2.65 | 236 | 1.54 | 204 | 300 |
| 1931 | 117 | 2.58 | 177 | 1.12 | 158 | 316 |
| 1932 | 117 | 2.53 | 223 | 1.42 | 197 | 312 |
| 1933 | 122 | 2.57 | 215 | 1.36 | 188 | 270 |
| 1934 | 120 | 2.50 | 214 | 1.34 | 186 | 268 |

*Sources*: Author's own elaboration with data from *Anuario Financiero y de Sociedades Anónimas de España*, [AFSAE]; *Sociedades de Aguas Potables y de Riegos*, Madrid, 1922–1934; *Anuario Financiero de Bilbao*, which includes the *Historial de los Valores Públicos y de Sociedades Anónimas de España* [AFB]; *Aguas*, Bilbao, Banco de Vizcaya, 1930–1934

companies—of great importance in Spain—were in the 11th place with 234 million pesetas of paid-up capital, that is, barely above the water companies. The 1920s show how water supply companies were at the same level as tramways, public works, insurance or electrical equipment companies. In 1930 their numbers increased, and their capitalisation also grew. This was their high point and from then on, they began to decapitalise and suffer the ravages of inflation.

Except for the electrical companies, banks, railroads and mining companies, which represented very high percentages in terms of capital (14.91%, 11.06%, 10.81% and 6.30%, respectively, in 1927), or new sectors such as telephones, which had 9.35% of capital, water supply companies moved within a large and numerous group which ranged from 1.04% for cement companies to 3.92% for textiles. These figures from 1927 show that, between the sixth place occupied by textile companies in terms of paid-up capital and the 22nd place for those firms dedicated to shipbuilding, there was a group of sectors made up of companies engaged in shipping, chemicals, machinery, steelworks, sugar, tramways, public works, insurance, cement and so on. The comparison with the tramway companies, a typically municipal service, shows that the water supply companies moved within similar parameters to those described in other public services. In other words, they were not out of step with other sectors that could to some extent be representative of the economic situation of the time (Martínez López 2008; Núñez and Buendía 2008).

These figures indicate that water supply companies were a group that had been on the rise since the second half of the nineteenth century. The number of companies and their capitalisation increased, and it was increasingly common for small or medium-sized towns to have a water supply company to manage the service. The peak was between 1930 and 1932, and it continued with small fluctuations until practically the civil war. From 1934 onwards, the loss of importance of the companies is observed, which became more acute and began to be felt especially after the civil war. During the conflict itself, companies such as *Aguas de Córdoba* were municipalised, and from then on the number of companies decreased and their decapitalisation continued unabated.

Gregorio Núñez has pointed to the presence of the public debt of a good part of the Spanish municipalities in the first third of the twentieth century as an indicator of the modernisation drive at the local level. In the same vein, José Luis Hernández-Marco has shown how local town councils resorted to private investment and emerging capital markets, both local and national, as well as to the modern financial institutions of the time (Hernández-Marco 2008; Núñez 2008).

Before 1900, the sources are not very precise, and it is difficult to know the exact number of companies. However, there are sufficient data to carry out a detailed study of the sector. The public companies, as an organisational model, provided the most significant support in the expansion of the water supply service in Spanish cities. The companies that did not adopt this typology were merely marginal in providing the service, limited to small neighbourhoods or the smaller towns.

In 1870 there were 22 water companies that were responsible for home supply, in 1890 there were 30, and by 1900 the number had already reached 48. From the latter date onwards, more specific data are available to help understand the situation and the evolution of the sector. The information has been extracted mainly from the *Anuarios Financieros*, the *Anuario Técnico Industrial de España* and the *Estadística de la Contribución de Utilidades de la Riqueza Mobiliaria* (ECURM). The data from the *Estadística de la Contribución* do not appear to be very exhaustive, given that for 1905 it only includes 19 companies and in 1910 it includes 37. These low figures may be related to the contributory nature of the source, which would lead many companies to try to avoid these responsibilities. However, the data provided by the same source for 1915 are already considerably more representative: 56 companies, and more in line with what is found in others from the same period, although their limitation is still apparent. The data from the *Anuarios Financieros* seem to be more complete, since they had a purely informative purpose. In 1913, a total of 70 companies were known to exist, and a significant advance was noted, from 101 companies in 1922 to 120 in 1934, with some small variations in those years, as shown in Table 9.2.

Observation of the business phenomenon between 1922 and 1934, the final years of the period of plenitude, shows the state of the sector in its maximum splendour. Both the number of drinking water supply companies and the amount of invested capital indicate that the sector occupied an important place in the group of Spanish public limited companies. It was one of the sectors with the highest number of companies, and although in absolute figures it increased throughout this period, its percentage compared to the rest of the sectors decreased progressively. The same occurred with the overall amount of capital invested: steady growth despite the appearance in 1931 of an ostensible decline in investment, which was the result of the political instability suffered that year. The restrictions imposed by the strengthening of interventions by the state and the refusal of local city councils to allow increases in water rates slightly delayed the sector in comparison with previous years. In 1930, when the sector was at its peak, the number of companies rose to 122, a fairly significant figure given the characteristics that prevailed in the sector: a tendency for companies to set up in large cities, local monopolies and taking advantage of economies of scale. The number of water companies is also significant when compared to the quantity of cities with more than 10,000 inhabitants at that time, which was 178, as it implies that just over 60% of communities of that size had some kind of water supply company. The same sources peg the number of water companies at 95 for 1950, a figure that indicates the decline these firms began to experience during the dictatorship.

**Table 9.2** Number of drinking water supply companies

| *Year* | *Number* |
|---|---|
| 1870 | 22 |
| 1890 | 30 |
| 1900 | 48 |
| 1905 | 19 |
| 1910 | 37 |
| 1913 | 70 |
| 1922 | 101 |
| 1926 | 110 |
| 1927 | 116 |
| 1930 | 122 |
| 1931 | 117 |
| 1932 | 117 |
| 1933 | 122 |
| 1934 | 120 |

*Sources*: Author's own elaboration with data from *Reseña Geográfica y Estadística de España* (1888); Dirección General de Contribuciones, *Estadística de la Contribución de Utilidades de la Riqueza Mobiliaria* [ECURM], Madrid, 1905, 1910 and 1915; Anuario Técnico e Industrial de España, *Empresas y sociedades de abastecimiento de aguas*, Madrid, 1913; Anuario Financiero y de Sociedades Anónimas de España, *Sociedades de Aguas Potables y de Riegos*, Madrid, 1922–1950; *Anuario Financiero de Bilbao*, which includes the *Historial de los Valores Públicos y de Sociedades Anónimas de España*, *Aguas*, Bilbao, Banco de Vizcaya, 1930–1934

## 9.3 The Investment Capacity of Drinking Water Supply Companies

The role played by investments in the process of urban transformation that Spanish cities experienced in the last third of the nineteenth century and first third of the twentieth century was very important. The share of fixed capital that the cities incorporated in the planning and development of road infrastructure, urban services and so on involved a substantial mobilisation of financial resources. The significant immobilisation of capital that had to be carried out and the slowness with which it could be recovered made it quite risky. Nevertheless, from the early stages and despite the inherent difficulties, entrepreneurs were willing to invest in the water supply business. But this involvement was made in response to a series of considerations, one of the most important of which was obtaining concessions under a monopoly regime (Bigatti 2014; Matés-Barco 2004, p. 169).

The existing data show that investment flows were significant in the 1880s. The same can be said of the first decades of the twentieth century, which saw a strong push by investors based on the good results obtained by the companies in the final stages of the nineteenth century. Some of these firms had been operating for quite some time and were earning profits which they, in turn, reinvested. It was common to resort to self-financing. At the same time, expectations of future profits were influenced by the results obtained in previous years. Business surpluses were a key determinant of capital formation. Investment also followed an upward trend from the late nineteenth century, which became more pronounced in the 1920s. As the scale of the water supply business grew, the use of borrowing became exponentially greater, as did the allocation of reserves.

Figure 9.1 shows the evolution of resources in the long term, specifically in the period 1903–1936. It shows rather timid growth, almost imperceptible, until 1915. The low level of investment is due to the economic recession at the end of the nineteenth century, and to the fact that the service was not yet very widespread in the smaller towns. This situation led to certain reservations on the part of investors. The final decades of the nineteenth century had been a hive of activity in the sector, at least in large cities like Barcelona. New companies emerged, and after a few months or years they ceased to exist. It was not surprising that investors were distrustful of the fact that companies were not yet well established in the market. On the other hand, except for a few very specific firms, the levels of profits and profitability were not very high either, providing an explanation for the reticence on the part of investors. It seems clear that demand was weak in these years and poorly consolidated.

From 1916–1917 onwards, there was a continuous rise in investment, which was not interrupted until 1934. Several factors indicate that the consolidation of the sector was taking place: the implementation of the service in a greater number of towns, an increase in the number of subscribers and, finally, higher levels of profits and profitability. This is the period of greatest expansion in the sector. The growth trend can be seen starting in 1922 and the peak was reached in 1930. From that year onwards, stabilisation began to be detected in the sector as a consequence of the interventionist influence that had been exercised for several years. With the civil war and the post-war period, investments entered an impasse

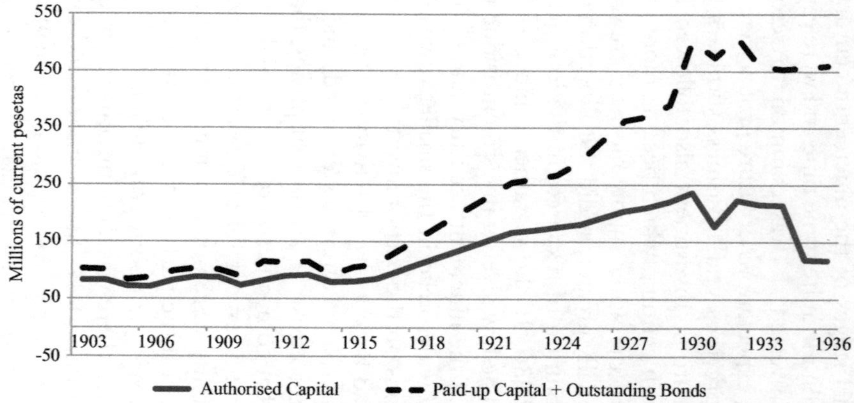


**Fig. 9.1** Drinking water supply companies: Evolution of invested capital (1900–1936). (*Sources*: Author's own elaboration with data from Dirección General de Contribuciones, *Estadística de la Contribución de Utilidades de la Riqueza Mobiliaria, Madrid*, 1905–1915. Anuario Técnico e Industrial de España, Empresas y sociedades de abastecimiento de aguas, Madrid, 1913. Anuario Financiero y de Sociedades Anónimas de España, *Sociedades de Aguas Potables y de Riegos*, Madrid, 1922–1936. Anuario Financiero de Bilbao que comprende el Historial de los Valores Públicos y de Sociedades Anónimas de España, *Aguas*, Bilbao, Banco de Vizcaya, 1930–1934)

to which no easy solution appeared. The economic crisis, inflation and the freezing of rates did the rest, and the paralysis of investment was constantly manifesting itself in the inability of water companies to increase their supply networks.

Two divergent trends can be seen in the size of water supply companies. On the one hand, the degree of investment per inhabitant was fairly homogeneous, since they tried to deal with the supply needs by providing a minimum service, intended only for home supply and with a basic technological level. On the other hand, investment in these companies was quite uneven and was usually closely related to the size of the city. These enterprises were not particularly noted for their large scale, since the structure of the supplies themselves led to the existence of a great variety of companies. Before 1880 it was common for small companies to appear, even in large cities, as the practice of creating monopolies was not yet very well established; however, between 1881 and 1900, the emergence of companies of considerable size began.

The known data on total assets refer, for the most part, to the most profitable and longest-running companies. Most companies had, at the peak of their activity—in the 1920s—total assets ranging from four to eight million pesetas. Logically, the two biggest companies in the sector, *Aguas de Barcelona* and *Aguas Potables y Mejoras de Valencia*, were much larger than this.

In the second half of the nineteenth century, many of these companies emerged thanks to the contributions of foreign capital—British, French and Belgian—which also contributed their knowledge, technology and industrial materials. As Fernández-Paradas (2009, p. 110; 2016) indicates, this phenomenon was not exclusive to water supply companies, but was the result of a trend that was occurring in some public services, most notably the railways and the first gas, tram and electricity companies.

According to data from Costa Campi, investments made in the nineteenth century by water companies, with the total or partial participation of foreign capital, amounted to 40,670,400 pesetas. French capital predominated with 48.6% of total foreign investment, followed by English with 34.56% and, finally, that of Belgian origin with 16.82%. More specifically, Table 9.3 shows the breakdown of investment and the percentage compared to total foreign investment in Spain (Costa 1981; Matés-Barco 2002; Castro-Valdivia and Matés-Barco 2020).

**Table 9.3** Investments by foreign water supply companies in Spain (nineteenth century)

| | *Total investment (pesetas)* | *Percentage of total foreign investment* |
|---|---|---|
| France | 19,768,750 | 23.71 |
| England | 14,057,900 | 28.57 |
| Belgium | 6,843,750 | 16.45 |

*Sources*: Author's own elaboration with data from Costa (1981, pp. 45–83), Matés-Barco (2002, pp. 301–316)

## 9.4 The Characteristics of the Drinking Water Companies

The information provided by the sources of the time and the data existing in the accounting records of some companies allow us to reveal several characteristics of the drinking water supply companies.

Firstly, it is worth noting the change in the concession regime for the supply of water to communities, which varied over the years. While in the early stages, 1840–1880, they were generally granted for an unlimited period of time, later concessions included the 99-year clause, which had been established in the Water Law of 1879. This was the predominant model, although in the early years of the twentieth century it became quite frequent to grant concessions for a shorter time period: 20, 25, 30, 40, 50, 60 and 75 years. Some specific cases are as follows: *Hidráulica Santillana* (1905), which obtained the concession for 50 years; *Aguas, Luz y Fuerza de la Segarra* (1912), for 25 years; *City of Las Palmas Water* (1913), for 60 years; *Aguas Potables de Ripollet-Sardañola* (1917), for 20 years; *Aguas de Argentona a Mataró* (1922), for 60 years; *Aguas de León* (1923), for 75 years; *Hidráulica Carpense* (1923), for 30 years; *Aguas de Villafranca* (1924), for 60 years; and, finally, *Aguas de Viladecans* (1931), for 40 years.[3] These modifications seem to be related to the progressive interest shown by town councils, from about 1900, in obtaining the reversal of the concessions.

Secondly, there was great instability in the companies at the early stages of the sector. This peculiarity allows us to divide the companies set up throughout the second half of the nineteenth century into three groups:

[3] Anuario Técnico e Industrial de España [ATIE], *Empresas y sociedades de abastecimiento de aguas*, Madrid, 1913, 19; Anuario Financiero y de Sociedades Anónimas de España, [AFSAE], *Sociedades de Aguas Potables y de Riegos*, Madrid, 1931, 129.

(1) those that lasted in the water market for little more than two or three years, (2) those that did not survive beyond 20 years and (3) those that managed to hang on for a long time, some until they reached the end of their concession period.

For the first case—companies with a very short duration—we can cite examples such as *Jean Bouchard*'s company, which was founded in 1860 to supply water to La Coruña and by 1861 had already discontinued the service. In the same city, the *Luis Petit* company was in charge of the supply between 1863 and 1866. This situation was repeated in other cities, both with national companies—*Compañía de Aguas Potables de Muntanya* (1883–1890) and *Compañía General Anónima de Aguas de Barcelona* (1881–1890)—and with foreign ones.[4] Examples of foreign water companies with a short duration include *Cádiz Water Works*, which operated between 1872 and 1876, and *Barcelona Besós Waterworks*, which operated between 1892 and 1895.

For the second group, companies that were not established in the market for more than 20 years, again the cases were repeated massively in Barcelona (Matés-Barco 2019a).[5] *Palau, García y Cía* was set up in 1857 and managed to maintain its supply until 1865, the *Compañía de Aguas de Barcelona* was in charge of the supply between 1867 and 1882; the *Empresa del Alto Vallés* supplied some areas of the city between 1869 and 1890, as did the *Compañía de Aguas de Sants* between 1869 and 1887; and finally, the *Compañía de Aguas de San Martí de Provençal* between 1878 and 1895. In other cities the problem was repeated; for example, the British company *Alicante Water Work* was in charge of the water supply in that city between 1883 and 1898.

Among the companies that remained in place over the very long term, several cases can be cited.[6] In Valladolid, the *Sociedad Industrial Castellana*, which had managed the supply since 1876, ceded its rights to the city council in 1959. Similar situations occurred with *The Seville Water Works Company* (1881–1957) and *Aguas de Alicante* (1898–1956). Other companies ceded their concessions some years before their termination dates;

[4] Anuario Financiero de Bilbao que comprende el Historial de los Valores Públicos y de Sociedades Anónimas de España [AFB], *Aguas*, Bilbao, Banco de Vizcaya, 408; AFSAE, 1927, 512–515.

[5] AFSAE, 1935, 278; AFB, 1948, 409.

[6] AFSAE, 1934, 339; AFB, 1950, 402.

for example, *Aguas Potables de Villafranca* (1881–1921), *Aguas Potables de Cádiz* (1885–1927) and *Aguas Potables de Córdoba* (1891–1938).

The existing statistics for the first decades of the twentieth century allow us to draw attention to other peculiarities. Of the 70 companies included in the 1913 *Technical and Industrial Yearbook of Spain*, some 23 had been founded before 1900, which shows that a third of the companies had managed to establish themselves in the business of water management despite the initial difficulties of the sector. However, this success is more nuanced when we learn that 82 companies were founded during the nineteenth century. A certain instability can be seen in many of the early initiatives, although it is observed that companies established in medium or large cities managed to survive. The estimate, made after considering those population centres with more than 10,000 inhabitants in 1900, is even more evident when the analysis is raised to those that were above 30,000 inhabitants.

Of the companies founded before 1900, only those that had made significant investments managed to survive, although it does not seem that their stability was as much due to the size of the company as to the conditions of the city. A small company in a medium or large city had significant growth potential, to the extent that it was able to cope with the investments needed to extend the supply network. The large investments of the big companies were mostly made at the end of the nineteenth century.

Before 1900, in almost all the large cities there was a household water supply network managed by a private company. The security provided by the term of the concessions, generally quite high and specified by the Water Law at 99 years, allowed these companies to be very stable. The history of some of these companies in their initial stages shows the instability they went through at the start, but it can also be seen how they endured with guarantees beyond 40 or 50 years. The relationship of some companies such as *Aguas de Jerez* (1868), *Sociedad Industrial Castellana* (1876), *Aguas del Gévora* (1878), *Aguas Potables de Cádiz* (1885), *Aguas Potables de Córdoba* (1891) or *Aguas de Arteta* (1893) with the length of their concession is sufficiently evident, since it was not until well into the 1920s that they began to suffer the effects of municipalist policies, and they remained profitable until then.

These data show that there were no considerable differences between companies based in large or small cities. Nor can it be forgotten that many of these companies went through periods of doubt and instability in the big cities. In the initial years, companies emerged that only lasted a few years, or even a few months, due to the inexperience and novelty that existed in the sector. Before the emergence of a strong company that could cope with the vicissitudes of the business, many attempts were made that did not succeed. What occurred in Barcelona, Cádiz, Valencia, Cartagena, Murcia, Pamplona, Córdoba and Valladolid are clear examples. In the big cities there were companies that managed to establish themselves in the market and survive for many years, perhaps much more easily than in the smaller towns. But at the start, the larger cities also suffered the appearance of water companies that lasted for just a short time in the market, and that can be said to have paved the way for other stronger firms. The difference, therefore, with the smaller towns was that the failures of the first companies in the big cities led to the appearance of larger companies, capable of managing the supply for many years, while in the smaller towns this dissolution soon left the service in the hands of the town councils. Everything points to the fact that by 1900–1905, the sector was coming of age, with an organisational, technical and business profile that enabled it to deal with all kinds of situations. This fact is confirmed by the abundant number of companies founded between 1900 and 1915.

## 9.5 The Nature of the Drinking Water Business

To a large extent, the characteristics of the water companies were determined by the nature of the business. This type of initiative was characterised by the fact that it was attractive to the small saver, symbolised by the father of the family who was looking above all for a stable, very predictable investment, but something more profitable than the securities of the state. The dividends from these investments, which were between 5% and 6%, were well above the 3% offered by government bonds and it was logical that this new alternative was chosen. In addition, companies tended to raise resources by issuing bonds because the market demanded it, but also because it was a way of limiting risk and providing a more secure income that would attract this type of investor. On the other hand, some of these investments came with the backing and prestige of major foreign companies, which contrasted with the much-maligned reputation traditionally granted to government securities throughout the nineteenth century (Castro-Valdivia et al. 2019).

In the early days, the family element was important in the organisation of the small companies, although over time they evolved into more modern type of businesses. Due to their specific characteristics, water supply companies grew from the second half of the nineteenth century onwards on the basis of an organisation in which small and medium-sized companies predominated, which were thinly capitalised and, on many occasions, had a family structure. The internal markets, with their relatively low levels of earnings, delayed the industrialisation process, and therefore generated a rather weak organisational structure in the water companies. The family element—without being the most predominant—is seen in the continuity that existed for several generations due to the control of some companies. Among various examples, there is the Carbonell family in *Aguas de Cerro Muriano*,[7] the Castelltor-Gabarró family in *Aguas de Rigat*,[8] Abarzuza in *Aguas Potables de Cádiz*,[9] the Guisasola family in *Aguas de León*,[10] the Pastor family in *Aguas Potables de Aspe*[11] and, finally, the clan made up of the various groups of the families Garriga-Nogués, Garí Gimeno, Garí Rossi, Más Sardá, Borrás and Calvell, which from around 1920 were gradually consolidated in the control of *Aguas de Barcelona*.

The predominance of small- and medium-sized companies based on a clearly family business structure was a fairly characteristic system in the final decades of the nineteenth century and the first third of the twentieth century. Despite this, there were companies that, due to their development and size, gradually incorporated more advanced forms of organisation, born of the separation between ownership and management, of which *Aguas de Barcelona* was the most significant example.

After carrying out an analysis of the payroll of directors and board members of the various companies, three essential points can be noted. The first is the interrelationship observed between the various business groups, as evidenced by the presence and control of various boards of directors. The process of business concentration that took place during the Francoist period can be seen in the years when the sector was at its peak. Valencia and Barcelona form part of these nuclei. In terms of the former city, the Spanish companies of *Abastecimientos*, *Aguas Potables y Mejoras de Valencia* and *Omnium Ibérico* emerged. This group became, in

[7] AFSAE, 1933, 340.

[8] AFSAE, 1931, 129; AFSAE, 1932, 169; AFSAE, 1933, 337; AFSAE, 1935, 278; AFB, 1950, 408; AFB, 1970, 95; Anuario Financiero y de Empresas en España [AFEE], *Aguas y Balnearios*, Madrid, 1983, 65.

[9] AFSAE, 1927, 512–515.

[10] AFSAE, 1930, 221; AFSAE, 1934, 339; AFB, 1948, 409; AFSAE, 1950, 402.

[11] AFSAE, 1930, 200.

1947, the property of *Aguas de Alicante*[12] and *Aguas y Saltos del Zadorra*. With regard to the city of Barcelona, *Aguas de Barcelona*, *Aguas Subterráneas del Río Llobregat*, *Aguas del Río Besós*, *Artesa*, *Empresa Artesiana de Riegos*, *Centro Levantina de Riegos y Captaciones*, *Aguas de Reus*, *Sorea* and *Saur*, would become another important conglomerate. This entire complex business world eventually ended up within the *Aguas de Barcelona* group when it took over the supply rights for Valencia and Alicante. The connection between the Valencian and Catalan groups was already evident in 1940, immediately after the civil war. The list of board members would be endless. The policy of controlling the market and absorbing competing companies was already far reaching in the case of *Aguas de Barcelona*. Shortly before the civil war, *Hidráulica Santillana* and *Aguas Potables y Mejoras de Valencia* also chose this course, although it seems that the impasse caused by the war dispelled these intentions.[13]

The second point can be glimpsed after a long-term chronological viewing of the members of the boards of directors. Two aspects stand out. First, in the early years there was a significant representation of foreign names. Second, one observes the presence of directors from *Aguas de Barcelona*, which was the most important business group in this field and was beginning to control a large part of the water supply market in the main Spanish cities.

Finally, it is worth noting the presence of a good number of small- and medium-sized investors, which can be detected in most of the companies and must have been very numerous in the large private firms. Even in a state initiative such as the *Canal de Isabel II*, it can be seen from the outset: in 1855 there were 872 subscribers, most of them small- and medium-sized bondholders. The same situation took place with the small companies that were able to offer shares at a cost of 50 or 100 pesetas, which sought to attract small savers.

## 9.6 Business Strategy and Control of the Market

Although the drinking water supply sector showed a preference for small- and medium-sized companies, not particularly integrated and very individualised due to the nature of the business itself, there were some business conglomerates that showed interest in extending their operations to other

[12] AFB, 1970, 121; AFEE, 1983, 65–69.
[13] AFB, 1950, 397; AFEE, 1983, 67.

cities and entering into other relatively similar activities. However, rather than talking about *business groups*, it is perhaps more appropriate to refer to the acquisitions and diversification practised by some companies (Matés-Barco 2019b).

The basic strategy of the companies was to exercise *control of the market*. For a sector like the supply of water, with its natural monopolistic characteristics, it was very important to dominate large areas. In addition, it had to have a diversified demand, free from any competition. The decision to invest was made after consideration of the size of the market or its future potential, and with knowledge of the expansion of demand. During the nineteenth century, entrepreneurs made great efforts to create their own market. Its growing size, thanks to the increase in population, was undoubtedly the main factor that encouraged the corporate structure, since demand skyrocketed and production benefited from economies of scale (Matés-Barco 2009).

One of the fundamental causes of this phenomenon can be found in the characteristics of the so-called *Unternehmergeschäft*. Peter Hertner has described this situation by referring to the actions of the large German electrotechnical producers before the First World War: they created their own markets by setting up local and regional electricity, tram and lighting companies in other countries (Russia, Italy, Spain and Latin America) and with those customers who were suffering from a chronic shortage of capital, especially the local corporations. The newly established companies were obliged to purchase electrotechnical supplies from their large industrial founding partners (Hertner 1990, p. 206). A relatively similar situation arose with some English or French producers of pipes and ferrous materials: they set up companies in third countries with the obligation to purchase their products and thereby develop their industries of origin.

As economies of scale were relatively low in the water supply sector, many entrepreneurs brought with them a substantial portion of their operational skills and a certain know-how, which had to be applied in a timely and tailor-made manner in each specific situation. These entrepreneurs also most likely provided privileged access to "mature" financial markets, such as those in Paris and Brussels. The same actions have been detected in some British cement manufacturers, who were also interested in developing this type of business that consumed their products.

These operations were a further step towards internalisation with the aim of reducing the risks of sales in foreign markets. Nevertheless, they did entail serious risks: the accumulation of a growing volume of capital in shares which the businesses were forced to keep in their portfolios, and which tended to dangerously reduce their liquidity. Foreign producers found the solution by creating financial holdings with major banks. These were responsible for acquiring the bonds and shares of newly created public utilities and holding them in their portfolio during the initial construction and development period. Once the business had "matured," they sought to sell much of the capital to small- and medium-sized investors or even to domestic "banking groups" to fill the gap left by the foreigners.

This process, which was often practised by Belgian, British and French companies, can be seen in particular in the *Compagnie Générale des Conduites d'Eaux*, of Belgian origin, and the *Crédit Général Liégeois* with the creation of the *Compañía Anónima General de Aguas de Barcelona* in 1867 (Matés-Barco 2018b).[14] Later, in 1882, French capital—through the *Société Lyonnaise d'Eaux et de l'Eclairage*—replaced the Belgian capital and brought about a change in the company, which became known as *Sociedad General de Aguas de Barcelona*. In 1898, the Belgian company repeated the same policy with the creation of the *Société d'Eaux d'Alicante*.[15] In the first case, in 1920, a group of Catalan bankers ended up acquiring the Barcelona company; and in the second, in 1926, the Alicante company was acquired by a company in the sector—*Aguas Potables y Mejoras de Valencia*—which was eventually integrated into *Aguas de Barcelona*.

Some companies, in order to control the market, looked to other types of strategies, for example, imposing limits on the entry of potential competitors. On many occasions, the companies requested the concession of a high volume of water, an amount above the flow needed to supply the population. In this way, in areas close to large markets, they ensured that they could expand supply in proportion to the growth in demand, and it was also a way of preventing other companies from being able to obtain concessions to supply areas of the community that had not yet been reached by the supply network. This strategy was used by *Aguas de Barcelona* (1882) right from its earliest days.[16]

Clashes and takeovers between companies occurred with some frequency in various Spanish cities. The cases of Madrid and Barcelona were

[14] AFSAE, 1930, 200.

[15] AFSAE, 1927, 512–515.

[16] AFSAE, 1922, 52–53; AFSAE, 1935, 278–302; Anuario Financiero de Valores Mobiliarios [AFVM], *Sociedades de aguas*, Madrid, 1917, 531.

the most significant, but they also occurred in others such as Pamplona.[17] Likewise, the eagerness of foreign companies to invest in the Levantine and Catalan area—mines, dissemination of their products and so on—seems to explain the concentration that occurred in the companies that succeeded them.

In Spain there was no price competition, as there was in England, as a strategy of some companies to increase market share. In some large cities, concessions were granted for very specific and limited areas of the city. In Barcelona, some companies were granted concessions to supply neighbourhoods or adjoining towns such as Sants, Hospitalet or some streets in the old town. The small size of these companies, a consequence of the limited areas they supplied, made them easy prey for more powerful companies.

In the early stages of implementation of the water supply service, there was the theoretical possibility of granting several concessions to different companies to supply one city. However, in small- and medium-sized cities, it was very rare for two water supply concessions to be granted, as the very dynamics of business eventually eliminated such a procedure. In the twentieth century, and especially from 1924 onwards, the specifications in which it was made public stated that the concession was exclusive.

The difficulties these companies encountered in integrating themselves in a given market in the early stages of development of the sector are noteworthy. It was common to find towns in which various companies were trying to establish themselves in the management of this public service. After successive failures, one of the companies—however small—always succeeded in achieving stability and taking over the market, usually lasting for quite some time. This trend shows that once the first period of uncertainty was overcome and the company was relatively consolidated, the possibilities of stability in the medium term were practically assured. This is a typical aspect of the sector, which itself is stable. But it can also be explained by the dominance that the companies had over the market; the existence of the monopoly ensured them, however small, of a certain level of profitability, and thus they managed to survive.

It was also often influenced by the contracts they had with the town council itself: water for public institutions, street cleaning, markets, slaughterhouses and so on. This allowed them to have an important client that ensured them, in a fixed way and in spite of the existence of special rates

[17] AFB, 1934, 388–413; AFSAE, 1935, 278–302; AFB, 1950, p. 408; AFEE, 1983, 65.

for these establishments, of part of their income. It was not the main factor that allowed these companies to move forward, but in the early years of their existence it must have been the anchor point that allowed them to enter the business and persist for quite some time. The figures fluctuate and change greatly over time.

One strategy that some water supply companies employed to grow was to diversify their economic activity and get into other types of business, such as electricity. This was the case for *Aguas de Barcelona*, which participated in *Compañía Española de Electricidad y Gas Lebón* and in *Electricidad de San Fernando y Chiclana*. In this same course of action, this strategy encouraged the vertical integration of companies dedicated to the manufacture of materials. The same strategies can be seen in companies in Valencia, Cadiz, Madrid and so on.[18]

In short, the normal evolution of the sector saw the most powerful companies displace others that were already established, acquiring their concessions and absorbing other companies that were set up as subsidiaries. An integral part of this strategy also consisted in entering into other businesses, especially the electricity business.

## 9.7 Conclusions

Water supply companies occupied an important place among the various sectors in the Spanish economy. Without reaching the level of the largest groups—banks, electricity providers and railways—they came to be situated among the top 20 business sectors that operated in Spain.

From the first stages, the number of water companies grew steadily, which explains the improved ranking among the business sectors. The large cities proved to be very attractive to private operators, who saw considerable commercial and business opportunities in managing a drinking water service. Slowly but steadily, the activity of the private companies was transferred to other medium and smaller-sized towns. Logically, there was a direct relationship between the size of the community and that of the water companies operating there. In spite of the difficulties encountered in the initial attempts to get a foothold in the water business, with the passage of time greater stability was achieved, and it can be seen that the most

[18] AFB, 1950, 406; AFB, 1960, 172; AFB, 1970, 121; AFVM, 1917, 531; AFSAE, 1932, 190; AFB, 1950, 408; AFEE, 1983, 67.

competitive and best placed companies were among those that had been operating for the longest time.

The water supply companies were of great importance, especially during the period of maximum expansion of the sector between 1900 and 1936. The regional distribution in its first years coincided with the Spanish industrial and urban map. There was a clear relationship between regions with a strong urban or industrial growth rate and the establishment of firms dedicated to the supply of drinking water.

The growing number of companies that began to emerge in the first decades of the twentieth century is evident, providing a palpable sign of the importance of the sector. The persistent legislation of this period was another important point, which led the town councils to see private sector actors as the agents capable of solving the water supply problem.

At the same time, the alignment of existing business strategies in Great Britain and France played a significant role. As the century progressed, foreign investment began to dry up—due to the conflict that broke out in 1914 and the subsequent legislation that appeared in Spain with a very nationalist slant—leaving a large part of the sector in the hands of Spanish capital. These years saw the period of maximum expansion and the opportunity for some Spanish businessmen to take control of these companies.

The very nature of the business—natural monopoly, regulated and controlled sector, pricing policy—explains to a great extent the functioning of these companies throughout the period. Among them, it is worth mentioning the withdrawal of competition, the control of the market and the progressive predominance of large companies. The trend led to the disappearance of smaller companies due to their acquisition by larger firms and the gradual municipalisation of the service by the town councils.

Finally, a large number of these companies are the result of the investment interest of foreign capital in Spain and of the initiatives promoted by local leaders with industrial interests. In some companies, small investors and the predominance of the family component are observed. The permanence of some of these companies over time—despite the ups and downs—shows that they enjoyed relatively secure profitability and stability.

## References

Anuario Financiero de Bilbao which includes the Historial de los Valores Públicos y de Sociedades Anónimas de España [AFB]. (1915–1972). *Aguas*. Bilbao: Banco de Vizcaya.

Anuario Financiero y de Sociedades Anónimas de España [AFSAE]. 1916–1977. *Sociedades de Aguas Potables y de Riegos.* Madrid.

Anuario Técnico e Industrial de España [ATIE]. 1913. *Empresas y sociedades de abastecimiento de aguas.* Madrid.

Bigatti, Giorgio. 2014. Da bere per tutti. Serivizi idrici e politiche dell'aqua in Italia tra Otto e Novecento. Uno sguardo di sintesi. *TST: Transportes, Servicios y Telecomunicaciones* 26: 110–126.

Castro-Valdivia, Mariano, Mercedes Fernández-Paradas, and Juan Manuel Matés-Barco. 2019. Las empresas extranjeras de agua y gas en España (circa 1900–1921). In *Los servicios públicos en España y México, coordinated by Juan Manuel Matés-Barco and Alicia Torres-Rodríguez*, 51–74. Madrid: Sílex.

Castro-Valdivia, Mariano, and Juan Manuel Matés-Barco. 2020. Los servicios públicos y la inversión extranjera en España (1850–1936): Las empresas de agua y gas. *História Unisinos* 24 (2): 221–239. https://doi.org/10.4013/hist.2020.242.05.

Costa, María Teresa. 1981. Iniciativas empresariales y capitales extranjeros en el sector servicios de la economía española durante la segunda mitad del siglo XIX. *Investigaciones Económicas* 5: 45–83.

Dirección General de Contribuciones. 1901–1933. *Estadística de la Contribución de Utilidades de la Riqueza Mobiliaria.* Madrid.

Estadística de Obras Públicas. 1895–1900. *Compañías concesionarias de abastecimientos de aguas.* Madrid: Ministerio de Fomento.

Falkus, Malcolm. 1977. The Development of Municipal Trading in the Nineteenth Century. *Business History XIX* 1: 134–161.

Fernández, Alexandre. 2014. La distribution de l'eau à Bordeaux de 1852 à 2011: singularité et exemplarité d'une économie politique des services techniques urbains. *TST: Transportes, Servicios y Telecomunicaciones* 26: 68–88.

Fernández-Paradas, Mercedes. 2009. Empresas y servicio de alumbrado público por gas en España (1842–1935). *TST: Transportes, Servicios y Telecomunicaciones* 16: 108–131.

———. 2016. La regulación del suministro de gas en España (1841–1936). *Revista de Historia Industrial* 61: 49–78.

Goubert, Jean Pierre. 1988. The Development of Water and Sewerage in France, 1850–1950. In *Technology and the Rise of the Networked City in Europe and America*, ed. Joel Tarr and Gabriel Dupuy, 116–136. Philadelphia: Temple University Press.

Guillerme, André. 1988. The Genesis of Water Supply, distribution and Sewerage Systems in France, 1800–1850. In *Technology and the Rise of the Networked City in Europe and America*, ed. Joel Tarr and Gabriel Dupuy, 91–115. Philadelphia: Temple University Press.

Hassan, John A. 1998. *A History of Water in Modern England and Wales.* Manchester: Manchester University Press.

Heredia-Flores, Víctor Manuel. 2013. Municipalización y modernización del servicio de abastecimiento de agua en España: el caso de Málaga (1860–1930). *Agua y Territorio* 1: 103–117.

Hernández-Marco, José Luis. 2008. La banca y la financiación de las infraestructuras urbanas: El Banco de Bilbao antes de la Guerra Civil española. In *La modernización económica de los Ayuntamientos: servicios públicos, finanzas y gobiernos municipales*, ed. Luis González-Ruiz and Juan Manuel Matés-Barco, 313–347. Jaén: University of Jaén.

Hertner, Peter. 1990. Estrategias financieras y adaptación a los mercados exteriores: la industria electrotécnica alemana y sus actividades multinacionales de 1890 a 1939. In *Empresas multinacionales, finanzas, mercados y gobiernos en el siglo XX. (I) Perspectiva histórica de las empresas multinacionales*, ed. Alice Teichova, Maurice Lévy-Leboyer, and Helga Nussbaum, 197–214. Madrid: Ministerio de Trabajo y Seguridad Social.

Lorrain, Dominique. 2002. Capitalismes urbains la montée des firmes d'infrastructures. *Entreprises et Histoire* 30: 7–31.

Martínez López, Alberte. 2008. El transporte urbano en A Coruña: del abandono del tranvía a la modernización del servicio, 1962–2005. In *La modernización económica de los Ayuntamientos: servicios públicos, finanzas y gobiernos municipales*, ed. Luis González-Ruiz and Juan Manuel Matés-Barco, 117–146. Jaén: University of Jaén.

Matés-Barco, Juan Manuel. 2002. Strategies of foreign firms in the sector of water supply in Spain (1850–1990). In *Transnational Companies, 19th–20th Centuries*, ed. Hubert Bonin, 301–316. Paris: Plâge.

———. 2004. The development of water Supplies in Spain: 19$^{th}$ and 20$^{th}$ Centuries. In *Urban Growth on Two Continents in the 19th and 20$^{th}$ Centuries. Technology, Networks, Finance and Public Regulation*, ed. Andrea Giuntini, Peter Hertner, and Gregorio Núñez, 165–178. Granada: Comares.

———. 2009. Las sociedades anónimas de abastecimiento de agua potable en España (1840–1960). *Revista de la Historia de la Economía y de la Empresa* 3: 177–218.

———. 2014. Las empresas concesionarias de servicios de abastecimiento de aguas potables en España (1840–1940). *TST: Transportes, Servicios y Telecomunicaciones* 26: 58–89.

———. 2016. La regulación del suministro de agua en España, siglos XIX y XX. *Revista de Historia Industrial* 61: 17–49.

———. 2018a. La distribution de l'eau dans les villes d'Espagne (1840–1936): Le rôle des compagnies privées. *Histoire, Économie & Société* 3: 14–29.

———. 2018b. De la Regulación a la Privatización y viceversa: la gestión del agua en España y Gran Bretaña. In *Agua y Servicios Públicos en España y México.*, Coordinated by Juan Manuel Matés-Barco and José Juan Pablo Rojas-Ramírez, 29–68. Jaén: University of Jaén and University of Guadalajara.

———. 2019a. El abastecimiento de agua a Barcelona (1850–1939): Origen y desarrollo de las compañías privadas. *Historia Contemporánea* 59–1: 165–194. https://doi.org/10.1387/hc.19434.

———. 2019b. Estrategia empresarial y control del mercado: la gestión del abastecimiento de agua potable. In *Empresas y empresarios en España. De mercaderes a industriales.*, Coordinated by Juan Manuel Matés-Barco, 223–240. Madrid: Pirámide.

Millward, Robert. 2007. La distribution de l'eau dans les villes en Grande Bretagne au XIX^e^ et XX^e^ siècles: le gouvernement municipal et le dilemme des compagnies privées. *Histoire, Economie, Société* 26: 111–128.

Núñez, Gregorio. 2008. Citadini-Creditori. Municipi e mercati finanziari in Spagna durante il primo terzo del XX secolo. *Storia Urbana* 119: 101–124.

Núñez, Gregorio, and Dionisio Buendía. 2008. Información financiera en España en la primera mitad del siglo XX: Las cuentas anuales de la sociedad de tranvías eléctricos de Granada. *De Computis, Revista Española de Historia de la Contabilidad* 8: 97–137.

Reseña Geográfica y Estadística de España. 1888. *Obras de abastecimiento*. Madrid.

*Revista de Obras Públicas*. 1851–1900. Madrid: Colegio de Ingenieros de Caminos, Canales, y Puertos.

Tomory, Leslie. 2015. London's Water Supply before 1800 and the Roots of the Networked City. *Tecnology and Culture* 56 (3): 704–737.

———. 2017. *The History of the London Water Industry, 1580–1820*. Baltimore: Johns Hopkins University Press.

Villar-Chamorro, Fernando, Mariano Castro-Valdivia, and Juan Manuel Matés-Barco. 2019. Crecimiento urbano y abastecimiento de agua potable en España: el protagonismo de las empresas privadas (1840–1950). *Posición* 1: 1–21.

CHAPTER 10

# The Railway Sector in Spain in the Long Term

*Miguel Muñoz Rubio and Pedro Pablo Ortúñez Goicolea*

## 10.1 Introduction[1]

This short study is directed towards an audience who may not necessarily be familiar with the topic addressed, namely, how the railway transport system has been organised in the long term and the main changes that have taken place in the over 170 years of its existence.

The principal railway companies involved over this long period have been the *Compañía de los Ferrocarriles del Norte de España* (Norte), the *Compañía de los Ferrocarriles de Madrid a Zaragoza y Alicante* (MZA), for

[1]While we were preparing this work, we received news of the death of Pedro Tedde de Lorca, a renowned historian and an even better human being. Both of this work's authors consider him to be a master amongst historians and, more immediately, for those of us who seek to shed some light on the history of transport and communication. We wish to dedicate this work to him by way of a tribute and as a reflection of our gratitude and admiration.

M. Muñoz Rubio (✉)
Spanish Railways Foundation, Madrid, Spain

P. P. Ortúñez Goicolea
University of Valladolid, Valladolid, Spain
e-mail: portunez@eco.uva.es



M. Vázquez-Fariñas et al. (eds.), *Companies and Entrepreneurs in the History of Spain*, Palgrave Studies in Economic History,
https://doi.org/10.1007/978-3-030-61318-1_10

the period of construction and private use of the network, and RENFE, a public company set up in 1941, and whose Spanish acronym means the National Network of Spanish Railways, and which on 1 January 2005 split the operations it had been carrying out up to that point between *Adif* (Administrator of Rail Infrastructures) and the Renfe-Operator. Herein, we provide a look at some of the main milestones that reflect the various adaptations and transformations that have taken place: the first major crisis of 1868, the so-called turn of the century crisis, the difficulties brought about by the Great War, the years of the Primo de Rivera dictatorship, the Spanish Civil War which started in 1936, the downfall of the autarchy in 1959, and Spain's entry into the EEC in 1985.

For many years now, railways have drawn the attention of a wide array of research disciplines given the all-round fascination they hold, and thereby offer a veritable kaleidoscope: engineering in its many areas of specialisation, the economy, as well as other experimental and numerical sciences, together with literature and art. Behind all of these lie history, and all of these fields have found a source of inspiration in this singular means of transport.

## 10.2 The Early Years: 1844–1890

The early years of the companies which began to operate on the Spanish railway network prior to the General Law of 1855 passed virtually unnoticed. This is true of both the effects they were able to generate and the actual reality of the institutions themselves. Following on from the fiasco of the public works policy applied by moderate governments, successive progressive governments after 1856 engaged in an economic policy in which the construction of the railway network became one of their core objectives. This goal was achieved, since the 54.1 km that were built each year between 1848 and 1856 increased to 458.5 km between 1857 and 1866, thereby extending the length of the track laid from 459 to 5044 km in only ten years.

Implementation of the General Law of 1855 helped to channel capital towards the railways and brought to the Spanish business scene Norte and MZA, two companies set up with mainly French capital and which later became the two giants in the sector. Both secured the concessions of the country's major transport axes and the centre for their exploitation in Madrid (Comín et al. 1998).

The first major crisis to hit the sector came in 1866. It was then that the companies found that the returns were not enough to pay off the debts they had run up during construction. Since most of their demand came from the primary sector, the situation was only exacerbated by the effects of the agricultural crisis which the Spanish economy suffered in the 1860s. All of this meant that some companies reported an operating loss at the end of the year.

Since the companies, in particular Norte and MZA, had already reached the limit of their possible debt, they were unable to do anything. The State was not in a position to help them out either, since it was immersed in its own budgetary crisis, with the Paris and London stock markets refusing to open their doors to the Spanish economy due to its habitual inability to pay. The effects of the international crisis also took their toll. The stock price of the railway companies began to tumble and railway bonds started to lose their value. This dragged down with it a large part of the Spanish financial system since its assets were mainly pegged to the railways.

Norte and MZA were able to weather the crisis thanks to the help received from their parent companies. They also managed to convince the State to set up a public fund to help them.[2] After that time, the Spanish railway system lay in the hands of the French financiers Rothschild (MZA) and Pereire (Norte). The creation of this duopoly, which received the State's blessing, was grounded on takeovers and mergers that led to the two companies going from holding a third of the whole network to two thirds.

In 1868, MZA boasted a network of 1428 km, which enabled it to have connections from Madrid to the Mediterranean and Andalusia. It was not until 1875 that it would once again experience an increase in the number of kilometres in operation, reaching 1557. From then until 1899, takeovers and mergers with other lines more than doubled its network, reaching 3679 km.

For its part, by 1868 Norte had reached 723 km thanks to its Madrid to Irun and Venta de Baños to Alar lines. This figure was to remain unchanged until 1874 when it increased to 878 km. By 1878, it had managed to double its network, reaching 1765 km, and it would continue to grow until it had 3581 km, parallel to the progression undergone by MZA. Increases in the initial networks were mostly due to newly laid

[2] Decree of 7 November 1868 (*Madrid Gazette* issue 313 of 8 November 1868, 1–2).

track. After 1874, however, following the takeover of the line from Alar to Santander, networks were mainly extended as a result of mergers and takeovers.

## 10.3 A New Century: 1890–1914

In the late nineteenth and early twentieth centuries, three companies, Norte, MZA and Compañía de los Ferrocarriles Andaluces (Andaluces), accounted for 75% of the broad-gauge track being operated in Spain, with just the first two alone accounting for almost 65% of the total. This percentage remained the same until 1936. Anes (1978, pp. 485–486) and (Broder 2012, p. 43) point out that after 1860, two French groups, Norte and MZA, shared the main Spanish railway axes. There was no new support from the State and the concentration of the sector in the hands of the major companies grew even stronger (Tedde de Lorca, 1978).

This period of change at the turn of the century has been defined in Spain as the "turn of the century" crisis. Its impact was felt most clearly by Norte and MZA. If we take freight transport as a reference, which is the goods most often affected in any economic crisis, Norte had multiplied the total volume of goods carried between 1890 and 1898 by 1.7%. During the same period, MZA had managed to double its volume. This represented a faster rate of growth than the increase in the network which they exploited during the same period. Yet between 1898 and 1905, Norte only multiplied the volume of goods transported by 1.1 and MZA by 1.3%. Very slow or indeed no growth is therefore evident in the long term. The only period which witnessed a drop in the tonnage transported was around the end of the First World War. This loss was offset by the spectacular rise in the total number of passengers using the railways. This increase had already begun to be felt at the turn of the century, although it was far more evident after the First World War. The fact that this number grew more in MZA than in Norte gives an indication of the unrelenting transformation of urban areas in the peninsula, particularly in the major axes that were linked by this company: Madrid, Seville, Alicante, Zaragoza and Barcelona (Muñoz Rubio and Ortúñez Goicolea 2013a).

A good way to take stock of these two early stages is to ascertain in which years the leading companies were not able to pay out any dividends to their shareholders. MZA was not able to do so until 1859, and indeed between 1864 and 1872, both years included, it did not pay dividends. Nor did it pay out any dividends in 1885, or between 1893 and 1898.

Between 1899 and 1905 dividend payouts were extremely modest, between 5 and 9 pesetas per share. Returns of around 24 pesetas per share were felt to be normal, a figure which was only achieved in 1912 and 1913. It is worth remembering that MZA was the most profitable railway company for its shareholders. Norte, for example, was unable to pay out any dividends between 1900 and 1906.

## 10.4 The Impact of the First World War

Even though Spain remained a neutral country during the Great War, it was still affected. Railway companies were severely impacted by the difficulties the conflict brought with it. For the Spanish railway sector, the war meant increased demand for transport, reflected in a greater density of traffic, a greater volume of goods carried, and a change in the nature of these compared to previous years. Infrastructure and transport equipment were subject to more intense use, which was not, however, compensated by increased investment in renewal and maintenance of carriages, engines and track. To a large degree, this was because the suppliers were also involved in the conflict.

There was an increasing number of complaints from users due to delays, accumulation of goods at the stations, damage to the material, greater repair costs, deteriorating infrastructure and difficulties getting this replaced; such were the consequences of those very difficult years. Norte made a loss in 1917 and 1918 and did not pay out any dividends between 1917 and 1919. MZA's results plummeted between 1917 and 1918, although it still managed to return a profit, albeit a small one, and was able to pay its shareholders a dividend every year. Andaluces also made a loss between 1919 and 1920 and reported disastrous results for the two previous years. It was time for those who were advocating that the sector should be nationalised by the State to make themselves heard.

The situation was extremely difficult for companies and State alike. The Royal Decree of 26 December 1918 authorised companies to increase fares by 15%. This had the effect of boosting income, although operating costs and financial costs also rose because of the inflationary effect, the application of the eight-hour day and a growth in staff numbers, together with the gradual adoption of other social improvements and the enormous cost of financing the debt.

On 3 April 1919, the eight-hour working day was introduced, which had a substantial impact on the railways. Faced with delays and company reluctance, in January 1920 railway workers went on strike. The government opted to resolve the problem by issuing provisional Royal Order of 23 March, and permanent Royal Order of 29 April. By implementing these measures, the State took care of the workers' wage demands without having to resort to raising fares. To do this, it granted the companies refundable advanced payments. This government solution saw the dawn of a new era in Spanish railway history since State interventionism increased after that point, finally leading to the nationalisation of the railways after the Civil War of 1936–1939. These advances provided by the State to cover the cost of wage increases were included in the liabilities of the company balances as debt, which was obviously deducted from the compensation companies received from the bailout payments for the support given in 1941.

In 1920 and 1921, the State thus opened up new lines of support for companies. The aim was to improve and modernise the sector and to allow for wage rises. State aid once more became available. The formula involved refundable advances, with favourable terms, which the major companies did their best to repay.

## 10.5 The "Roaring Twenties" of Spanish Railways: 1923–1931

The 1920s posed fresh challenges for companies. The new political regime in Spain after the military uprising of General Primo de Rivera intensified State interventionism. Companies forfeited financial autonomy and the capacity to make decisions. Shortly after coming to power, the government approved the so-called Railway Statute by Royal Decree-Law on 12 July 1924.

Railway companies were forced to adhere to the Statute. Indeed, this was the requirement if they were to be granted access to the foreseen financial support. Through a body set up specifically for the purpose, the so-called Railway Fund, which was financed via public debt, the State agreed to bankroll the investments required to modernise both transport infrastructure and material. In this regard, one may speak of the "Roaring Twenties" as the title of this section: companies had never had it so good and had never had so many resources to invest.

The State was making an enormous financial effort and, as can be seen from the outcome, one which was highly necessary: there were improvements in returns for shareholders, traffic conditions and transport figures. However, it proved impossible to maintain such a high level of public debt over time. Between 1922 and 1930, the increase in passenger numbers was insignificant in Norte and very small in MZA (0.9% mean annual cumulative). Nevertheless, the tonnage being moved did increase in both companies by a mean annual cumulative rate of over 4%. As a result, operating revenue increased: 3% in Norte and 1% in MZA. The problems were the costs, particularly the financial costs, even though the Railway Fund bore a large part of the investment. Taking into account all of the costs and repayments, the final results in Norte and MZA fell between 1922 and 1930 at a mean annual accumulative rate of 5%.

The total investment in railways made by the Railway Fund between 1925 and 1930 amounted to some 1600 million pesetas.[3] It was a huge sum that was designed to solve the lack of investment the sector had been suffering and which, according to the most common interpretation of the time, was the cause of the problems that were affecting it and which had increased during the Great War years: disappearance of freight, delays, a slow service, high prices and so on. This decided support from the State towards the sector also pursued another objective. Once these difficulties had been overcome, thanks to the increased investment, in theory on 31 December 1928 the companies which had agreed to the Statute would sign up for what the Statute called the "definitive period", a stage which would lead to the repayment of State aid, to the reunification and concentration of the network, and to making the sector able to survive on the revenue derived from fares. Yet this definitive period never materialised. Before the proclamation of the Republic, and in the grip of an international economic crisis and an institutional crisis in Spain, the State declared to Norte and MZA that it could no longer continue to provide the railways with support and that it was the companies themselves which would have to find the resources from then on, at the worst possible moment.

[3] Included are normal gauge and narrow gauge, private and public ownership, and new constructions.

## 10.6 After the "Roaring Twenties" the Great Depression: 1931–1936

The 1930s posed a large number of problems for railway companies. Their chances of obtaining financial resources in the market had been dealt a severe blow following the previous period. The fact that the oldest and most important concessions were about to expire did not help since this complicated the guarantees that could be given to any new debt. The figures for the amounts being transported soon began to plummet and, with them, the revenue from operating costs; losses soon followed. Competition from the roads was also beginning to emerge. In addition, institutional, international and domestic instability only served to further exacerbate the impact of all these aspects.

Between 1930 and 1935, the number of passengers carried by Norte fell at a mean annual cumulative rate of 3%, and the company's revenue fell by a similar amount. In MZA, there was a 2.1% drop, a figure which was slightly higher in the case of revenue from this concept, which fell by 3.2%. There was an even greater decline in freight transport, where the rate was 5.6% in Norte and 6.1% in MZA. As pointed out earlier, a logical consequence was the arrival of the loss in results from 1931 in the two companies. From 1931 to 1935, MZA was able to pay out to its shareholders 10 pesetas per share for the returns which the company's private assets had generated, far removed from the 28.50 pesetas they had been able to pay out between 1927 and 1929. This accumulation of problems was now beyond repair and, with the outbreak of the Civil War in 1936, there was no time to redress the situation.

The sector, which was shackled by the indecisive decisions taken by the previous dictatorship, had left an enormous hole in the Republic's treasury, thanks to the debt issued by the Railway Fund. In addition, many of the works undertaken in the form of construction were still eating away at the available resources, such that they had to be discontinued, with the works eventually being abandoned in order to put a stop to the spending. Calls for nationalisation increased. Having done so would only have worsened the chaotic situation for the public coffers, as a result of which Indalecio Prieto, the Minister of Public Works, would not hear of it. In the meantime, the companies continued to bleed to death and investment was again halted. Everything possible was done to amortise vacant posts and to retire workers. Norte cut its workforce but MZA did not.

Company reaction to such a complex situation was very limited and restricted in scope. Action sought mainly to influence successive governments with two basic goals in mind: to secure a fresh increase in fares and to obtain authorisation to issue new debt bonds that would be backed by the State. In order to compete with the roads, there were requests for a reduction in taxes or to have those applied to road transport equated to those paid by the railways. The outbreak of the Civil War brought a tragic end to these years (Muñoz Rubio and Ortúñez Goicolea 2013b).

## 10.7 The Civil War Years and the Early Franco Period: 1936–1959

The Civil War substantially altered the institutional framework in the railway sector. In the Spain which came under the republican government there was a process of public interventionism which ended with nationalisation and the corresponding creation of a public company in 1938. In the areas controlled by Franco's troops, the railway companies were seized, and although it did not quite reach that point, and probably in order to take advantage of the concessionaires' know-how at such a crucial time, the Burgos government laid the foundations for subsequent nationalisation in 1941 (Barquín and Ortúñez Goicolea 2019).

Once the war was over, the new regime made the State the main architect of the industrialising policy. The era of public companies had begun. The change brought about by this new economic policy proved to be a turning point for the railways. In 1941, through the Law Establishing the Bases for the Organisation of Railways and Road Transport, a new institutional framework was created by replacing private with public management. Prior to nationalisation, the Iberian wide-gauge railway network had reached 12,364 km, accounting for 70.9% of the total, whilst the narrow-gauge networks, with their 5080 km, made up the remainder. The vast majority of the network was in private hands, since only 5% was being run by the State.

This change was confirmed, on the one hand, through the creation of Renfe as a public company charged with operating and managing the wide-gauge railway system (Muñoz Rubio 1995) and, on the other, by merging narrow-gauge public railways into a federation, which also entailed nationalising several companies (Muñoz Rubio 2005a). Nationalisation was the basic instrument of the transport policy designed by General Franco's regime. Its aim was to make railways the preferred means of transport.

This change gave rise to an organisational structure of the transport system which was enormously hierarchised and bureaucratised. The tip of the pyramid was the presidency of the government itself, on which depended the Ministry of Public Works, as well as the ministries of the Treasury, Military, Government, Labour, and Industry and Trade, as did the recently created Delegation for the Organisation of Transport (DOP) and the Commissary for Railway Material (CMF). Although the level of power was asymmetric, it should be highlighted that whereas the task of the Higher Railways Board (JSF) was to ensure the consistency of the transport market by removing any kind of competition, the CMF emerged as the maximum authority for controlling industrial production destined for the railways and the DOP assumed authority for controlling transport, particularly the distribution of raw materials.

Moreover, the Renfe president held a casting vote with regard to the decisions taken by his board. Production was organised so that it continued to use private companies: in other words, a system which established on the one hand the five major divisions—operations; material and traction; track and works; electric power; and the commercial division—as the central axis,[4] and, on the other, the director general as its key figure, since all of these areas depended directly and hierarchically on him.

Despite the fact that the literality of the new institutional framework—and of its intentions—made the railway the dominant form of transport, this was to become yet another victim of the two principal shortcomings suffered by the Spanish economy during the crazed autarchy: the lack of financial resources, and the inexistence of the technological capacity required to replenish production factors. Indeed, the Spanish economy, wracked by inflation, was in the grip of an acute shortage of its own resources, a situation which was aggravated by foreign investment grinding to a complete halt and by the decline in domestic saving.

The situation could not have been worse, not only vis-à-vis financing the recovery of fixed railway capital, which was the number one priority at

[4] Complemented by ten services not related directly to operations (technical secretariat, legal advice service, stockpiling and warehousing, fuels, general accounting, complaints and enquiries, transport coordination, general expenditure, commissary and staff and social assistance).

the time, but also in terms of ensuring its gradual capitalisation. This therefore meant that the investments received by Renfe were insufficient to keep facilities and equipment up to ideal standards. In fact, until 1947 the railway network experienced a veritable disinvestment which was not to be reversed until 1950. Although there was net positive investment in the years that followed, it continued to prove insufficient with regard to raising technological standards.

## 10.8 The New "Liberalising" and "Planning" Winds of Change: 1960–1975

When making the State the universal operator in 1941, the aims of the regime focused on maintaining the railways at their optimal operating level by using only national industry, which it sought to strengthen. Nevertheless, it was forced to resort to foreign industry to ensure the supply of equipment and facilities. Failure reached such a scale that in 1960 national industry was unable to guarantee the sector's demands other than by resorting to imports.

In sum, by 1960 the railways were totally obsolete due to the scant investment received, investments which, to make matters worse, had been used to maintain technologies that were out of date or that were soon to disappear. All of this gave rise to two major problems. First, the railways came to a standstill in terms of production, which, once the tepid reforms of the 1950s had been introduced and once the alternative of road transport had returned, caused its share of the market to plummet. While rail passenger transport in 1950 accounted for 59.9% of total demand, by 1960 this had fallen to 30.6%, whilst in the case of freight transport the figure had dropped from 57.6% to 30.1%. Second, Renfe suffered enormous losses which, between 1941 and 1963, amounted to 18,655 million pesetas due to the fact that, while operating costs multiplied ninefold, revenue only increased sevenfold.

This "railway failure" was nothing more than the failure of the autarchic project itself, which, much to its chagrin, forced the dictatorship to make a strategic U-turn that became official through the approval of the 1959 Stabilisation Plan. There thus emerged a new period of change that was ultimately designed to partially replace radical public interventionism with a system which opted to channel resources towards private initiative in an effort to continue promoting industrialisation. As on previous occasions, this decision was to have major repercussions for the railway sector.

The Ministry of Public Works drew up the 1964–1973 Ten-year Modernisation Plan (PDM) for Renfe in an attempt to overhaul the company and adapt it to the new situation. The first change took place at an organisational level by making sweeping changes designed to endow Renfe's governing bodies with greater decision-making capacity.[5] In other words, the autarchic bodies responsible for financial intervention were dissolved and their main powers transferred to the executive, which took over responsibility for devising railway policy, the running of the companies' governing bodies, and the decisions which affected its material integrity. The Ministry of Public Works took charge of most of JSF's duties. The Inspectorate Division and the Treasury Ministry regained control of matters related to the companies' financial affairs. In addition to what it was already responsible for, Renfe also took over the tasks that had been assigned to the CMF and DOP, namely renewing equipment and facilities, as well as the overall management of freight transport.

The Board of Administration remained as Renfe's main internal organisation body, and continued to be headed by its president who, after 1969, also assumed the post of government delegate, which heightened the company's presidential nature. It should, however, be noted that Renfe's statutes, approved by decree on 23 July 1964, endowed the company with a substantial degree of independence to run the public transport service and to engage in whatever commercial and industrial activities might be related to the duties it was charged with carrying out.

The PDM also undertook action that changed the structure of some production forces which, in certain aspects, had remained unchanged since the early days of the railways. Electrification of the lines, adapting the rails, introducing automated blocking and communications systems, phasing out steam traction and basing the system on railcars, replacing conventional freight cars with railcars, and changing the types of carriages were the structural changes that took place during those years. All these changes heralded more than just a modernisation, since they entailed the most

[5] The report of the World Bank concluded that urgent changes to Renfe's organisation were required in order to solve its three main problems: the existence of a plethora of administrative bodies within Renfe itself, which divested responsibility and paralysed the controlling authority; constant State intervention in the details of the railway administration system; and the fact that Renfe lacked the power to take certain key decisions.

radical structural modification that rail facilities and equipment had witnessed since the railways had been born.

The plan meant that any action would depend on obtaining financial resources, which would only be granted if the conditions imposed by the World Bank for financing the plan were met. The investment that Renfe received over those years amounted to 2182 million dollars at today's prices, and was principally funded through direct contributions from the State, although, once again, loans were taken out. The first of these was signed with the International Bank for Reconstruction and Development in July 1964 and amounted to 65 million dollars and the second in August 1967 for 50 million dollars. To finance the 1972–1975 Renfe Plan, the successor to the PDM, a final agreement was signed in 1971 for the amount of 90 million dollars. Since then, this mechanism has regularly been used to such an extent that in 1980 it represented 26.6% of total revenue.

The gradual normalisation of financial flows meant a qualitative leap in investments compared to previous decades, since, of the capital received for this purpose between 1941 and 1980, 11.8% was provided in the 1960s and 85% in the 1970s. Thanks to this, Renfe's production underwent its most important modernisation since 1848. Worth noting here is the benefit which taking advantage of this relative delay implied, since, whereas other European countries had modernised their railway networks using the technologies of 1945, the Spanish railway network did so using the technologies developed in the two decades in question. Despite this, however, it was not sufficient to enable Renfe to meet the sharp rise in demand for transport which the boom in the Spanish economy brought with it between 1964 and 1975. The gradual increase in national rent, coupled with industrialisation and the liberalisation of overseas trade, which demanded the movement of huge amounts of raw materials and goods, together with demographic evolution (30 million people in the 1960 census compared to 37.5 million in the 1980 census) are among the principal causes which explain this phenomenon.

Demand in units of traffic of all kinds in terms of passengers rose from 13,732 million in 1950 to 28,867 million in 1960, to 99,577 million in 1970, and to 144,461 million in 1975. This rise in demand is unparalleled in any of the records for any of the previous eras. The principal beneficiary was, without doubt, road transport. Replacing rail transport with road transport as the dominant means had already started during the 1950s if we take into account that in 1950 the market share for railways was 60%

(52% for Renfe and 8% for FEVE) whilst the share for roads was 39%. This trend accelerated considerably in the following ten years, since 1970 closed with the figures standing at 31% (25% for Renfe) and 68%, respectively. By 1975, this distribution was far more favourable for the roads, which accounted for 87%, whereas in the case of Renfe it failed to reach 9% (Muñoz Rubio, 2005b; 2013).

This explains why, despite the progress made by the railways thanks to the modernisation it underwent, Renfe's financial performance over the years proved to be so unsatisfactory, even though the operating account showed a profit in certain years. Between 1964 and 1969, ordinary income did not cover operating costs, which ran at a loss of 11,237 million pesetas. The situation improved over the following five years and the company made an operating profit, which up until then had been unheard of, and which reached a peak in 1973 of 3014 million pesetas. Nevertheless, the joy was short lived as losses returned in 1975, amounting to a figure of no less than 6077 million pesetas. As a result, the operating ratio went from 114.2% in 1964 to 111.3% in 1967, to 105.2% in 1969, to 97.8% in 1970, and to 115.9% in 1975.

If we add industrial repayments and financial interest[6] to the operating results, the final balance reflects considerable losses. Renfe's total losses over these twelve years came to 58,858 million pesetas, and were covered through contributions from the State via budget subsidies which represented between 2% and 3% of the State's general budgetary expenses.

In addition to the above, application of the PDM led to the first major reduction in staff to result from a planned action: in this case, the conditions imposed by the World Bank for financing to be granted. Whilst Renfe ended 1962 employing 126,467 workers (which already meant it had shed 11,155 jobs compared to 1954), this was to be the starting point for a process that would extend over the following ten years and which entailed a gradual reduction in staff. Between 1962 and 1973, the mean number of jobs lost came to 4843 per year, which meant an overall reduction amounting to 53,270 jobs; in other words, the 1973 workforce stood at 57.9% of what it had been in 1962.

[6] In other words, the bonds issued between 1946 and 1957, foreign loans prior to 1964, loans from the IBRD and other foreign loans taken out since 1964.

## 10.9 Political Transition and Membership of the European Economic Community: 1976–2012

Democracy in Spain would, sooner or later, mean joining the EEC. As a result, there was a new scenario of change which was to affect the railways, whose institutional framework was forced to adapt to the new rules which the Union of the Democratic Centre (UCD) government brought forward to 1979 when drawing up the White Paper on Transport. This opted for a transport policy based on a free market, yet which also accepted the need for public interventionism that would strike a balance between the different trends of each means of transport involved. It established a series of principles, with a differing number of variations, that would provide the grounding for all the transport policies applied up to the present day: freedom to participate; each modality specialising in the market segments where it held the best comparative advantages; fiscal neutrality (possible taxes for the use of infrastructure); exclusive subsidies for public services; preferential use of railways in passenger services in commuter trains and in the major population corridors, whilst coordination with the roads would be left to the weaker lines of traffic, with air traffic catering to long distances; and preferential use of the railways in freight services for large volumes over long distances, while the use of roads would be encouraged for medium-distance transport.

If respective UCD governments failed to enjoy the necessary stability, the following governments of the Spanish Socialist Workers' Party (PSOE) did, as well as the time required to put these principles into practice. Nevertheless, once it came into power, and bearing in mind the previously mentioned major crisis that affected the railways as a result of the investment in the transport market between 1960 and 1975, the socialist PSOE government had no choice but to adopt an immediate strategy aimed at trying to halt this downward trend. This took five years and, consequently, it was not until the 1987 enactment of the Law Organising Land Transport (LOTT) that the new phase truly got under way.

The new law established neutrality as a guiding principle for all means of transport and, as an immediate consequence thereof, forced railway operators to adapt to the market, and even admitted private operators in the handling of certain services. It also distinguished between the concepts of public work and public service and announced its intention to grant Renfe greater independence in its powers.

Its consequences made themselves felt when the LOTT saw Renfe as fulfilling three distinct functions: as transport operator, as provider of goods and services, and as maintainer of infrastructure. Each of these entailed clearly differing levels of organisation and management criteria. As an operator, Renfe took on the task of transporting passengers and goods, for the running of which different business units were used depending on the characteristics imposed by the market: long haul, regional, high speed and commuter, in passengers; and with full loads and fractional loads in freight. In addition, different criteria were established with different management depending on market behaviour, since all the business units needed to operate on a profit-making basis, except for regional and commuter activities given their nature as a public service, although this did not imply foregoing the possibility of obtaining supplementary funding from other public authorities. As a provider of goods and services, Renfe would take charge of managing traction, rolling stock and a series of services for stations, ticket offices, cleaning and so on, which were given the status of public service, as was to happen with the third function mentioned, namely maintenance of infrastructure and transit.

Renfe's statutes, approved by Royal Decree 28-I-1994, confirmed this type of organisation, endowing the business units with a series of clearly defined powers and objectives over a short period which were to be assessed by the extent to which these goals were accomplished and by its own profit-and-loss account. The aim was to provide for better functioning: better adapting supply to demand, and thereby enhancing the quality of the service; tighter control over spending by making each of them responsible for their profit-and-loss account; and a clarification of the commercial relations between the company's own production units. This legal framework went even further since it afforded the possibility of the organisation units becoming legal entities in their own right should there be reasons requiring them to do so, subsequent to the necessary approval by the ministry.

Spanish government commitment to building high-speed lines, after the successful inauguration in 1992 of the Madrid-Seville line, hastened the institutional changes brought in through previous laws. The most significant stemmed from the need to create a new public company to administer whichever railway infrastructures it was felt required intervention, in particular the high-speed lines. Law 13 enacted on 30 December 1996 set up the Railway Infrastructures Management (GIF), which was born as a public body with its own legal status and own assets and distinct from the State's assets.

In any case, the institutional framework imposed by the LOTT was to last only 17 years, as in October 2003 the Spanish government enacted the Law on the Railway Sector (LSF), which heralded a major step in the policy of liberalising the railway market that had been in place since 1985. This measure split Renfe into two new public companies so that, respectively, they could maintain infrastructure and provide transport service: the Administrator of Railway Infrastructure (ADIF) for the former and Renfe-Operator for the latter.[7]

The law also split the Renfe-Operator into state mercantile companies (Royal Decree-law 22/2012, of 20 July, adopting measures in the matter of rail infrastructures and services). Specifically, one was created devoted to providing the passenger transport service stemming from its "Travellers" operating area; another would handle freight traffic; another would take charge of activities undertaken by the operations area of manufacturing and maintenance; and the last would manage "leasing operations and others related to railway material assets and, as a subsidiary, sales and other forms of transactions involving said material and facilities".[8]

## 10.10 Final Considerations

The institutional framework proves key vis-à-vis understanding the Spanish railway sector. As such, more than the weight of market needs at the time, it was the General Law of 1855 that spurred the development of the railway network. The economic crisis of 1866 prompted the start of a process of business concentration centred around the two large railway companies: Norte and MZA. When the process had concluded, the sector had become a duopoly.

The First World War triggered another important change by opening the door to greater public interventionism in the system. Railway companies sought to maintain the private nature of Spanish railways, something

[7] It was ADIF which inherited the brand of Renfe. This decision involved the most complex business change the railways had witnessed since nationalisation in 1941. In spite of this and despite that fact that it had to be applied with a change in government in between, it was conducted in exemplary fashion since the service provided did not suffer in any way.

[8] Narrow-gauge public railways, which had been operated since 1965 by FEVE (Decree-Law 11/1965 of 23 September) were closed down and became part of ADIF and Renfe-Operator by virtue of the Royal Decree of 20 July 2012.

which proved impossible, however, because of institutional changes, the Railway Statute of 1924, and the economic crisis of the 1930s. When the Civil War ended in 1939, any attempt to maintain a model that had been created almost a century earlier was both anachronistic and impossible, and even more so bearing in mind the lengthy period of no investment and the destruction caused.

Nationalisation and the creation of Renfe in 1941 emerged as the most decisive institutional changes to take place in the history of the railways in that they inverted a trend that had been in place since 1848. Although their consequences were catastrophic for the railways, it was the failure of Franco's economic policy that gave rise to a fresh change which, although it enabled a much needed modernisation of the railways and their organisational systems, proved unable to cope with the competition from motorised transport and Renfe's rampant deficit.

The arrival of democracy found the railways in a critical situation, yet a new institutional change—Spain's entry into the EEC—altered all the rules of the game. Although the transport policy set down in Brussels was implemented over a number of decades, its consequences are still very much in evidence today.

## References

Anes, Rafael. 1978. Relaciones entre el ferrocarril y la economía española (1865–1935). In *Los ferrocarriles en España*, vol. 2, coordinated by Miguel Artola, 355–541. Madrid: Banco de España.

Artola, Miguel. 1978. *Los ferrocarriles en España*. 2 vols. Madrid: Banco de España.

Barquín, Rafael, and Pedro Pablo Ortúñez Goicolea. 2019. El sector del transporte en la guerra civil española. In *El impacto de la Guerra Civil española en el sector terciario*, coordinated by Mercedes Fernández-Paradas and Carlos Larrinaga, 131–152. Comares: Granada.

Broder, Albert. 2012. *Los ferrocarriles españoles (1845–1913): el gran negocio de los franceses*. Madrid: Fundación de los Ferrocarriles Españoles.

Comín, Francisco, Pablo Martín Aceña, Miguel Muñoz Rubio, and Javier Vidal. 1998. *150 Años de Historia de los Ferrocarriles Españoles*. Madrid: Anaya-Fundación de los Ferrocarriles Españoles.

Muñoz Rubio, Miguel. 1995. *Renfe (1941–1991). Medio siglo de ferrocarril público*. Madrid: Ediciones Luna.

———, dir. 2005a. *Historia de los Ferrocarriles de Vía Estrecha en España*. Madrid: FFE.

———. 2005b. La contribución de RENFE a la economía española durante la segunda mitad del siglo XX: una primera aproximación. *TST* 8: 54–81.

———. 2013. El ferrocarril español durante la segunda mitad del siglo XX. In *Vie e mezzi di comunicazione in Italia e Espagna in età contemporanea*, ed. Carlos Barciela Lopez, Antonio Di Vittorio, Giulio Fenicia, and Nicola Ostuni, 321–349. Cantanzaro: Rubbettino Editore.

Muñoz Rubio, Miguel, and Pedro Pablo Ortúñez Goicolea. 2013a. Los transportes y las comunicaciones: la transición de modelos tradicionales a industriales. In *Historia Económica de España*, coordinated by Agustín González Enciso and Juan Manuel Matés-Barco, 209–241. Barcelona: Ariel.

———. 2013b. Los transportes y las comunicaciones en la España de la primera modernidad. In *Historia Económica de España*, coordinated by Agustín González Enciso and Juan Manuel Matés-Barco, 551–591. Barcelona: Ariel.

Tedde de Lorca, Pedro. 1978. Las compañías ferroviarias en España (1855–1935). In *Los ferrocarriles en España*, Vol. 2, coordinated by Miguel Artola, 9–354. Madrid: Banco de España.

CHAPTER 11

# The Pioneers of the Spanish Travel Agency Business Before Mass Tourism

*Carlos Larrinaga*

## 11.1 Introduction

Although the background of tourism goes back to the Modern Age, with phenomena such as the Grand Tour and spas, it was actually in the nineteenth century when it gained greater importance. Along with the Industrial Revolution, there was also a first Tourist Revolution, in which transport, and therefore travelling, underwent great transformation. More specifically, in the cradle of industrialisation, in the United Kingdom, the transition from a minority tourism to one with a greater social base was brought about by the spread of railways and steamships. These means of communication made large-scale leisure travel possible. This expanded mobility also gave rise to a new way of travelling, favoured by

This study forms part of the research project HAR2017-82679-C2-1-P, financed by the Minister of Science, and Innovation of the Government of Spain and the FEDER/ERDF Fund.

C. Larrinaga (✉)
University of Granada, Granada, Spain


M. Vázquez-Fariñas et al. (eds.), *Companies and Entrepreneurs in the History of Spain*, Palgrave Studies in Economic History,
https://doi.org/10.1007/978-3-030-61318-1_11

intermediation. This was the great success of Thomas Cook in the mid-nineteenth century, founder of the first travel agency and therefore creator of organised trips. Cook, in short, sold a service, taking care of transportation, accommodation, support and so on. Therefore, travellers did not have to worry about such details. In summary, it was about offering a product to its customers. And here lies the origin of travel agencies, although it is true that the vast majority of trips continued without an intermediary.

However, customers who used a travel agency paid a certain price in exchange for services and the guarantee of reduced uncertainty. The user bought tangible but also intangible services such as trust, security or comfort (Vallejo and Larrinaga 2018, p. 724, 2020, p. 2). Hence the success of travel agencies, some companies, many of them family-owned, that began to emerge in the second half of the nineteenth century (Visentin 1995, p. 303). Spain was no exception, although the birth of the first properly Spanish travel agencies occurred a few years later, at the beginning of the twentieth century, when the first Spanish tourist system began to take shape. And the development of the business of travel agencies must be linked to the birth of modern tourism—in other words, tourism conceived as an industry, in which we are going to have different companies, or entrepreneurs, dedicated to tourism in its different aspects. Here we must then place the first Spanish travel agencies, among which Viajes Marsans (first called Viajes Marsansrof) and Viajes Cafranga stand out. We will focus on these companies in this work, although, as will be seen, they were not the only ones.

## 11.2 The Beginnings of Intermediated Travel in Spain

The period between 1900 and 1914 must be considered the embryonic years of the establishment and development of travel agencies in Spain, a period in which certain characteristics stand out. First, the importance of traditional operators: foreign and national railway companies as well as foreign (Booth Line, Real Mala Inglesa, etc.) and national (Trasatlántica, Transmediterránea) shipping companies which expressly worked in "tourism" or incorporated tourism travels into their business. Second, the appearance of foreign travel agents moving their clients to Spain or stopping over in Spain. Third, some of these foreign operators made the leap to Spain through two routes. The first was by opening one or more offices in the country, just as Cook did from 1892 onwards in Madrid (Vallejo and Larrinaga 2020, p. 9). The second way was to open a strictly national branch or subsidiary after signing an agreement with a Spanish agent. This was the strategy followed by Maurice Junot, from the Société Française de Voyages Pratiques (later Exprinter), with the newspaper *La Correspondencia de España*. A fourth characteristic was that large events were an extraordinary motivation for some tourist intermediaries to decide to operate in Spain. The fifth feature would be the birth of the first Spanish travel brokerage companies.

Although it was not the only one, Viajes Marsansrof (1910) stood out, emerging as a section of the Marsans Rof e Hijos banking house with its headquarters in Barcelona.[1] Undoubtedly, Marsansrof's first challenge was to create tourists, foster a love for travel and, at the same time, facilitate itineraries, transport and accommodation. That is, the classic middleman tasks of a travel agency. And for this its location in Barcelona was a comparative advantage, both from a geographical point of view, due to its proximity to France and the existing contacts with this country, and also thanks to its character as an economic engine. At the time, Catalonia was the spearhead of the travelling movement in Spain (Viajes Marsans 1986, p. 84). In addition to its industrial appeal in Barcelona, its urban, cultural and artistic appeal should also be noted, to name but a few of its features (Palou 2012, chap. 2). Thinking specifically about its customers' trips abroad, in 1912 it launched a very innovative payment system at the time in Spain, traveller's cheques, then called *giros de viaje* or money orders, a device that had already been introduced by American Express in 1891. These money orders or cheques were issued by the J. Marsans Rof e Hijos bank in francs and included a list of the equivalences in different European currencies and in dollars. The aim was to prevent travellers from frequent abuse in currency exchange (Viajes Marsans 1986, pp. 85–86). Here we have a clear example of the connections between businesses, banking and travel.

This first expansion of the business of intermediated travel in Spain was aborted by the First World War. The lack of foreign market (inbound and outbound) in those years led some agencies to focus their business on the

[1] Banca Marsans was a family bank founded in 1892 by José Marsans Rof. In 1902, his son Luis Marsans Peix and son-in-law Francisco Casas Negre joined the company, under the name J. Marsans Rof e Hijos (translator's note: J. Marsans Rof and Sons). However, it was not until 1919 that it became a Public Limited Company when new associates entered the business (Viajes Marsans 1986, p. 82).

domestic market, as was the case with Viajes Marsansrof, which focused, above all, on the so-called circular trips in Spain, that is, the organisation of circuits (Viajes Marsans 1986, p. 86). After the Great War, we can recall the formative years and the boom of travel agencies in Spain, coinciding with an expansion of tourist activity after the war years. When the battle was over, and, above all from the early 1920s, Spanish travel agencies had a greater national and international presence. These agencies became an important pillar of the Spanish tourism system of the time, occupying a prominent role in the tourism industry. More specifically in this context it is worth mentioning the emergence of an entrepreneur, Eusebio Cafranga, who, over the years, would become one of the key figures in intermediated travel in Spain. Of Asturian origin and established, at least since 1916, in the small town of Mendaro (Guipuzcoa), he would soon settle in San Sebastian. In fact, during the Great War he devoted himself to international trade and banking. Here it should be remembered that many tour operators had the basis of their origins in this type of business (transport, banking or travel). These were the cases of the aforementioned José Marsans Rof, from Viajes Cafranga, and, a little later (1930), of Viajes Baleares, to name just a few examples (Vallejo and Larrinaga 2018, p. 727, 2020, pp. 9–10). With this logic, Cafranga would diversify his business, soon becoming a travel agent. In 1922, he began to participate with the Genoese company Navigazione Generale Italiana in organising a trip to South America. In fact, this would not be his only collaboration with this company. The following year he began working with the Italian official operator Ferrovie dello Stato through the travel and tourism offices of the Ente Nazionale Italiano per il Turismo (ENIT). Still in 1926, Cafranga continued to operate with outbound tourism, especially to France, this time as an agent of Turismo Internacional (Paris) (Larrinaga 2019, p. 285).

At the same time, there was a renewed interest from European travel agencies in Spain, not so much as a tourist destination (although this was also the case), but as an outbound market. It should be borne in mind that neutrality had enriched the country with more disposable income from the classes with greater purchasing power, while the strengthening of the peseta in the 1920s favoured Spanish travel abroad (Vallejo and Larrinaga 2018, p. 751, 2020, p. 11). Consequently, foreign agencies considered the Spanish clientele a business opportunity.

But there were also Spanish agencies. Viajes Marsans shows the positive situation of Spanish travel agencies through this important fact. In its

1924 report and balance sheet, the expansion of the travel agency was mentioned thanks to having obtained the corresponding banking services of American Express (along with what this implied as regards North American tourists) and the opening of its first branch outside of Catalonia, in Madrid, with a second one planned in Seville and others in the rest of Spain.[2] The following year, it also opened offices in Seville and Vigo and branches in Palma de Mallorca, Zaragoza and Valencia.[3] It even started a new business strategy incorporating a nationalist discourse, very typical during those years of the Primo de Rivera dictatorship. Everything seems to indicate that this Spanish manoeuvre was market-oriented whereby the large foreign travel agencies had considerable weight.[4] Responding to this strategy, in 1927 it presented itself as a "genuinely Spanish agency", at a time of expansion throughout the national territory (Vallejo and Larrinaga 2018, p. 755, 2020, p. 13).

In the summer of 1928, the travel agency achieved the autonomy of the parent bank, becoming Viajes Marsans, S.A.[5] Its founders were José Luis Marsans Comas and Pelayo Miguel Banús, representing Banca Marsans, S.A. Its purpose was to make and issue tickets for individual or collective trips by sea, land and air in any country and in combination with and apart from railway, maritime or air companies; to promote tourism in all its manifestations, preparing and making excursions and visits to cities and monuments or to fairs and exhibitions; to establish services for travellers on their own or for others; to publish loose leaflets, brochures and advertising and guidebooks; and to carry out all the secondary and banking operations of transportation and consolidation with and without agreement with other companies. In short, it could be dedicated to any lawful business that directly or indirectly was related to a travel and tourism company. The registered office was established in Barcelona but it could set up branches, agencies, subsidiaries and representations anywhere in Spain or abroad. The company was born indefinitely and with a capital of 1,010,000 pesetas, represented by 1010 bearer shares of 1000 pesetas each. This capital was disbursed by the founders at the time of creating the company. In this constitution, the first Board of Directors was appointed (Table 11.1),

[2] 1925. La Ilustración Financiera, February 22, and 1925. El Financiero, March 20 (includes the balance sheet).

[3] 1925. "VI Congreso de la Federación Internacional". La Vanguardia, October 22.

[4] This nationalist discourse would be reinforced even further after the 1929 crisis. See, for example, 1930. "El veraneo, el turismo y el valor de la peseta". Nuevo Mundo, June 27.

[5] Madrid Commercial Register, 3 September 1928, Sheet 60,680, 1st inscription.

**Table 11.1** First Board of Directors of Viajes Marsans, S. A.

| | | |
|---|---|---|
| President | Francisco A. Ripoll Fortuño | lawyer and entrepreneur[a] |
| Members | Juan Salvans Pascual | textile entrepreneur[b] |
| | Francisco Corbera Puñet | financer[c] |
| | Francisco Salvans Armengol | textile entrepreneur and financer[d] |
| | Bernardo Corbera Puñet | financer and entrepreneur[e] |
| | José Guix Ribas | entrepreneur? |
| Secretary | José Luis Marsans Comas | financer and entrepreneur |

Source: Madrid Commercial Register, 3 September 1928, Sheet 60,680, 1st inscription. Author's own elaboration

[a]http://dbe.rah.es/biografias/100976/francisco-de-asis-ripoll-y-fortuno. Accessed on 5 March 2020
[b]http://dbe.rah.es/biografias/65677/francesc-salvans-armengol. Accessed on 5 March 2020
[c]1928. La Vanguardia, January 26
[d]http://dbe.rah.es/biografias/65677/francesc-salvans-armengol. Accessed on 5 March 2020
[e]1943. Obituary. La Vanguardia, December 5

while the General Management of the company was taken on by José Dalmau Castiñeira, who held the position until his death in 1953.[6] José Luis Marsans Comas (the grandson of José Marsans Rof) was appointed as Chief Executive Officer representing Banca Marsans, owner of the majority of the shares (Viajes Marsans 1986, p. 87).

On 12 February 1931, Viajes Hispania merged with Viajes Marsans. This was a horizontal merger between two companies in the sector and demonstrated the strength of the company, which that year had, in addition to the parent company, nine branches and agencies in different Spanish cities and "various" delegations throughout Spain.[7] Based on the data in Table 11.2, everything seems to indicate that this merger responded to the restructuring that the sector was undergoing at that time. The period 1930–1931 were years of crisis in the tourism sector in general, greatly affected by the serious global crisis of 1929. The rising number of travel agencies in Spain, against the backdrop of international exhibitions in 1929, was drastically interrupted in those years and began to pick up again in 1932. This crisis of the travel agencies coincides, in addition, with the crisis of the tourist activity of those first years of the decade of 1930 (Ogilvie 1933).

The Hispania and Marsans merger was not the only one during this period in this sector. In fact, Viajes Baleares, as already mentioned, was founded in 1930 from the merger of three businesses: banking, railways

[6] 1953. La Vanguardia, March 19.
[7] 1931. La Vanguardia, February 12.

**Table 11.2** Contributing travel agencies in Spain per Industrial and Commercial Contributions, 1927–1933[a]

| | *Barcelona* | *Madrid* | *Other provincial capitals* | *Cities with over 20,000 inhabitants* | *Places with under 20,000 inhabitants* | *Total* |
|---|---|---|---|---|---|---|
| 1927 | 4 | 5 | 7 | | 1 | 17 |
| 1928 | 10 | 5 | 14 | | 6 | 35 |
| 1929 | 13 | 8 | 15 | 2 | 8 | 46 |
| 1930 | 11 | 7 | 17 | | 4 | 39 |
| 1931 | 8 | 5 | 22 | | 4 | 39 |
| 1932 | 11 | 6 | 26 | | 4 | 47 |
| 1933 | 16 | 7 | 29 | 1 | 8 | 61 |
| 1927–1933 (Average) | 10 | 6 | 19 | 2 | 5 | 41 |

Source: *Estadística de la CIC* (Statistics on Industrial and Commercial Contributions), 1927–1933. Collated in Vallejo y Larrinaga (2018, p. 734), and Vallejo and Larrinaga (2020, p. 7). Author's own elaboration

[a]Does not include travel agencies in the form of PLCs

and tourism. The Crédito Balear Bank was the majority shareholder and leader of a new agency, with 85 per cent of the subscribed capital. Rafael Blanes Tolosa, a board member of Ferrocarriles de Mallorca, represented railroad interests for Viajes Baleares. Eventually, the tourism business was represented through Viajes Catalonia, a travel agency belonging to Banco de Cataluña. Therefore, Viajes Baleares was closely associated with Viajes Catalonia and in fact acted as its representative in the islands. But scarcely a year after the creation of Viajes Baleares, the owners acquired Viajes Catalonia in order to organise a network of travel agents which would cover the entire country. Viajes Catalonia had a single office in Spain, in Barcelona, and another office in Paris. The acquisition of Viajes Catalonia and its greater objectives made it necessary to change the name Viajes Baleares to Viajes Iberia in 1932 (San Román 2017, pp. 55–56).

## 11.3 The International Dimension of Spanish Travel Agencies and FIAV Congresses

The *Federación Internacional de Agencias de Viajes* (FIAV) (the International Federation of Travel Agencies) had been created in 1919 and from the following year onward organised its annual congress. Three were held in Spain, in 1925, 1928 and 1934, proof of the power and hold which Spanish travel agencies were beginning to have. Therefore, the VI Congress was held in October 1925 in Barcelona, with Viajes Marsans being the main protagonist. Its objective was to promote the development of tourism in Spain and consequently it invited many foreign travel agencies from both Europe and all over America. The representatives for Spain were Mr Blateau from Viajes Prácticos, the director of the Agencia Sommariva de Madrid and the directors of branches of Viajes Marsans in Madrid, Seville and Vigo, as well as the subsidiaries of Palma, Zaragoza and Valencia. Nine representatives of the railway companies also took part.[8] Thus, the *Federación Nacional de Agencias de Viajes* (National Federation of Travel Agencies) was also constituted, integrated into the International Federation.

A few years later the IX FIAV Congress was also held in Spain (October 1928), organised by the association of Spanish travel agencies, under the auspices of the *Patronato Nacional de Turismo* (PNT) or National Tourist Board (NTB). Eusebio Cafranga was the congress president, and his secretary, Maurice Junot, also representing the French Federation and the Exprinter agency, attended on behalf of the FIAV. The Assembly brought together delegates from the 31 participating agencies and the many agencies represented.[9] On the eve of the Exhibitions in Seville and Barcelona, this congress was the ideal setting to publicise the great modernising advances that had been taking place in Spain since Primo de Rivera's accession to power. In fact, the congressmen not only visited Madrid, but also the two venues of the exhibitions, seeing the rhythm of the works and Spain's tourist potential. Naturally, infrastructure, hotels and the issue of passports were also analysed.[10] Additionally, they discussed the advantage that Spanish railway companies were comparable to foreign ones as regards the organisation of services and tourist excursions.[11] In short, as a result of the congress, the participating travel agencies committed to promoting Spain as a tourist destination, especially Barcelona and Seville (Table 11.3).

[8] 1925. "VI Congreso de la Federación Internacional". La Vanguardia, October 22.

[9] 1931. "El Congreso de las Agencias de viajes". ABC, October 27.

[10] Risquet. 1928. "El Congreso de Agencias de turismo". El Imparcial, October 25. 1928. "El Congreso de la Federación de Agencias de Viaje". La Época, October 25. 1928. "El IX Congreso internacional de Agencias de Viaje". La Vanguardia, October 26.

[11] 1928. "El congreso Federación de Agencias de Viaje". La Voz (Madrid), October 26. 1928. "Reunión del Congreso de la Federación internacional de agencias de viajes". El Heraldo de Madrid, October 27.

**Table 11.3** Receptive or Inbound tourism in Spain, 1912–1934

| | *Total number of visitors* | *Tourists (in thousands)* | *Bookings* | *In transit* |
|---|---|---|---|---|
| 1912 | | 198.7 | | |
| 1925–1927 | | 213.3 | | |
| 1929 | 362,716 | | 276,468 | 86,248 |
| 1930 | 440,552 | | 277,912 | 162,640 |
| 1931 | | | 187,220 | |
| 1932 | | | 201,914 | |
| 1933 | | | 200,346 | |
| 1934 | | | 190,830 | |

Source: Fernández Fúster (1991, p. 277), and Vallejo et al. (2016, p. 147). Author's own elaboration

Note: Tourists (thousands): these figures are taken by Vallejo, Lindoso and Vilar (2016, 147), comparable to those of Bookings for 1931–1934

Taking advantage of the momentum of the 1928 congress and, above all, while the Barcelona and Seville Exhibitions were still being held, in March 1930 an important meeting took place in Barcelona, chaired by José Luis Marsans and attended by Eduardo Lesperut on behalf of Viajes Hispania of Alicante, Eusebio Cafranga for Viajes Cafranga of San Sebastian and Fernando Baquera for Viajes Bakumar of Málaga. In this meeting, a decision was made to communicate, through the FIAV bulletin, that these events were still open to promote travel, more specifically, in a context marked by the 1929 crisis. It was then agreed that a large amount of advertising would be sent both to the national and foreign federations to distribute it amongst their associates. Approval was also given to submit a request to railway companies to grant tourists as many facilities as possible. They would also send another letter to the PNT so that, in line with foreign travel agencies, it would intensify advertising about Spain. They also asked the PNT for permanent contact with the Federation of Travel Agencies of Spain, requesting the participation of one of its members within the Board of trustees, a fact that was accepted by the Government a short time afterwards.[12] Finally, they went to the *Cámara*

[12] 1931. "La Federación de Agencias de Viajes de España". La Correspondencia de Valencia, December 24. In fact, in the Provisional Regulations of the PNT, approved on 12 February 1932, it was established that the Federation of Travel Agencies of Spain was part of the General Council of Tourism, an advisory body of this institution. 1932. Boletín Oficial del Estado [Official State Gazette], January 14, pp. 365–367.

**Table 11.4** Federation of Spanish Travel Agencies in 1932

| *City* | *Agency* |
|---|---|
| Barcelona | Viajes Internacional Express |
| Barcelona | Viajes Marsans, S.A. |
| Barcelona | Italia-América |
| Barcelona | Viajes Catalonia |
| Madrid | Carco, S. A. |
| Malaga | Viajes Bakumar |
| San Sebastian | Viajes Cafranga |
| Valencia | Valencia Express |

Source: 1932. La Época, May 25. Author's own elaboration

*Oficial Hotelera*, the Official Chamber of Hospitality, to agree on issues related to national tourism.[13] Thus, with these four agencies, this business federation was launched, although that same year Viajes Internacional Express of Barcelona joined. In its organisation chart, at the meeting in December 1930, José Luis Marsans was named president, Eusebio Cafranga vice president and Eduardo Lesperut secretary.[14] In 1932 there were already eight federated agencies (Table 11.4). In 1933, Cafranga was elected president[15] and, soon afterwards, a member of the PNT.[16]

In addition, some of the members of the FAVE created a public limited company capable of launching itself to attract tourism directly in the European outbound markets. In fact, in 1933 the "Fave Travel PLC was created, with a capital of 250,000 pesetas, to channel international tourism in Spain, Portugal and Morocco". With its registered office in the French capital, it had its "first office in Paris, at the premises of the PNT", in order to take advantage of "this body's work for the advertising carried out Abroad".[17] Marsans, Cafranga, Iberia and Carco were part of FAVE, S.A.[18]

[13] 1930. La Vanguardia, Mars 19.

[14] 1930. El Heraldo de Madrid, December 26.

[15] 1933. La Vanguardia, December 28. In fact, as vice president and by representing the Federation, he took part in the International Tourism Congress of Brussels in 1932 (1932. El Sol, October 28).

[16] 1934. El Sol, May 6. We must remember that the General Council of Tourism was abolished by the decree of 31 January 1934, hence modification of the PNT regulation. 1934. Boletín Oficial del Estado [Official State Gazette], January 31, p. 810.

[17] 1933. El Heraldo de Madrid, January 3. See also Moreno (2007b, pp. 212–213).

[18] 1936/2. Barcelona Atracción, 302.

In this new context of clear recovery of tourism, in 1934 the last of the FIAV congresses (no. XV) was held in Spain before the outbreak of the Civil War. Specifically, the congressmen embarked in Barcelona on 29 October to go from there to Mallorca, where the sessions were held, and the congress was inaugurated on 30 October. The objective was to debate particularly significant aspects for Spanish tourism, but, above all, for tourism in Catalonia and the Balearic Islands (Palou 2012, Buades 2004 and Cirer 2009), which reveals the importance that these two regions already had in the national tourism panorama.[19] Almost 100 attendees gathered,[20] with 75 foreign delegates. They remained on the island until 3 November when they returned to Barcelona, where the closing ceremony took place. It is important to point out that by then Eusebio Cafranga was already the President of FIAV.[21] This should be interpreted not only as a great personal success, but also a success for Spain's travel agents, having become important players both on the national and international stage.

In this sense, the territorial expansion of Viajes Marsans, for example, has already been seen, although this was not the only case. Bakumar had been founded in 1921 and by 1929 there were seven branches (Malaga, Barcelona, Valencia, Alicante, Seville, Cordoba and Cadiz). As for Viajes Cafranga, by 1934 there was a branch in Bilbao and a delegation in Oviedo. In 1935, two delegations joined in Pamplona and Santander (Larrinaga 2019, p. 293). In 1933, when the crisis seemed to be over, other agencies emerged, proof of the dynamism of the business in the years before 1936 (Vallejo and Larrinaga 2018, p. 756, 2020, p. 14). In turn, Viajes Iberia, in addition to the Barcelona and Palma offices, opened another in Madrid but this closed in 1936 (San Román 2017, p. 60).

## 11.4 The Early Years of the Franco Regime

The Civil War put an end to all this congressional dynamism and, to a large extent, to the tourist activity which had occurred until then. For example, almost all of Viajes Marsans' employees were soon mobilised, travel-related activities were paralysed, most offices closed their doors and,

[19] 1934. "El fomento del turismo". La Vanguardia, October 26, and 1934. "El XV Congreso internacional de Agencias de viaje". La Vanguardia, October 27.

[20] 1934. "El XV Congreso de la Federación Internacional de Agencias de Viajes". La Vanguardia, October 30.

[21] 1934. La Vanguardia, November 4.

hoping to maintain some commercial activity, the management decided to dedicate their shops in Barcelona and Valencia to the sale of books, although this had little success (Viajes Marsans 1986, p. 87). Both Marsans and Cafranga joined the rebels, but since the cities where they lived, Barcelona and San Sebastian, did not join the uprising, they were forced to flee. Cafranga resorted to his Portuguese passport, having been first Vice Consul and then Honorary Consul of that country in San Sebastian, returning shortly after the war to this capital after his capture by the Franco side (13 September 1936) (Larrinaga 2019, p. 294). Everything seems to suggest that Eusebio Cafranga soon recovered his economic activity.

In the area controlled by the Franco regime, by an Act of 30 January 1938, the National Tourism Service (NTS), dependent on the Ministry of the Interior, was created. This was headed by the journalist Luis Bolín, who settled in San Sebastian. Enrique Marsans Comas, José Luis's brother, was chosen so that, from the General Secretariat, he would be in charge of structuring its organisation.[22] The NTS launched the War Routes for that summer. These were tourist itineraries initially through northern Spain, and later through Andalusia. The two fundamental objectives were to obtain foreign currency and to advertise the Franco cause (Holguín 2005, p. 1.400; Correyero and Cal 2008, pp. 250–273; and Concejal 2014, p. 260). These itineraries were a monopoly of the state and could not be carried out freely, but through the purchase of coupons from certain travel agencies authorised by the NTS in collaboration with different foreign financial entities when it came to foreign visitors. They were therefore intermediated trips, and hence the need to collaborate with travel agencies. Indeed, Viajes Cafranga, based in San Sebastian, was one which collaborated most actively with the NTS. Although these routes were not a great economic success, they served to maintain some hospitality businesses (Bolín 1967, p. 315). For his part, Eusebio Cafranga saw the opportunity that these War Routes offered, since some of his competitors saw their business paralysed by the battle. Thus, at his headquarters in San Sebastian, he soon added two more branches that same summer, one in Bilbao and the other in Zaragoza, two very significant cities in northern Spain and therefore with potential clients.[23]

[22] http://dbe.rah.es/biografias/85508/enrique-marsans-comas. Accessed on 5 March 2020. Later he would become the head of the Foreign General Tourism Directorate. 1940. La Vanguardia, August 23.

[23] 1938. Advertisement by Viajes Cafranga. El Diario Vasco, July 2 and August 24.

Shortly after the war ended, the Central State Administration was reorganised through the Act of 8 August 1939, by which the former *Servicios Nacionales* (National Services) were renamed *Direcciones Generales* (General Directorates). The NTS was now renamed the GDT, General Directorate of Tourism, with Luis Bolín again at the forefront. The GDT was created with the general coordination of all the tourist aspects related to the private sector. In fact, through the Franco dictatorship's desire to control the private sector, the GDT carried out an intense legislative activity that revealed the clearly interventionist policy of the regime in tourism matters (Correyero 2005, pp. 62–63; Moreno 2007a, pp. 152 and 159–160). The DGT always tried to collaborate in the reconstruction of Spain, stimulating the country's promotion and its preparation to welcome national and foreign tourists, while aspiring to achieve international recognition of Spain, when, at the end of the Second World War, it was prone to significant isolation by the triumphant democracies over fascism and Nazism. For this, it had no qualms carrying out remarkable propaganda work, relying mainly on the private sector, specifically in the Spanish Federation of Trade Unions of Initiatives and Tourism (FESIT in its Spanish acronym) and in travel agencies (Correyero and Cal 2008, p. 302). More specifically, those who had collaborated from the outset with the regime benefited extensively.

According to Bolín, it was very important to have the support of travel agencies as they knew the markets and had experience in managing tourism and selling Spain to foreign tourists (Vallejo and Concejal 2018, p. 399). In fact, the new functions of travel agencies in Spain were regulated in the Decree of 19 February 1942,[24] which aspired to take full control of their activity to avoid competition with the state. Tourism as such was the exclusive competence of the state, so that travel agencies were reserved, according to article 2, for the following purposes and business: selling tickets and reserving seats in all kinds of regular transport, booking hotel rooms and services, and organising package tours, group tours, excursions and city visits.

The decree further classified the agencies into two groups. Group A would be made up of those agencies which, dedicated to the activities indicated in article 2, fulfilled the following requirements: (1) be depositories and issue tickets of the International Union or, failing that, of three

[24] 1942. Boletín Oficial del Estado [Official State Gazette], May 6. Transcribed by Fernández Fúster 1991, pp. 484–486.

European nations; (2) be concessionaires for the sale of combined coupon tickets of the National Network of Spanish Railways; (3) be concessionaires for the sale of tickets of the Spanish Air Companies; (4) be authorised to sell tickets from the main Spanish Navigation Companies; and (5) have civil liability insurance arranged to cover the risks of both group and individual travel. Therefore, those agencies that did not comply with these conditions would infill Group B, acting as intermediaries between the public and those of Group A, only providing the tickets and bonds issued by them.

Once the decree had been issued and disseminated, the applications submitted were studied so that, from the month of December onward, the classifications or licences, granted to Group A agencies appeared in the *Boletín Oficial del Estado* (Official State Gazette) as shown in Table 11.5. At the same time, the first classifications were also awarded to Group B agencies, that is, to those agencies which were intermediaries between the main Group A companies and their clients. Taking into account Table 11.6, we see a territorial increase in these agencies and therefore an expansion of the business, and, at the same time, that the first three of Group A (Marsans, Internacional Expreso and Cafranga) were the agencies that had more intermediaries, which allowed them to strengthen their presence in certain areas of the country. Furthermore, the changes between one and the other with respect to the same Group B agency are also interesting, which makes us aware of a certain conflict between the large agencies of the sector at a difficult moment of reconstructing the tourism business after the Civil War and the Second World War. Indeed, the fact that some of these agencies ceased to trade is clear proof of this.

Likewise, the DGT created an Advisory Commission, made up of the 12 largest agencies operating in Spain, coinciding with those in Table 11.5. As its name indicates, this Commission had a merely advisory function. Ricardo Jaspe, representing the GDT itself, occupied the secretariat of an institution, known as the commission of twelve, which lasted until 26 February 1963 (Correyero and Cal 2008, p. 398), when it was abolished in a new stage of further liberalisation of the Spanish economy after the launch of the 1959 Stabilisation Plan and a greater opening of the Spanish economy to the outside world, which, in tourist terms, materialised in a real boom in the sector. The Permanent Commission of Travel Agencies,

**Table 11.5** The top 12 agencies in Group A (in authorisation order between 1942 and 1944)

| *Classifications* | *Name* | *BOE* | *Central office* | *Branches* |
|---|---|---|---|---|
| 1st | Viajes Marsans, S.A. | 3-12-1942 | Barcelona | Madrid, Palma, Sevilla, Valencia |
| 2nd | Viajes Internacional Expreso | 3-12-1942 | Barcelona | Palma |
| 3rd | Viajes Cafranga | 7-12-1942 | San Sebastian | Bilbao, Irún, Oviedo, Pamplona, Zaragoza, Vitoria. |
| 4th | Viajes Iberia, S.A. | 11-12-1942 | Palma | Barcelona |
| 5th | Wagons-Lits Cook | 23-12-1942 | Madrid | Agencies: Madrid (H. Palace), Barcelona, Seville, Malaga, Granada, Algeciras, Valencia, Palma, San Sebastian, Bilbao, Irún. Sub-agencies: Alicante, Badajoz, Cadiz, Santander, Zaragoza, Cartagena, Canfranc, Gijon, Oviedo, Valladolid, Jerez de la Frontera, Cordoba, La Coruña, Vigo y Valencia de Alcántara. |
| 6th | Viajes Bakumar, S.A. | 14-1-1943 | Malaga | Alicante, Barcelona, Cádiz, Córdoba, Palma, Madrid, Sevilla, Valencia. |
| 7th | Viajes Hispania | 14-1-1943 | Alicante | Barcelona, Valencia. |
| 8th | J. Meliá y cía. | 14-1-1943 | Valencia | |
| 9th | Deutsche America Linie | 14-1-1943 | Madrid | |
| 10th | Agencia General de las Compañías Hamburguesas | 14-1-1943 | Madrid | San Sebastian, Las Palmas de Gran Canaria. |
| 11th | Viajes Sommariva | 9-2-1944 | Madrid | |
| 12th | Viajes Vincit | 21-6-1944 | Pamplona | |

Source: Boletín Oficial del Estado (Official State Gazette), General Archive of the Administration, GAA, (03)049.002TOP.22/44.203-52.704-box 12.423, and Fernández Fúster (1991, pp. 486–487). Author's own elaboration

**Table 11.6** Agencies of Group B (in authorisation order between 1943 and 1950)

| *Classifications* | *Name* | *BOE* | *Head office* | *Intermediary of* | *Ceased trading (BOE)* |
|---|---|---|---|---|---|
| 1st | Pedro Jiménez y Jiménez<br>Viajes Castilla | 25-9-1943<br>18-6-1945 | Valladolid | Viajes Iberia<br>Cafranga (1944) | 12-5-1946 |
| 2nd | Viajes A.B.C. | 25-3-1944 | Barcelona | Viajes Marsans, S.A.<br>Cafranga (1947) | |
| 3rd | Viajes Galicia Expreso | | Vigo | Cafranga | 25-9-1946 |
| 4th | Viajes Sanmillán | 20-5-1945 | Castellón | Viajes Marsans, S.A. | |
| 5th | Jerez Expreso | 14-2-1946 | Jerez de la Frontera | Viajes Marsans, S.A. | 6-8-1947 |
| 6th | Viajes Horizonte | 20-3-1946 | Madrid | Viajes Marsans, S.A.<br>Internacional Expreso (1947) | 8-5-1948 |
| 7th | Viajes Elcano, S.A. | 28-9-1946 | Madrid | Wagons-Lits Cook | |
| 8th | Viajes Metropol, S.L. | 21-10-1946 | Las Palmas | Viajes Marsans, S.A. | 05-04-1952 |
| 9th | Viajes Viamar | 28-7-1947 | Palma de Mallorca | Viajes Iberia, S.A. | 5-04-1952 |
| 10th | Viajes Galicia Expreso | 2-11-1947 | La Coruña | Internacional Expreso | 19-10-1950 |
| 11th | Viajes Gerona | 12-03-1950 | Gerona | Viajes Baixas, S.A. | 5-04-1952 |
| 12th | Viajes Ibero-Alemán | 4-4-1950 | Barcelona | Internacional Expreso | |
| 13th | Viajes Orpag | 21-7-1950 | Sevilla | Cafranga | |

Source: Boletín Oficial del Estado (Official State Gazette). Author's own elaboration

**Table 11.7** Board of Directors of Viajes Marsans, S. A., 1955

| | | |
|---|---|---|
| President | Enrique Marsans Comas | Madrid |
| Members | Luis Figueras Dotti | Madrid |
| | Juan Claudio Güell | Madrid |
| | Federico Díez-Isasi | Madrid |
| | Antonio Navarro Reverter | Madrid |
| Secretary | Cirilo Genovés Amorós | Madrid |

Source: Madrid Commercial Registrer, 29 April 1955, Sheet 60,680, 5th inscription. Author's own elaborations

created on 10 December 1943, was more decisive. This was made up of Group A travel agencies and those other sectors interested in solving various problems of the time which affected tourism activity in Spain (DDT, RENFE, merchant marine, airlines or the *Sindicato Vertical de Hostelería*, to name but a few).[25]

In short, despite the crisis which the tourism business and travel agencies experienced in general (particularly during the war years), shortly after the war ended, the travel agency sector began to recover following the Decree of 19 February 1942. This decree served to regulate and reorder the sector, as well as to lay the foundations for its future action. The most important travel agencies managed to position themselves in the sector, so that, at the beginning of the 1950s, a denser implementation of these agencies was observed throughout the country. The intermediated trips were becoming increasingly important within the tourist activity of the 1950s. In 1955, Viajes Iberia S.A., for example, had eight offices: four in the Balearic Islands (Palma, Ibiza, Pollensa and Mahon) and another four in the peninsula: Barcelona, Madrid, Valencia and San Sebastian (San Román 2017, p. 66). By then Viajes Marsans had set up an empire, with offices in 15 countries and 50 in Spain (Viajes Marsans 1986, 130). This coincided, incidentally, with a very significant change in the company originating from the agreements taken at the extraordinary general meeting of 23 November 1953 (Table 11.7).

In those years, even the organised trips of Spaniards abroad began to become a reality.[26] Undoubtedly, it was a reflection of the strong tourist

[25] GAA, (03)049.002TOP.22/44.203-52.704-box 12.423.

[26] For example, for the summer of 1953 Viajes Marsans offered trips to Germany-Belgium-France-Switzerland, Scandinavian countries or a great cruise through Ceylon and India. *La Vanguardia*, 28-06-1953, 12. However, a few years earlier, in 1949, José Meliá had created the Coach Tours in Europe, even opening two offices in Paris and New York. Galindo (2000, 445).

expansion that began to be experienced in those years and which accelerated even further in the 1960s. The distribution of travel agencies allows us to recognise the most significant tourist regions in Spain, although, in the early 1950s, there had still not yet been any radical changes from the previous years (Barke and Towner 1996, p. 17).

## References

Barke, Michael, and John Towner. 1996. Exploring the History of Leisure and Tourism in Spain. In *Tourism in Spain*, ed. Michael Barke, John Towner, and Michel T. Newton, 3–34. Wallingford: CAB International.

Bolín, Luis. 1967. *España. Los años vitales*. Madrid: Espasa-Calpe.

Buades, Joan. 2004. *On brilla el sol. Turisme a Balears abans del boom*. Eivissa: Res Publica.

Cirer, Joan Carle. 2009. *La invenció del turismo de masses a Mallorca*. Palma: Documenta Balear.

Concejal, Eva. 2014. Las Rutas de Guerra del Servicio Nacional de Turismo (1938–1939). In *Visite España. La memoria rescatada*, 259–273. Madrid: BNE.

Correyero, Beatriz. 2005. La Administración turística española entre 1936 y 1951. *Estudios turísticos* 163–164: 55–79.

Correyero, Beatriz, and Rosa Cal. 2008. *Turismo: la mayor propaganda de Estado*. Madrid: Vision Net.

Fernández Fúster, Luis. 1991. *Historia general del turismo de masas*. Madrid: Alianza.

Galindo, Pedro. 2000. José Meliá Sinisterra (1911–1999). In *Cien empresarios españoles del siglo XX*, ed. Eugenio Torres, 444–450. Madrid: Lid.

Holguín, Sandy. 2005. National Spain Invites You: Battlefield Tourism During the Spanish Civil War. *The Amerivan Historical Review* 110 (5): 1399–1426.

Larrinaga, Carlos. 2019. El empresario Eusebio Cafranga y el negocio de las agencias de viajes en España antes del turismo de masas. In *Empresas y empresarios en España: de mercaderes a industriales*, coordinated by Juan Manuel Matés Barco, 281–301. Madrid: Pirámide.

Moreno, Ana. 2007a. *Historia del turismo en España en el siglo XX*. Madrid: Síntesis.

———. 2007b. L'Office de Tourisme Espagnolde París (1929–1939). Política y turismo en los años treinta. *Cuadernos de Historia Contemporánea* 29: 199–228.

Ogilvie, Frederick W. 1933. *The Tourist Movement: An Economic Study*. London: P. S. King.

Palou, Saida. 2012. *Barcelona, destinació turística*. Bellcaire d'Empordà: Viltel·la.

San Román, Elena. 2017. *Building Stars*. Madrid: Grupo Iberostar.

Vallejo, Rafael, and Eva Concejal. 2018. La política y la Administración turística durante la Guerra Civil. In *Los orígenes del turismo moderno en España. El nacimiento de un país turístico, 1900–1939*, ed. Rafael Vallejo and Carlos Larrinaga, 381–420. Madrid: Sílex.

Vallejo, Rafael, and Carlos Larrinaga. 2018. Las agencias de viaje: operadores turísticos. In *Los orígenes del turismo moderno en España. El nacimiento de un país turístico, 1900–1939*, ed. Rafael Vallejo and Carlos Larrinaga, 723–762. Madrid: Sílex.

———. 2020. Travel Agencies in Spain During the First Third of the 20th Century. A Tourism Business in the Making. *Business History* (ed. on line): 1–20. https://doi.org/10.1080/00076791.2019.1685503.

Vallejo, Rafael, Elvira Lindoso, and Margarita Vilar. 2016. Los antecedentes del turismo de masas en España, 1900–1936. *Revista de la Historia de la Economía y de la Empresa* 10: 137–188.

Viajes Marsans. 1986. *75 años de turismo en España. Marsans 1910–1985*. Madrid: Viajes Marsans.

Visentin, Claudio. 1995. Nuovi viaggi e nuovi viaggiatori: la nascita delle agenzie turistiche in Italia (1878–1914). *Storia in Lombardia* 1–2: 297–311.

CHAPTER 12

# Menorcan Entrepreneurs of Footwear and Technological Innovation: Pons Quintana and Mascaró

*Juan Hernández Andreu*

## 12.1 Introduction

In Menorca an important manufacturing activity, including modern industrial activity, took place in the strict sense since 1850. Thus, its peculiar economic diversification meant that the island did not develop fully in tourism until the 1960s, after Mallorca. Today tourism predominates, which coexists with activities from other sectors, somewhat reduced, compared to yesteryear. Likewise, new industries are promoted through a technology park, with public sector support for private initiatives. Menorca has always had great entrepreneurs in different economic sectors.

Menorca, despite its small population, has had an active economy, at least since the mid-eighteenth century. Entrepreneurship was able to overcome the difficulties derived from the smallness of the island territory and the isolation of the markets, technology and universities, having registered

J. Hernández Andreu (✉)
Complutense University of Madrid, Madrid, Spain
e-mail: jhandreu@ccee.ucm.es


M. Vázquez-Fariñas et al. (eds.), *Companies and Entrepreneurs in the History of Spain*, Palgrave Studies in Economic History, https://doi.org/10.1007/978-3-030-61318-1_12

difficulties for job learning. All in all, throughout history, menorquines have known how to take advantage of opportunity costs and situation income to boost Menorcan economic development, particularly during the 1960s. Afterwards, economic integration in the European market, globalization, and development of tourist activities were important.

Most of the companies belonging to a selected number of 35 outstanding Menorcan entrepreneurs were or are of a medium size; that is, they are companies with between 50 and 100 workers. After the Spanish Civil War, companies organized as Sociedad Anónima or Sociedad Limitada became predominant on the island. Most of the capitals come from the island, frequently with family origins, or from local connections.

The most frequent entrepreneurial qualities, among the aforementioned sample, among Menorcan entrepreneurs, are their work ability (in 20.7%), followed by their innovative capacity, to face risks and work in teams (17.2%); we also observed the analytical skills (10.3%) and the entrepreneurial character (6.9%), among other less significant qualities, such as the diversification of activities and the facility for social relationships. We observe a balance between values outside (vision, social relations) of the company and those inside (teamwork and work ability).

## 12.2 Technological Innovation

Technological innovation is the predominant factor in entrepreneurship, whose diverse nuances and characteristics appear in the personality of the two Menorcan businessmen that I am going to highlight in a sector of atavistic tradition, in the Menorcan industry. Currently, from a numerical point of view, many that were important in the past have disappeared, and those who knew how to win international markets, such as Santiago Pons Quintana and Jaume Mascaró, persist, with internationally recognized success.

I understand technological innovation in the broad sense, as accepted in the scientific community. I also consider as such a new business organization on its own physical and human resources, which increase productivity, competitiveness and profits. Along with the theory of the innovative entrepreneur (R. Cantillón, J. Garnier or J.A. Schumpeter), the theory of entrepreneurship has arisen, imputing to the company the causality of growth. We are talking about total productivity, which includes the factors of labor and capital, and, of course, the importance of entrepreneurs' education to interpret economic growth is also pointed out.

It has to be pointed out the importance of the causality principle of the factor "company culture", empirically valued, as the predominant factor for business profitability. According to recent studies, where the entity of the company is related to its own history, principles and philosophy of the organization, symbols, values and customs shared corporately are raised, which is decisive for winning the future of the company.

## 12.3 Don Santiago Pons Quintana (1929–2020)

Santiago Pons Quintana was born in *Alaior* (*Minorca*) on June 29, 1929, in a simple home, and recently passed away at the age of 90. He has been one of the leading shoe manufacturers in Spain and was a pioneer in the manufacture of women's slippers, the famous ***babuchas.***

Santiago was a very active, open, direct young man, a friend of his friends, loyal to his commitments; he always had a vision for the future, in addition to being a born fighter. He had a great sense of humor, a little sly. He started working in a small factory of his uncle Quintana. There he cut the "cuts", bought the leathers and was in charge of shipping the shoe boxes; and studied high school at night, passing three courses in a single year.

Don Santiago was fortunate to be able to perform military service in Menorca, which allowed him, during this time, to continue to be linked to his work, his studies and also playing football. A cinema fan, he collaborated in the diffusion and projection of the films in what would be the future cultural center of *Alaior*, where Santiago would become its president in full maturity. At the time, he also followed a pattern-making course and thus learned the art and secrets of drawing shoe patterns. Santiago was always very close to his parents; and his two sons, Santiago (born February 3, 1957) and Magdalena (born February 11, 1961), have become the effective continuators of his entrepreneurial work, when his father reached retirement, although without completely detaching himself of its great footwear company, *Pons Quintana, S.A.* (P.Q.). Starting in 1953, he began to market *Chicarro* children's shoes for an Icelandic firm, first, and for the Spanish market, later—starting point of what is today one of the main shoe factories on the island and perhaps in Spain.

One day, some Icelanders took an interest in the child's shoes that were on the counter of the store where Santiago's girlfriend, Inés, who would later become his wife, worked. It was the Löowik company that had an agreement with the State to sell cod to Spain and buy glasses, Alella wine and shoes here. Connected with Santiago, through Inés, an agreement was reached between them. The Icelanders advanced 200,000 pesetas to Santiago so that within a month he would send them 1220 *Chicarro* shoes. The deal worked perfectly and Banesto Bank made the corresponding payments to Santiago, following instructions from the Icelanders. Two months later, Santiago received a million pesetas of credit to make some 6000 pairs of shoes.

Icelanders' orders grew and Santiago gave Uncle Quintana the opportunity to collaborate with productions in his open and growing shoe market. That worked until 1955, and it became known afterwards that so many shoe boxes sold were re-exported to the USSR, where indeed there was a great demand for children's shoes.

To continue, Mr. Pons Quintana prepared the sample book and went to sell his shoes to the main Spanish markets. The sample included the children' shoes made by him and the shoes produced by his uncle Quintana's factory. In Bilbao, in "Calzados La Palma", after passing the test, he opened the market. The "chicarrones" of the north bought the *Chicarro* shoes. In Madrid, he managed to sell in "Los pequeños suizos", specialized in children's shoes, closing an order for 300 pairs. He also formalized sales to "Calzados la Imperial" and to "Joaquín de Pablos". In Barcelona he placed his productions at "Calzados Grimp". Sales were going well, although there was a setback with "Calzados La Imperial", as its various stores were ruined and Pons Quintana was caught with a loss of 300,000 pesetas, at that time a fortune.

Customers went to the Pons Quintana factory to place their orders, as was the case with the "CasaTorrens" in Barcelona. On August 11, 1956, Santiago Pons Quintana married Inés, his girlfriend forever, and he bought a house to live and found his own family. In 1957 the factory had 20 workers. Customers paid 30 days religiously and a time of economic euphoria began. The balances were beneficial and the children came. In 1961, they bought a new headquarters for the factory, which, although their own, would soon be small. There were already 35 workers. Santiago invested in heritage and acquired the *Rafal Fort* property (1962) and a villa (1963) in the port of Mahón.

A great mercantile operation had taken place in 1956 when Don Santiago introduced the sales of his shoes in "El Corte Inglés". Since then, this company has not stopped buying from it in an increasing way, season after season. They were also the beginnings of "El Corte Inglés," located on *Preciados* Street, and Santiago made the deal with Ramón Areces himself, a businessman who had come from Cuba; Pons Quintana was the first to sell slippers and Areces the first to ask the Menorcan manufacturer for women's slippers, since Santiago began to manufacture this type of product at the request and initiative of the smart Mr. Areces.

After a trip by the Minister Mr. López Bravo to Menorca, which encouraged the Menorcan industrialists to be competitive, Santiago bought a plot, for the new factory headquarters, of 800 square meters only on the ground floor, with a basement, first floor and others outbuildings that opened in November 1968.

However, the first customer, by volume of orders, was "El Corte Inglés" and continued to be so. On one occasion, the order went from 10,000 to 18,000 pairs in a single day, after a run-in with Ramón Areces and provoked by him, without further explanation. The owner of El Corte Inglés later clarified that he wanted to check the safety of the manufacturer. *Pons Quintana, S.A.* is the 147th supplier to "El Corte Inglés", and there is an excellent relationship with those responsible for these department stores.

In the early 1970s, Pons Quintana strengthened the market for its products thanks to the invention of the model that was the result of a new type of manufacturing, consisting of double turning the leather. The Catalan market for sneakers grew due to a change of representative there. Santiago began to attend the *Italian Preselection* that was held twice a year in Bologna and continued to frequent Paris with other Menorcan manufacturers. He began the adventure of exporting to the United States, obtaining large orders for "slippers" from the "Charlless" firm, which owned department stores. Exports were then driven by the State with a 10% tax relief, which was good for the sector and the situation exposed for the United States lasted for some years. A Barcelona shirt shop, "J. Roca", which had several branches on the Costa Brava, was also a good customer, with orders for 5000 pairs of men's shoes for the summer season.

The depression of the 1980s forced a rethinking of what the market needed in this situation. This moment was key for the company, since it laid the definitive foundations of what Pons Quintana is today. In 1980, P.Q.'s shoe sales declined, and the company's bottom line that year was poor. Santiago's reflection and drive led him not to succumb, and he took the right steps to get out of the rut, already counting on the effective collaboration of his son "Santi", a graduate in Business Studies, who was already working at the company and had good commercial sense, having expanded the market in Andalusia.

An exhaustive market analysis led Santiago to invest in the application of new technologies for the factory, thus having the most advanced machinery—which is essential to offer excellent collections, both in terms of new trends and in their materials and finishes—. New products made up the 1982 sample, which turned out to be a surprise and a success at the same time, especially with a new article, "Frontis de crepé".

The Pons Quintana came up with the smart solution by going to the State controllers, a consultancy from the public sector carried out by officials expert in controlling the work of the companies, who taught to accelerate the pace of work, counting on the collaboration of all the staff of the factory. This came back and increased productivity. The daughter, Magda, had joined in 1982 to run the factory. Since 1983, the company has grown steadily. The pattern designer was in permanent contact with Milan, where he spent a season, and the teachings of two Italian modelers in the factory launched the fashion both in braid and leather. The design, production and marketing direction were passed on to Santi, Jr. and Magda's boyfriend, Juan Carlos, who married her, also joined the office as an expert in new technologies.

In 1985 and 1986, with the braided shoe, the Pons Quintana company received another great push. In Germany, his sales took the palm, and his proclaimed collection was the best-selling; there were also many requests from France, Belgium, the Netherlands, Austria, Switzerland and the United States (Las Vegas); in short, for the Pons Quintana a world without borders was opened. In 1990 they had 90 employees, the work was not lacking and they decided to renew the machinery (automatic belts, with their corresponding ovens, reactivators, refrigerators and with the return of furnaces on the same belt and a lot of other machines), investing 75 million *pesetas* in it. Production effectiveness increased greatly and the investment was a success. The years 1993 and 1994 were difficult, but the workforce increased to 104 workers and the planned budget was executed. That last year Santiago turned 65 and retired.

Don Santiago Pons Quintana was the founder and director of the company until his retirement. He also was the Chairman of the Board of Directors. The company's business strategy rests on two fundamental management points: the factory and the commercial network. Regarding the input of its products, the leathers used by Pons Quintana are exclusively manufactured by the company by 60% and their origin is both national and foreign. All the materials such as leathers, *becerritos*, gemstones, soles, heels and platforms used are manufactured exclusively for the brand. Regarding output, Pons Quintana's commitment was to apply new technologies, where Santiago was a pioneer, to implement advanced production systems and to experiment with new materials. Likewise, design, crafts, tradition and technology have been the keys that led Santiago to business success.

Regarding the commercial aspect, 60% of the production of Pons Quintana is exported to the European market: France, Germany, Belgium, Italy, as well as to the United States, Australia and Asian markets. The company highlights its points of sale in New York, Melbourne, Venice or Neyron (France) and participates in international footwear fairs: Dusseldorf, Milan, New York, Hong Kong, Munich, Las Vegas, Tokyo, Madrid, Benelux Euroscarpa, London and Paris. In Spain it has representatives by areas: Catalonia, Center, Aragon-Cantabria, the Basque Country and Asturias-Castilla-León-Galicia.

After Santiago's retirement, the management of the company has been in the hands of his sons, Santiago and Magdalena, whose management stands out for his know-how in governing the company as a team. "Santi" is the director of design, production and commercialization, and "Magda" is the financial economic director. The company has about 100 operators. One of the most appreciated traditions of Pons Quintana continues to be the handcrafted manufacture of braiding, whose own design draws different motifs and colors, making the shoe a unique, different and high-quality item that marks the latest fashion in footwear, combining this with natural materials and braiding, which gives them a different personality and great quality.

Don Santiago has received awards and recognitions for his business work; thus, the Italian prize of the Italian consortium of the Footwear Board of Trustees with the "San Crispino e Crispiniano" award, and plaques from the Menorca Footwear Manufacturers Association, the National Footwear Federation and the Alaior Agricultural and Mercantile Cultural Center, respectively. Don Santiago Pons Quintana has held positions of responsibility representing the interests of the footwear industry. He has been the president of the Menorca Footwear Manufacturers Association (1970) and president of Pyme Menorca (1992). Since 1975 he was the vice president of the Executive Board that promoted the construction of the Alaior Industrial Estate (PIASA) and that was inaugurated by the Minister of Industry Bayón in 1982. He has also held political positions as deputy mayor of Alaior, elected on behalf of the Independent Group who attended the municipal elections of April 3, 1979. He was also the president of the Alaior Agricultural and Mercantile Cultural Center, elected in 1977, which he endowed with new headquarters, through the Procensa Joint Stock Company, created for this purpose. In 1972 he was the president of the Alaior Red Cross. Magdalena, the daughter of Santiago Pons Quintana, has been the president of the Menorca Chamber of Commerce, Industry and Navigation.

## 12.4 Don Jaime Mascaró (1939–2014)

Let's see next the profile of another great Menorcan footwear businessman. In the autumn of 2014, businessman Jaime Mascaró died, after having successfully created and developed one of the most outstanding footwear companies not only in Menorca, but also internationally.

Don Jaime Mascaró Pons was born in Ferrerías (Minorca) on November 18, 1939 and married Doña Francisca Coll Pons. Since he was a boy he worked in the manufacture of footwear, in a family business; and in 1980, his father having passed away, he would create a new factory that was a spectacular take-off for the firm, which, in recent decades, has become a great footwear company; his daughters, Lina and Úrsula, who are currently the managers of Grupo Mascaró, S.A., played an important role in the international expansion, with Don Jaime presiding over the Board of Directors.

Jaime Mascaró did not have an education beyond the primary studies, but he was instructed by his father in practical teachings, who instilled in him the custom of working in various trades. As an assistant to his father in electricity tasks, in the 1950s, he used to go to every house in the town every month to do the consumption reading of the electricity meters and then do another round to collect the bills, which was then paid in cash. On Saturday and Sunday mornings, Jaime worked as a barber's assistant, and when he left they gave him five pesetas. And many days at seven in the morning he would distribute bread for a bakery, and at the end, they would give him a loaf of bread. For many years he combined the work of an electrician with that of a shoemaker, which were the trades that his father also practiced.

The family history of making shoes dates back to 1918. Then, Jaime Mascaró's father, Pedro Mascaró Allés (1906–1974), 13 years old, combined the job of an electrician at Ferrerías with working with his 17-year-old brother, Jaime, in the workshop of his uncle, his mother's brother. This great uncle of Jaime Mascaró, who was called Pericás Vey, was a man completely dedicated to the manufacture of shoes.

When Jaime turned 20 (1960), he first went to the peninsula to sell the shoes of the family business. He walked the shopping centers of all the cities in Spain with a bag full of sneakers, since most of the clients did not want to see the entire collection. A short time later he was already working with the best clients from each Spanish city. At that time he had the precious help of his sister María, who combined his teaching studies with the administrative tasks of the company's secretary.

I had the privilege of knowing Jaime's rich personality and his effective implications for social service as an industrial company man with a large volume of manpower, intelligent, user of technological innovations in physical capital (machinery, facilities, design, knowledge, work and ... work for his fellow citizens), also a great fighter and market winner; therefore, a man of industry far removed from strictly financial "entrepreneurship". Mascaró was a model businessman.

Winning customers was for Jaime the courtesy of inviting them to some other lunch. Jaime once commented about it: "It is still curious to have to eat lobster, in order to take chickpeas home".

In Jaime's opinion, working on several things at the same time is good teaching for being an entrepreneur. His father was a man who imposed a lot of self-demand on him in the fulfillment of work obligations and also rigor in his personal behavior, closely following him. The job offers were few, and in the face of any minimal breach, the father threatened Jaime with taking him to work as a "peasant", which was about to happen on occasion.

When Jaime began to travel as a representative of shoes and the sneakers that his family manufactured, his father instilled in him that he lead an austere life in the performance of his tasks; however, his behavior was always smart, while still being sober. He learned to face the setbacks of the profession, the comment of an experienced Catalan clothing representative, who confessed a golden rule, helping him on the way: "Do not be discouraged, if one day you do not sell; good dinner, good wine, good drink and the best cigar".

Already in the 1970s, there was such a high demand that Jaime, being off the island, flew to Menorca, just after the sales season began, to request that the factory be machined to increase productivity—proof of Jaime's commitment to technological innovation. So, paying attention to his father, Pedro, with his cousin Juan Mascaró Florit, Jaime went to Mallorca to buy machinery and thus gave a positive turn to the company. Jaime understands that an entrepreneur must never stop investing in his own company. The father would die in 1974.

In 1976 Jaime's relatives, Antonio Mascaró Allés, his sons and other members of the Mascaró Pons family formed "Calzados Ferrerías, S.A.". The factory had changed the production of sneakers for semi-sport shoes, sandals and boots, which had required a new mechanization. In 1998 it would have 58 workers, producing about 200,000 pairs of shoes per year, 90% of which were sold in the national market.

For his part, Jaime Mascaró, already in 1980, at the age of 40, had created a new factory, with the name "Jaime Mascaró, S.A.", which underwent a notable upward career, starting from the foundations laid long ago by his deceased father. It was a decision agreed amicably with his uncle and cousins, but risky, where Jaime played a lot personally and family-wise, but also financially.

Don Jaime Mascaró's stage as a commercial coincided with the years of the greatest economic expansion in Spain in the entire twentieth century, the 1960s, in terms of growth rate. Later, the consolidation of its specific business projects took place in the 1980s, which followed the international oil crisis and it was a difficult stage, at least until Spain's entry into the European Union, in 1986, which opened new commercial channels to Spanish companies until the 1992 crisis, whereby, after three devaluations of the peseta, the Spanish economy would begin to grow again. However, Don Jaime Mascaró overcame short-term difficulties and configured the large company, endowing it with a consolidated prestige and goodwill, establishing the right conditions to reach a starting point for the introduction of Mascaró shoes in international trade, also in line with the opening of the Spanish economy to European countries. In short, it transformed the workshop into a design and quality shoe factory.

Years later, the third-generation family, made up of Jaime's daughters Lina and Úrsula, successfully won multiple international markets. Jaime says that his daughters did with the conquest of foreign markets something analogous to what he had done by winning the Spanish markets, giving the saga an exemplary continuity. I believe that this led to the formation of the Mascaró Group, which would include, along with pre-existing initiatives, new specialized firms created by the daughters.

At the beginning of the 1990s, Lina and Úrsula, being very young, began a punctual and effective collaboration with their father in the government and management of the company, whose active and fruitful task would consolidate a true footwear multinational that the Mascaró Group has become, made up of its various brands. The integration of Lina and Úrsula to the company breathed new industrial and commercial air into the business dynamics, also driven by a constant innovative process in the design of footwear from an essentially creative platform that makes the shoe a work of art; all this based on an adequate administrative and financial organization.

Although both sisters have comparative advantages in their respective business tasks, their works are harmoniously assembled in the shared objective of always offering magnificent products in the footwear market, both within Spain and in the multitude of international destinations served by the Group, where the greatest business and commercial success lies, of the Mascaró sisters, true winners of the world market for the different types of shoes that the company manufactures, thus continuing the parental teaching profession.

Lina is a woman of character well established in her Menorcan roots and adopts the attitudes of her ancestors before work; thus, a simple and direct personality emerges in this way of being and conversing, which inspires confidence. Her talents of rational government are combined with an inspired sensibility to understand her work in detail and the demanding quality of the products that the company sells, the foundation for her harmonious journey as a citizen of the world, meeting and developing internationally with ease and poise. Lina is the Commercial Director and, therefore, she also watches over the Group's administrative and financial management, having adequate financial training for this. Since 2007 she is the president of the Menorca Footwear Manufacturers Association, integrated into the Federation of PIME *(Federació de la Petita i Mitjana Empresa de Menorca)*.

Úrsula is the General Director of Product of the Mascaró Group and in this lies her comparative advantage. She has innate artistic conditions, inherited from her father, which has improved with intellectual efforts, through certain specific techniques of reflection and drawing in the service of the beauty that rounds the original design of the shoe, elevating it to artistic work. Naturally those techniques have to do with the thinking and creative guidelines of an era that offer solutions and answers, always at the forefront, that Úrsula was able and knew how to capture in the right places and times, transforming those breaths into concrete models, into shoes that make fashion, the result of generational concerns. Úrsula studied interior design, fashion and shoe pattern-making in Milan for six years, at this time when she designed her first models and collections, following in her father's footsteps.

Úrsula Mascaró's creativity is also due to her experience and studies in London or New York, where she continued her training. She does not consider intuition as something sudden, but as the result of thoughtful work, which she applies to her own lines not only of shoes, but also of bags and accessories. Her designs have been introduced in Europe, and are spread in the United States and the Asian world. In Úrsula's creations, the classic Menorcan artisan tradition converges with solutions inspired by contemporary trends, occasionally obtained from tribal times with ancient details, or with Asian influences. The company has also brought out masculine lines, both classic and party-night forms with a more daring style.

The complementary contributions of Lina and Úrsula to the company crystallized in what is today the multinational group Jaime Mascaró; however, all the factories are in Ferrerías and Ciudadela (Minorca), employing the inhabitants of the island, in accordance with the express wishes of Don Jaime Mascaró. The company has become an industrial and commercial complex that has six factories, where some 350 people work. It has some 50 of its own stores, scattered in numerous points of sale, where some 150 more people work, with very important centers in the main squares, such as Madrid or Barcelona, but also in France, the United Kingdom and the United States; in addition, it has showrooms in these countries, and also in Germany, Australia, Canada and Taiwan. It also has commercial points in Italy and Japan.

Don Jaime Mascaró understood that the good results of the company depend on a combination of work, intuition, that is, creativity, and a favorable situation. In the company there is a sign that says: "Work poorly done has no future, work well done has no borders". With this philosophy, the commercial dynamism of the company continues at the international level, establishing stores, granting franchises and making timely use of the virtual market for a certain type of shoe.

The Group or business company Mascaró S.A. includes the different brand-name production units that have been founded since its creation in 1918: Jaime Mascaró, Úrsula Mascaró and *Pretty Ballerinas*. The first two offer a wide range of footwear for every occasion. Internet sales have been successful for the *Pretty Ballerinas* brand products, since they are simpler sales because they are only "dancers" with a wide variety of models, unlike the collections of other footwear, which offer a great complexity of variants. Internet sales are widely accepted abroad.

The "dancers" have great recognition in the specialized press and among celebrities such as Claudia Schiffer or among personalities such as Queen Leticia. In addition to the boom in their virtual market sales, the *Pretty Ballerina Boutiques* in New York, London, Madrid, Barcelona and in Canada are also very successful.

The presence in New York also serves to take a pulse and create a brand. The magic formula for success lies in the family experience and the goodwill of the company; in the entrepreneurial spirit, of overcoming, demanding daring and sensible perception of the social reality and the sector; in the balance between quality, design and prices; and in notable units within the organization of the company, which collaborate with Lina and Úrsula, such as the press officer, the store director and the technical product director. The Jaime Mascaró collections respond to the current, elegant and sophisticated women's style. The Úrsula Mascaró collections offer more avant-garde designs and involve constant research of new materials; they are very dynamic collections of footwear and daring accessories, young and innovative (purses, belts, jackets, fur coats, travel items and briefcases). Jaime Mascaró is the matrix of all brands.

A new contribution is the development of the design department, whose work precedes the assembly of artisan elaboration with the most advanced technology in production processes. The design department is made up of 30-year-old Menorcan personnel, who are up to date with everything that happens in the fashion world, taking advantage of the informative standardization of today's society and who regularly travel to Milan and other centers where fashion designer creativity is promoted.

Another thing is the transport and logistics expenses that the insularity originates, but they are neutralized by the design, product quality and efficiency of a team focused on a family nucleus that shares the same objectives and contributes to the production of 2500 pairs of shoes every day.

Jaime Mascaró was recognized as the exemplary businessman in the entire Balearic Islands. Lina and Ursula visit the main shoe fairs, which take place all over the world (Dusseldorf, Munich, Copenhagen, Barcelona, Madrid, New York, Paris, London, Milan and Tokyo, among others) and the business name Jaime Mascaró is an outstanding value of the Menorcan,

Spanish and European industry, which knows how to grow, opening prestigious journeys, in a practical and metaphorical sense, with its innovative shoes, the result of manufacturing industrial art, the splendid legacy of a well-executed family past. The Jaime Mascaró company is paired with firms such as Inditex in recognition given by the main international design and fashion magazines.

## 12.5 Main Sources

Interview with Santiago Pons Quintana, 2013.
Interview with Magda Pons, daughter of Santiago, 2013.
Interview with Jaume Mascaró, 2013.
Interview with Lina Mascaró, 2013.

## References

Cabana, Francesc. 2006. *Cien empresarios catalanes.* Madrid: Lid.

Casasnovas Camps, Miguel Ángel. 2002. La industria del calzado en Menorca, 1400–2001. In *Las islas del calzado. Historia económica del sector en Baleares (1200–2000)*, directed by Carles Pau Manera. Palma de Mallorca: Lleonard Muntaner.

Collins, James, and Jerry I. Porras. 1996. *Empresas que perduran. Principios básicos de las compañías con visión de futuro.* Barcelona: Paidós.

García Echevarría, Santiago. 1994. Respuesta del *Management* a los cambios de las culturas corporativas competitivas. *Alta Dirección* 174: 43–62.

Grant, Robert M. 2006. *Dirección estratégica. Conceptos, técnicas y aplicaciones.* Madrid: Thompson-Civitas.

Hernández Andreu, Juan, and Alfons Méndez Vidal. 2013a. Entrepreneurship and Development: The Minorcan Modal (Eighteenth–Twentieth Centuries). In *Entrepreneurship and Growth. An International Historical Perspective*, ed. Gabriel Tortella and Gloria Quiroga, 175–195. London: Palgrave Macmillan.

———. 2013b. *Treinta y cinco empresarios menorquines.* Madrid: Delta Publicaciones.

Hernández-Andreu, Juan, and Eva Asensio. 2008. Explicaciones sobre la 'Golden Age' de Europa. *Revista de Historia de la Economía y de la Empresa* 2: 305–320.

Juan y Peñalosa, Javier De (coord.). 2010. *Del Empresario al emprendedor. Cincuenta testimonios y cien ideas de éxito empresarial.* Madrid: JdeJ.

Méndez-Vidal, Alfons, and Juan J. Hernández-Andreu. 2010. *Trenta-cinc empresaris menorquins. Èxit individual i progres social.* Mahón: Institut Menorquí d'Estudis.

Pons Quintana, Santiago. 1996. *Libro de mi vida.* Mahón: Menorca.

———. 2003. *Pons Quintana. 50 aniversario* (1953–2003).

Ruiz, García, José Luis, and Pier Angelo Toninelli. 2010. *The Determinants of Entrepreneurship: Leadership, culture. Institutions.* London: Pickering & Chatto.

Sastre Genestar, María Ángels. 2008. *Els bens de character industrial a Menorca: El mapa de la sabata.* Menorca: Rotger.

Torres Villanueva, Eugenio. 2001. Los empresarios españoles del siglo XX. *Revista Empresa y Humanismo* 4 (2): 375–406.

Tortella, Gabriel, and Gloria Quiroga, eds. 2013. *Entrepreneurship and Growth. An International Historical Perspective.* London: Palgrave Macmillan.

Vidal Olivares, Javier. 2005. *Cien empresarios valencianos.* Madrid: Lid.

CHAPTER 13

# The Path to Success of MAPFRE

*Leonardo Caruana de las Cagigas*

## 13.1 Introduction

Founded in 1933, *Mutualidad de la Agrupación de Propietarios de Fincas Rústicas de España* (MAPFRE) was a small mutual insurance company that developed accident insurance for farmers. This is hardly surprising, since the agricultural sector accounted for 22.34% of Spain's GDP. Fear of nationalization of the accident insurance industry pushed MAPFRE to move to the automotive industry, where it became the market leader in 1983.

Another major development was international expansion. In 1984 MAPFRE entered the Latin American market, and then expanded to the United States, Europe and Asia, thus becoming a world player in the early twenty-first century.

The last development was the shift from a mutual company to a stock company, with a view to improving global business management, because Spanish legislation for mutual companies imposed numerous restrictions to investment abroad.

L. Caruana de las Cagigas (✉)
Faculty of Economics, University of Granada, Granada, Spain



M. Vázquez-Fariñas et al. (eds.), *Companies and Entrepreneurs in the History of Spain*, Palgrave Studies in Economic History,
https://doi.org/10.1007/978-3-030-61318-1_13

## 13.2 MAPFRE's Growth: From a Small Company to the Market Leader in Spain

The foundation of MAPFRE took place within a legal framework that made workers' and farmers' insurance compulsory. Under the Law on Industrial Accidents, passed on 30 January 1900, and its regulation of 28 July 1900, industrialists had to insure factory workers. The Law on Agricultural Accidents, passed in 1932, extended insurance to farmers.

Within this context, MAPFRE was set up on 16 May 1933 by a small number of farmers who decided to create a mutual company, which was called *Mutualidad de la Agrupación de Propietarios de Fincas Rústicas de España* (MAPFRE). The company's core business was accident insurance (80%), although it also operated in other insurance sectors: fire and hailstorms. The company went through financial difficulties during the Spanish Civil War and the postwar period. In 1955 it was saved from bankruptcy by a young manager, Ignacio Hernando de Larramendi, who appointed a new Board of Directors and focused on the major change that culminated in the sixties (Tortella et al. 2009). This change was the focus on car insurance. Nonetheless, other options such as the fire sector were examined. However, the fire sector grew slowly as compared with others. The crystals, theft and furniture insurance markets were very narrow as compared with the car insurance market, which grew by over 10% every year. Finally, in the life and transport insurance markets there was fierce competition. The main rivals were as follows: *La Unión y El Fénix Español, Banco Vitalicio, Mutua General de Seguros* and *Ocaso.*

Fear of nationalization pushed the management to focus on car insurance as the core business in the early 1960s. This decision was one of MAPFRE's major strategic successes. In 1966, under Franco's regime, the insurance of labour accidents was nationalized. This nationalization process resulted in the creation of two companies: FREMAP, which managed accident insurance and was under state control, and MAPFRE, which developed the other types of insurance, car insurance being the most successful business. The staff had to decide whether to stay in the accident insurance company or in the company run by Larramendi.

The strategic change from accident insurance to car insurance was driven by a rapidly changing economic environment ("the happy sixties"), marked by a strong growth of the Spanish economy. Moreover, the insurance market was moving in this direction in line with the emergence of the automotive industry which aimed to cater for the demands of a growing middle class who wished to purchase a car, specifically a SEAT 600. In contrast, life insurance and fire insurance policies were aimed at the upper class. The management was aware that prospective customers needed to insure their car, because the risk of accidents was very high at the time. The great number of claims and the high price of cars encouraged many people to take out an insurance policy.

It was difficult for MAPFRE to break into the car insurance market, since it had provided accident insurance for farmers for over 30 years, and was therefore virtually unknown in the most developed or industrial areas of the country (the Basque Country) and in Spanish cities such as Madrid and Barcelona, while it was well established in rural areas. However, one advantage for the company was that in the early 1960s car insurance was underdeveloped in Spain because there were few cars. There were only three companies: *Omnia*, the insurer of the Royal Automobile Club of Spain; *La Mutua Madrileña*, which operated exclusively in Madrid; and *Mutua Nacional del Automóvil*, which operated in Barcelona. The three firms operated in a market where the car was a luxury good that only well-off people could afford.

In this context, MAPFRE entered the car insurance market in the early sixties. The first strategic aim was the city of Barcelona, which had a long tradition in the automotive sector. Firstly, it is in Barcelona that the popular Hispano Suiza car had been launched in 1904. Secondly, the state-owned company SEAT was headquartered in Barcelona. Finally, Barcelona, along with Madrid, ranked first in the number of car registrations in the early 1960s.

In order to promote MAPFRE as a car insurance company, an advertising campaign was launched in local newspapers and weekly magazines, since the cost of advertising in national newspapers was too high. At the time it was unusual for Spanish insurance companies to invest in advertising. Other promotional media were brochures and billboards and posters in football pitches. MAPFRE also sponsored local youth football teams that participated in local tournaments. Finally, MAPFRE offered its clients an Automobile Guide.

In order to attract more clients, MAPFRE designed a new logo. The image of the truck, which had stood for modernity in the 1950s, was replaced by a red circle with a clover inside.

Another way of getting publicity and building up a customer base was the creation of a car drivers' club linked to the company. It was called the *Club 600*. The club provided a wide range of additional insurance services such as discounts in car repair, garages and automotive accessory stores, as well as credit facilities. In Barcelona, the Club was founded by MAPFRE's clients. Its main rival in the city was *Mutua Nacional del Automóvil.* The president of this Club, José María Torra, was very well known—he was the CEO of the Bank Torra—. In much the same way, MAPFRE's clients in Valencia and Madrid founded the Club, while in cities such as Bilbao, Malaga, San Sebastián, Seville and Zaragoza, it was the company that promoted the creation of the Club.

As a result of the advertising campaign, MAPFRE's product portfolio was extended and the number of car insurance premiums increased five-fold between 1960 and 1964 (Tortella et al. 2009, p. 372). The company also provided driver assistance across the country.

The company's goals at the time were the following:

(a) To cut labour costs due to the recruitment of engineers. MAPFRE trained its workforce in the complex management of car accidents so that the company would not need to employ engineers for this task.
(b) To reduce the premium rates to attract more clients.
(c) To lower the cost of claims.

> At the beginning, the company outsourced two services to CAP, a specialized company: claims for damages and legal defence. However, in the early 1960s it was agreed that MAPFRE would provide these services in order to cut costs. As Larramendi remarked (Larramendi 2000, p. 295), one of the keys to MAPFRE's success was to provide the whole range of services in car insurance.

Further developments took place in the 1960s:

1. Car repair garages that facilitated spare parts worked with MAPFRE.
2. Insurance cover was extended abroad. MAPFRE signed agreements with foreign companies to provide cover (MAPFRE 1983, p. 115): Glanbacher Feuerver-Sicherungs-Aktiengesellschaft from Germany, Versicherungsantalt Der Osterrichischen Bundelslander from Austria, Assurances Du Boerenbond Belge from Belgium, Onderlinge Waarborg Maatschappij from the Netherlands, Societa Cattolica di Assicurazioni from Italy, Secura from Switzerland,

Mutualidade from Portugal, Caisse Centrale des Mutuelles Agricoles from France and the National Farmers Union from Great Britain.

3. MAPFRE developed the Automobile Expert Plan that allowed decentralizing the payment of claims in order to speed up the claims process and cut costs. In each office two experts who received continuous training were under the supervision of experts in the head office in Madrid. This method allowed for writing detailed reports on each claim. In this way the service provided was better, faster and cheaper. Costs were further reduced when claims under 3000 pesetas (€478.93) were handled by clerks.
4. A network of offices was opened in all large towns with a population of over 30,000 after a feasibility study. They were located in strategical places that could be easily noticed. The rationale was to be as close to clients as possible. This feature distinguished MAPFRE from other insurance companies, which had the largest number of offices. Thus costs rose.

Market competition spurred the company's growth. Its main competitor was Mutua Madrileña Automovilista, founded in 1930. This company was unrivalled in Madrid. Since Mutua Madrileña Automovilista did not employ any sales representatives, the company was more efficient and premiums were cheap. However, it only operated in Madrid. By contrast, MAPFRE had a network of offices with sales representatives who offered different types of insurance.

As the number of clients and claims increased, MAPFRE introduced a computer system and claims were handled by telephone. The introduction of the computer was not easy, but it was really advantageous, as all information about drivers was available. Good drivers, who had no accidents, were quickly rewarded, whereas bad drivers, who were scarce, could have their car insurance policy cancelled quickly.

As early as 1967, MAPFRE signed up agreements with 100 European insurance companies which provided cover in other European countries ("the green card"). Although the green card was scarcely used, it gave great prestige to the company. In the 1960s MAPFRE moved from the 36th to the 17th position in the Spanish car insurance market thanks to good management, balanced growth and technical training at all levels.

One of the key elements that contributed to the firm's success was the cancellation of fast high-risk policies, which involved less income, but obviously less costly claims. Another reason for MAPFRE's fast growth, in addition to the reduction in the price of premiums, was the provision of additional services: offices, car rent, car sale, car payment financing, technical advice, crane services, sale of spare parts and accessories, car repair garages, care in particular hospitals, ambulances and medical services, legal advice, repair financing, deferred payment, recovery of stolen cars, regular car checks, including collection and delivery, and so on.

Despite MAPFRE's growth, in the early 1970s premiums did not cover claims expenses. Client selection, known as *risk selection*, elimination of unnecessary expenses and investigations of possible fraud began more systematically in 1972.

MAPFRE adopted a cost-cutting policy. First, instead of employing engineers as experts, the company hired industrial technical engineers, thus saving two thirds of total salaries. Second, MAPFRE created the Centers for Expertise and Fast Payment (*Peritación y Pago Rápido* [PPR]) aimed at decentralizing claims management and thus cutting costs. The first PPR was created in Madrid in 1978. In 1990 the number had reached 97 across Spain.

Following a report submitted to the Board of Directors on November 17, 1978, MAPFRE made a 62.4 million pesetas (€375,031) pre-tax profit from 1972 to 1976. It was 321 million-peseta loss (€1,929,249) in technical result, and 384.1 million-peseta (€2,308,487) in financial result. So the financial result made the difference to make it possible to achieve profit.

The poor technical result led MAPFRE to try to reduce claims costs.

The company continued growing as its customer based increased. In 1975, according to the official report of the sector, the National Insurance Union, MAPFRE ranked third, only surpassed by La Unión y El Fénix Español and Mutua Madrileña Automovilista. It surpassed very big companies such as La Estrella or Mutua Nacional del Automóvil.

One of the keys to MAPFRE's success was the development of an accident data bank, which compiled information about all Spanish clients. This reliable information was updated automatically and allowed for developing an incentive system for both mutualists and local managers. It also enabled the sales workforce to identify and select clients on the basis of the number of claims reported (risk selection). Thus, the price of the policy depended on the car value and the risk of each driver.

Similarly, computerization allowed conducting customer satisfaction surveys. For example, in 1973, 1300 mutualists from Málaga, Murcia,

Granada and Almería were interviewed to know their degree of satisfaction with the treatment received at MAPFRE's offices.

Therefore, MAPFRE moved from a policy consisting in gaining clients in the early 1960s to a policy consisting in selecting clients and building customer loyalty through reasonable insurance rates, good service and advertising. Great damages were transferred to a licensee, while good drivers—the majority of MAPFRE's clients, obtained discounts. This new policy enabled the company to make a technical profit in 1974.

In 1975 the geographical distribution of MAPFRE's clients was as follows: Madrid (21.2%), Catalonia (13.6%), Andalusia (12.5%), Community of Valencia (9%), Basque Country (8%), Galicia (5.5%), Castilla and Léon (5.5%), Canary Islands (5%), La Mancha (4.5%), Asturias (4%), Aragón (3.2%), Navarra (2.4%), Extremadura (2.3%), Murcia (1.6%) and Balearic Islands (1.3%). For more than 20 years Andalusia had been MAPFRE's first marketplace. It was in this region that the company first provided agricultural insurance.

In 1983 MAPFRE became the market leader in the car insurance market. Market dominance drove the management to look for new formulas for growth. Expansion abroad was the solution.

## 13.3 MAPFRE's International Expansion

There was a heated debate among the Board of Directors about MAPFRE's international expansion. While some believed that it was unnecessary and too risky, the majority thought that MAPFRE had to expand, following the example of the leading companies in other countries. Pro-expansion directors argued that global expansion would allow pendular growth. On the one hand, the company would project a better image in the home market if it became a multinational. On the other hand, operating in other markets would enable MAPFRE to develop further and learn from the more developed countries that were reinsured by MAPFRE. Finally, Spanish companies already operating abroad would be likely to be insured by MAPFRE if MAPFRE broke into foreign markets.

The integration of Spain into the European Economic Community (EEC) allowed for expansion. José Manuel Martínez, member of the Board of Directors, advocated MAPFRE's expansion (Martínez 1987). Although he realized that the size of the company in world markets was small, that entering foreign markets was arduous and that investments would be profitable only in the long term, he believed that the company had reached a high level of qualification, professionalism and operational capacity that made it very competitive, and that international expansion would also generate profits in Spain because MAPFRE would become a multinational. Although it was risky and maybe unprofitable, global expansion was a success.

MAPFRE's global expansion was achieved in three ways:

1. By opening new offices.
2. By buying a stake in a foreign company.
3. By working as a reinsurance company for a foreign company. The advantage was that the start-up capital was small.

The area of the initial expansion was Latin America. Although investment in these countries was risky (less economic development, weak currency, political instability), the Latin American market was less competitive, and thus market entry was easier. In 1984 MAPFRE had considered investing in Italy or France, where it already operated with the green card and where it enjoyed good reputation. Nevertheless, European markets were highly competitive and MAPFRE would make less profit.

Another problem was person risk. Cultural problems could arise as a result of cultural differences. Moreover, there were sharp differences between MAPFRE's corporate culture and Latin American countries. Such cultural conflict could be an obstacle to expansion.

MAPFRE's entry in the Latin American market was a success. It first established itself in Colombia, a country which, according to Larramendi, had strong cultural ties with Spain and was the most "Spanish" Latin American country. MAPFRE bought a 24% stake in a medium-sized company, Seguros Caribe. Two years later, in 1986, it bought a 75% stake in Aconcagua, a medium-sized Argentinian company, and a 45% stake in a Chilean company, Co. of Euroamerica General Insurance. In the following years MAPFRE made investments in the majority of Latin American countries and in the United States (Florida). The biggest investment was made in Puerto Rican-American Insurance Co. (PRAICO), owned by the American company Continental. MAPFRE had reinsured PRAICO since the 1970s. José Manuel Martínez took advantage of the poor financial performance of Continental in 1989 to buy PRAICO. Table 13.1 shows the list of the Latin American companies in which MAPFRE bought a stake or owned by MAPFRE (Caruana and García 2009).

**Table 13.1** Companies in America in which MAPFRE bought a stake or owned by MAPFRE, 1984–2000

| *Company* | *Year* |
|---|---|
| MAPFRE General Insurance of Colombia (Caribbean Insurance) (Colombia) | 1984 |
| MAPFRE Aconcagua (Argentina) | 1986 |
| Aconcagua (Paraguay) | 1986 |
| MAPFRE Chile General Insurance (Euroamerica) (Chile) | 1986 |
| Amstar (United States) | 1989 |
| Praico (Puerto Rico) | 1989 |
| Praico Life (Puerto Rico) | 1989 |
| Tepeyac Insurance (Mexico) | 1991 |
| MAPFRE Guarantees and Credi (Chile) | 1991 |
| Senalic (United States) | 1992 |
| Vera Cruz Seguradora (Brazil) | 1992 |
| Vera Cruz Vida e Previdência (Brazil) | 1994 |
| MAPFRE Uruguay (Uruguay) | 1996 |
| MAPFRE Aconcagua ART (Argentina) | 1996 |
| Insurance Security (Venezuela) | 1997 |
| Afore Tepeyac (Mexico) | 1997 |
| MAPFRE Peru (The National Sun) (Peru) | 1997 |
| MAPFRE Peru Life (Peru) | 1998 |
| MAPFRE Aconcagua Life (Argentina) | 1998 |
| Inc. Commercial Credit Insurance (Colombia) | 1999 |
| MAPFRE Colombia Life (Colombia) | 2000 |
| Finisterre Corporation (Peru) | 2000 |
| MAPFRE Chile Life (Chile) | 2000 |
| MAPFRE Guarantees and Credit Insurance (Brazil) | 2000 |

*Source*: Author's own elaboration on the documentation available in the MAPFRE Archive

MAPFRE initially invested 2% of its capital in Latin American countries because the Latin American market was risky. In 1997 the investment was 12,664 million pesetas (more than €76 million). However, the Latin American insurance business was half of the total company business in 2005.

In September 1998 MAPFRE made an €8.5 million loss in the Latin American market. To try to reduce losses, the company adopted several measures. A successful measure was the creation of specialized companies in each insurance sector. Another widely used way of reducing losses was to use dollars (hard currency) rather than the local currency.

Problems also arose in the United States. Natural disasters such as *Hurricane Georges* and *Hurricane Mitch*, which killed thousands of people in 1998, meant huge technical losses for MAPFRE, as the company had more claims to pay. These problems led the company to set up a reserve fund that could be used in such situations. Such know-how encouraged the Board of Directors to intensify international expansion, focusing on new markets. MAPFRE increased its presence in more competitive markets such as the United States. The company managed to enter the American market, which was strictly regulated, through the acquisition of Chatham Re, a reinsurance company, in 1999. Given the internal situation of the company, it was a friendly takeover, Chatham Re was a subsidiary of Shelter Re, which was owned by Ecclesiastical, a company linked to the Anglican Church. Chatham Re was renamed MAPFRE Reinsurance Corporation of the United States, which allowed it to enter the American market as another company operating in the United States on equal terms.

MAPFRE also developed business in Asia—China, the Philippines, India, Turkey—and Europe—the United Kingdom, France, Germany, Portugal, and Italy—.

In conclusion, in 2000 the Spanish market accounted for 32% of MAPFRE's business, European markets accounted for 21%, Latin American markets accounted for 34%, the American market accounted for 9% and the Asian market accounted for 4%.

In 2001, non-life insurance policies issued by MAPFRE America were worth over €1500 million. The insurance business was concentrated in Mexico (€311 million), Venezuela (€300 million), Brazil (€285 million), Puerto Rico (€223 million) and Argentina (€220 million). In 2010, MAPFRE dominated the non-life insurance market in Latin America. MAPFRE's leading position in Latin America is reflected in the number of employees in 2000: 1494 employees in Mexico, 977 in Venezuela, 1137 in Brazil, 515 in Puerto Rico and 626 in Argentina. The total workforce in Latin America was 6090 in 17 countries, while it was 153 in the United States.

The reinsurance company, MAPFRE Re, founded in the late 1980s, had accepted 23,583 million pesetas (€142 million) in 1990 and increased to 104,478 million pesetas (€628 million) in 2000, which shows a growth of 400%.

## 13.4 The Change from a Mutual to a Joint-Stock Company

MAPFRE continued expanding in Latin America until 2006. International expansion posed financial problems which were solved through alliances with banks, the most relevant one being Caja Madrid.

The financial problems that MAPFRE faced as a result of expansion explain its transformation into a stock company.

Along with the success in the field of car insurance and global expansion, the last major development in MAPFRE's history was the transformation of the mutual company into a joint-stock company between 2006 and 2008. The change in status encouraged international expansion, because the regulation of Spanish joint-stock companies is less tight than the regulation of mutual companies, whose funds are under strict control (Caruana 2015).

The transformation of MAPFRE into a joint-stock company was possible thanks to the essential role of the MAPFRE Foundation. Like other foundations, it develops non-profit activities and its funds come mainly from the company. In 2006, all the company's business lines were integrated within MAPFRE S.A. It is worth noting that, following MAPFRE's statutes, the Foundation had a majority stake in the joint stock. This ensured the company's control by the Foundation and prevented it from being taken over by another insurance company.

The five million mutualists were able to decide whether to buy shares from the corporation or to receive a sum of money equivalent to their cash value. The majority chose the second option. Only half a million bought shares from the stock company.

To back MAPFRE's change into a joint-stock company, at the 2006 Annual General Meeting, the company's president, José Manuel Martínez, referred to the speech made by Larramendi about the future of the MAPFRE Insurance Group at the General Meeting held on February 28, 1970: [I]t is considered appropriate to propose the creation of a coordinated insurance group in which insurance operations involving the risk of mass coverage are carried out by the mutual insurance company [...] while insurance operations with very specific technical or commercial characteristics are separated from it to be arranged through limited companies, coordinated with the mutual insurance company but with assets and a legal structure better adapted to its type of operations and clients. It should also be pointed out that, given MAPFRE's desire to extend its operations and working methods to Latin America at the right time, considering this the logical expansion of an insurance group with substantial internal importance, it is necessary to be in a position to provide the reinsurance service and to retain control of the Group within the mutual company or entities of an associative-foundational nature."

## 13.5 Conclusions

MAPFRE's history reveals the management skills of some directors who succeeded in adapting the company's core business to market demands and the legislation of each country. The shift in the core business from accident insurance to car insurance is a clear instance of adaptability, training and good performance of managers who overcame all the difficulties that were encountered. The same holds for the internationalization process of a medium-sized company in the late 1980. MAPFRE ventured to compete with multinationals in Latin American markets, so that after 20 years it became one of the insurance market leaders. Obviously, it is necessary to have big financial resources to compete in an increasingly globalized market. This is the reason why MAPFRE took a big leap forward and became a joint-stock company after a long history as a mutual company.

## References

### MAPFRE Archive

Caruana de las Cagigas, Leonardo. 2015. The Insurance Demutualization Process Develops in Spain with MAPFRE. In *Corporate Forms and Organizational Choice in International Insurance*, ed. Robin Pearson and Taku Yoneyama. Oxford: Oxford University Press.

Caruana de las Cagigas, Leonardo, and José Luis García Ruiz. 2009. La internacionalización del seguro español: el caso de MAPFRE, 1969–2001. *ICE, Información Comercial de España* 849: 143–158.

Larramendi, Ignacio Hernando de. 2000. *Así se hizo MAPFRE*. Madrid: Actas.

MAPFRE. 1983. *Cincuenta años de MAPFRE hacia el futuro*. Madrid: MAPFRE.

Martínez, José Manuel. 1987. Internationalization of Insurance and Reinsurance. The Spanish Case. Conference at the *V Inter-European Meeting of Reinsurance*, Madrid, September.

Tortella Casares, Gabriel, Leonardo Caruana de las Cagigas, and José Luis García Ruiz. 2009. *From Mutual Fund to Multinational*. Madrid: MAPFRE.

CHAPTER 14

# Spanish Businesses and the Negotiations for Spain's Entry into the European Economic Community

*Jorge Lafuente del Cano*

## 14.1 Introduction

Spain's entry into the Economic European Community is one of the most important events in the country's recent economic history. It has had a long-lasting impact on the country's economy and has also gone hand in hand with a number of other seminal events such as the political transition following the death of Franco and the international economic crisis which started in 1973. Spanish entrepreneurs were both witness to and indeed played a key role in some of the changes which took place after the 1970s. The pivotal role they played, which has often been overshadowed by political figures in early studies into the period, has only just begun to emerge (García Crespo 2019; González Fernández 2012; Cabrera and Del Rey 2011; Díez Cano 1991).

J. Lafuente del Cano (✉)
University of Valladolid, Valladolid, Spain
e-mail: jorge.lafuente@uva.es



M. Vázquez-Fariñas et al. (eds.), *Companies and Entrepreneurs in the History of Spain*, Palgrave Studies in Economic History,
https://doi.org/10.1007/978-3-030-61318-1_14

The period saw a change in regime, with the transition to democracy after the death of Franco in November 1975. It was a time of uncertainty as well as of progress and setbacks, yet it also spawned a period of hope that Spain's future democracy could be on par with that of other European countries. As in a number of other aspects, the end of the dictatorship and the passing of the Law on Political Reform led to a gradual liberalisation of the old Francoist employer-based structures. Despite the fact that affiliation to the Spanish Trade Union Organisation, the *Sindicato Vertical*, had granted entrepreneurs more flexible participation than was afforded to workers (González Fernández 2004), it was the laws passed on 4 March 1977, governing working relations, and on 1 April 1977, concerning the right to trade union membership, which were ultimately to grant the right to freely form associations. Their coming into force gave rise to a proliferation of business organisations at a national, regional, and sectorial scale and which pursued an array of differing aims and objectives (Gutiérrez Álvarez 2001, pp. 71–78). However, it was not until a few months later, in June 1977, that the organisation of organisations was formed which, since then, has represented the interests of the Spanish employers' associations: The Spanish Confederation of Business Organisations (Spanish acronym-CEOE). It was set up as a large-scale platform of associations with a specific purpose, to make the voice of Spanish business heard in Spanish public life and to defend the free market economy (Cabrera and Del Rey 2011, pp. 356–357).

This desire on the part of business people to become involved in public life also reflected an ever increasing concern; namely, a certain mistrust towards the ruling class which, since the death of the dictator, had focused on political issues—on transforming the regime into a democratic system—and which seemed to be paying insufficient attention to the economic situation, which was particularly delicate in 1977, with alarming increases in inflation, deficit, and unemployment (Hernández Andreu 2006, p. 786). After over a decade of rapid economic growth, made possible thanks to the approval of the 1959 Stability Plan, the 1973 oil crisis had burst onto the Spanish economic scene. It had done so somewhat later, given that the Francoist authorities of the time had failed to take the necessary measures to deal with it, perhaps fearing that strong social unrest might threaten a political system which was already beginning to falter due to Franco's ill health. It was therefore the early democratic governments that were faced with the difficult situation and who strove to remedy it by seeking political consensus. This led to the signing of the Moncloa

Agreements in October 1977 which sought to bring about economic stability (Maluquer de Motes 2014, p. 367). It should be pointed out that only representatives of the parliamentary powers, and not businessmen and women, were present when the agreements were signed.

In this uncertain political and economic situation, a third factor came into play; namely, Spain's membership of the EEC. This had been a long sought-after objective, but had proved impossible for political reasons. The transition to democracy seemed to suggest that such a goal finally lay within reach. This chapter focuses on the issue of Europe and, in particular, on the role played by businesses in the early negotiations, when the government finally gave them the chance to voice their opinions on Spain's entry into the Common Market. Our aim is to ascertain and analyse their views, concerns, and proposals, marking the outlines of their position. Our goal is to find links as well as conflicts of interest with the stance adopted by the first Spanish negotiating team (1978–1980). Although both groups were united by common interests, they did not, as shall be seen, adopt either same tone or the same priorities. The near on three years the first group was together provide us with an insight into the positions that were embraced in the early days of the negotiations, negotiations which, it must be said, were expected to be far swifter than they ultimately proved to be. The negotiating team's desire to maintain contact with business representatives allows us to examine their initial ideas and how these evolved over time. It also gives us an understanding of the Spanish government's economic strategy, how this could be conveyed, and what the result was. The personal archive of Leopoldo Calvo-Sotelo, the first Spanish negotiator, has provided the main documentary support.

## 14.2 The Return to Europe

Joining the EEC was one of the most important events in Spain's economic history in the second half of the twentieth century. Not only did it reflect an economic need but also the desire to chart a new political and strategic course for Spain's recently established democracy. The passing of the years, coupled with the perspective afforded by over 30 years since Spain's entry, have enabled us to widen the scope of study and to focus on the agreement's impact on an economy that has changed radically from the early days of the transition up to the first decades of the twenty-first century.

It should be remembered that during the accession process, the Spanish government acted as the only interlocutor. The negotiating team, as shall be pointed out later on, sought to reflect the opinions of all the actors involved, yet at no point did it ever delegate its tasks or permit the involvement of any "outside observer". An awareness of the major economic implications of Spain's entry ran parallel to the certainty that it was politics and above all the political decisions of the Common Market member countries which would ultimately grant admission: hence, the desire to seek the internal unity of all sectors of Spanish society in an effort to speak with one voice at the negotiating table.

The desire to speed up Spain's accession soon became apparent. Only a few months after the June 1977 general elections, the newly elected government submitted its formal application to Brussels. In order to conduct the negotiations, in February 1978 the president of the government set up a new Spanish administrative body to pilot the process: The Ministry for Relations with the European Communities. Its first head was Leopoldo Calvo-Sotelo, a businessman who had been working in private industry for 25 years, but who had at the same time developed a keen political vocation. In December 1975, he was appointed Minister for Trade and later became one of the architects of the electoral coalition which served as a platform for Adolfo Suárez's Centre Democratic Union.

Since its inception, the Ministry adopted a two-fold strategy (Lafuente del Cano 2017, p. 66): the outward strategy, geared towards dealing with EEC member countries as well as with EEC bodies and agencies in order to commence the accession negotiations; and the domestic strategy, aimed at bringing Europe closer to Spaniards and, specifically, to those economic sectors which might be most affected by Spain's entry into the Common Market. As part of this domestic strategy, the new ministry undertook a number of initiatives in which it was in direct contact with the leading businesspeople and economic agents in an effort to convey the government's perspective on the matter vis-à-vis the reality of the EEC, the negotiations, and the consequences of Spain's entry. Between February 1978 and September 1980, over 50 activities which pursued such a goal have been documented.[1]

[1] Leopoldo Calvo-Sotelo Archive (hereinafter ALCS), Relations with the EEC, 51, 10. List of talks, meetings, round tables, symposiums, conferences, assemblies, etc. in which the Ministry for Relations with the European Communities was involved. Madrid, 17 May 1979.

An analysis of these meetings provides an insight into two key topics for historiography: on the one hand, the major deep-rooted issues that were raised in the early days of the economic negotiation and which subsequently proved to be decisive vis-à-vis Spain's joining the EEC, and on the other, the role played by businesspeople in the negotiation and their various positions on the matter. For this, we posit a two-pronged approach which pinpoints the positions and priorities of both the ministry and the businesspeople involved.

## 14.3 The Position of the First Spanish Negotiating Team

Together with the initial positions of the members of the negotiating team, it is interesting to note how they were able to convey their message to their interlocutors. It is also worth asking to what extent the latter's concerns managed to fit in with the plans of the negotiating team. We then look at a series of key ideas that were present on numerous occasions and over a prolonged period of time. Broadly speaking, the message conveyed did not appear to change in any way, although it is true that, in the early days of the official negotiation (February 1979), the timeline for Spain's possible entry into the EEC was a recurrent theme.

Two different levels emerge in this series of arguments. The first concerns the theoretical issues: the outline of the negotiation, the timeframes in which it would be conducted, and the need to involve businesspeople, while the second addressed more practical matters, by analysing the sectors and products that would be directly affected by accession.

### *14.3.1 Initial Arguments*

First, there was the actual essence of the negotiation; in other words, explaining the key aspects of Spain's accession as well as the various stages involved. Both in the internal departmental reports and in the first public appearances made by the minister, the same idea which explained this need emerged time and again: in Spain, there was parliamentary and social unanimity concerning Spain's entry into the EEC.[2] Yet it was by no means clear that it could be inferred from such unanimity that there was a

[2] ALCS, Relations with the EEC, 51, 10. Note on possible ministry activities in the upcoming months, May 1978.

sufficient degree of information concerning the Common Market, both amongst the economic and social sectors as well as amongst the Spanish population as a whole. Indeed, as had occurred in other countries, any debates or exchange of ideas on the matter of Europe had been avoided since they were felt to be superfluous. The ministry thus deemed it necessary to convey, as a mantra, that the negotiations were not in fact negotiations in the strict sense, since Spain had taken as read a series of norms which the EEC had been furnishing itself with over a number of years and which made up the famous "*acquis communautaire*". As a result, the terms could not be negotiated; rather, it was more a question of when to embrace them into Spanish legislation, in other words, what the transition periods involved would be. This was in fact one of the main concerns of Spanish businesses. Likewise, it was considered imperative to explain the various stages involved in the negotiation process and which, following the precedent of the first EEC enlargement, had been set down. Nevertheless, negotiations with Spain did entail certain novelties, prominent amongst which was splitting the whole negotiating process into two parts: the initial stage (the joint vision) in which the two negotiating teams would examine the situation of each economic sector; and a second stage during which the various chapters would be closed. This strategy was at times seen as a delaying tactic on the part of France, designed to attune Spain's entry to fit in with its neighbouring country's various electoral events—notably, the 1981 presidential elections—(Bassols 1995, p. 220).

Whatever the case, the negotiating team was concerned that a lack of understanding of the process might trigger a feeling of frustration, were the negotiations to drag on longer than anticipated. Inversely, this same idea (a delay that might lead to possible disenchantment with Europe in Spain) was also used on various occasions by the Minister for Relations with the European Communities, Calvo-Sotelo, on his early trips to the EEC capitals to try to speed up the steps that would enable negotiations to get underway as quickly was possible. This led to a recurrent theme that was conveyed to businesses: despite the need to overcome the various technical hurdles, the political impetus of the member countries to speed up the negotiations could prove to be key.

Second, albeit closely linked to the previous question, was the idea of defending the timing of Spain's application to join. This matter was also one of the concerns running through the minds of businesspeople. The issue of whether Spain, in the grip of an economic crisis, had chosen the right moment to apply for EEC membership was extremely pertinent. In the eyes of the negotiating team, the answer was most definitely yes, not only due to economic and political needs, but also because Europe had been forged "by dint of crises", in the famous words of Jean Monnet, a phrase that the minister would repeat on a number of occasions to his former colleagues.[3] Three arguments sought to support this claim. The first was the negotiators' own experience with the EEC: Europe was a work in progress, even though at times there were conflicting attitudes, delays, and uncertainties that called into question the viability of the EEC project. The second was the need to display political coherence, between domestic democratic reform and by joining up with European countries who upheld the same values. If entry into the Common Market was to be seen as final proof that democracy had arrived, Spain could not back down merely because it was going through a tricky economic situation. The third was the practical element: the longer accession was delayed, the greater the number of interests there would be in the EEC and the more difficult it would therefore prove to join. Europe had been forging its identity without Spain, and now was the time for the country to make itself heard on the European stage.[4] In all of this, however, there was a need to maintain a pragmatic approach, since in no way could accession be seen as a panacea or the immediate solution to all of Spain's problems: it was more a matter of perspective, of shifting from the national to the European.[5]

Thirdly, there was the need to encourage businesses to become involved in the negotiation. Engaging economic representatives in the ongoing negotiations was a way to understand and ultimately reflect their demands at the bargaining table. Particularly illustrative in this regard was Leopoldo Calvo-Sotelo's involvement in the study meetings on Spanish business and the future of the European Economic Community, held on 11 April 1978, barely two months after he was appointed. It was the first time he would have occasion to speak to his former professional colleagues, whom he

[3] ALCS, Relations with the EEC, 84, 2. Note for the minister: Study meetings on "Spanish businesses and the future of the European Economic Community", 7 April 1978.

[4] ALCS, Relations with the EEC. 72, 3. Address by the Minister for Relations with the European Communities in the course of Spanish integration in the EEC organised by the Official Chamber of Commerce and Industry and the Zaragoza Confederation of Business, 16 May 1980.

[5] ALCS, Relations with the EEC, 85, 3. Address made by Leopoldo Calvo-Sotelo during the closing act of the talk "The New International Economic Order and Cultural Values" organised by the Institute for Intercontinental Cooperation on 14 June 1978.

asked to become involved in the process and not to let the immediate issue (the economic crisis) take precedence over the key issue (Spain's future in the EEC).[6] A practical question was also to emerge after the request for participation. The members of the negotiating team constantly referred to an idea that could put Spain's entry into the EEC in its true perspective: the same efforts, reforms, and sacrifices that accession would require from certain areas or sectors were identical to those that would have to be made in any case to deal with the economic crisis the country was experiencing.

### 14.3.2 *Practical Arguments*

From this perspective, the idea which was deemed basic was that of unity in the negotiation. The aim was to show that the Spanish economy was negotiating en bloc, rather than defending any particular sectors more than others and without sacrificing the quotas of certain products in order to benefit others. The goal was to avoid any resentfulness or misgivings between sectors with conflicting interests and that might emerge during the negotiating process. Indeed, the theoretical outline with which official negotiations began, on 5 February 1979, followed this very procedure: a general study of the Spanish economy during the first stage of a joint vision and then closing the various chapters sector by sector during the second stage, even though this did not eventually prove to be fully the case. The address made by the president of the French Republic before the Agricultural Chamber in June 1980 in the short term led to an interruption of negotiations with Spain and, in the medium term, a veto on some of its chapters, specifically the most complicated, when Spanish interests came into conflict with those of other countries. Agriculture proved to be a particularly exemplary issue and despite Spanish efforts to study and negotiate the matter as soon as possible, it was relegated to virtually the final part of the negotiation, with a new government and a new negotiating team. The address had a major impact on Spanish society and politics at the time, and was soon dubbed by the media as the "giscardazo" (or the Giscard "issue"), and the term has since passed into Spain's recent history.

Secondly, there was a need to conduct an analysis of the sectors and products vis-à-vis the negotiation as well as the possible impact which Spain's entry into the Common Market might have. Before holding any

[6] ALCS, Relations with the EEC, 84, 2.

meetings with the business sector, the ministry issued reports in an effort to learn beforehand the principal concerns of the areas being visited. Irrespective of the place or sector in question, the reports always reflected certain common elements: The Preferential Agreement of 1970 and the tariff issue.

The Preferential Economic Agreement of 1970 was one of the trump cards which the various negotiating teams played up until the very end, such that it appears time and again in the reports issued by the Ministry for Relations with the EEC. In this regard, it should be remembered that with the first enlargement of the EEC, Spain felt that its rights had been affected with regard to the agreement and demanded its adaptation.[7] The EEC position varied between supporting Spain's request and rejecting it, and included the suggestion that a new industrial treaty be signed, since it was believed that the agreement had undervalued Spanish industry. Whatever the case, the situation took on a new dimension subsequent to Spain's application to join in July 1977. After that point, all of the EEC's requests to renegotiate the agreement or to reach a compromise were rejected by the Spanish negotiating team, who only saw the accession agreement as a goal, with no intermediate stages involved. This process, and Spain's determination not to alter its position, are highlighted in the documents used to prepare the meeting with Spanish businesses.[8]

Tariff issues also emerge as a major concern. In this aspect, the Spanish negotiating team did not prove to be as resolute as in the previous instance since, due to their nature, some of the matters under negotiation held an uncertain future. One clear example of this are the issues related to fishing or the iron and steel industry, which were being negotiated in the EEC. Territorial fishing waters were being extended to 200 miles, which meant changes not only in the Common Market but in other countries as well, who would see their room for manoeuvre in EEC waters cut, a matter which was particularly important in the case of Spain due to its large fishing fleet. After the iron and steel crisis of the mid-1970s, the EEC had implemented a new policy which involved approving maximum

[7] AMAE (Archive of the Spanish Ministry for Foreign Affairs), EEC-Spain, 9, 15573. Unsigned report from the General Directorate for International Economic Relations: "Content of the possible protocol to be signed with the EEC as a step towards integration", Madrid, 26 January 1976.

[8] ALCS, Relations with the EEC, 72, 5. "Official visit by the minister to Barcelona". 22 November 1978.

production quotas for member countries, and which was linked to the requirement that third countries should restrict their exports to the EEC.

As a result, the negotiators strove to convey a message of calm. Entry into the Common Market would be beneficial from the economic standpoint, and a balance would be sought between the various sectors in an effort to ensure that no one in particular would lose out, despite the expected sacrifices and cutbacks that would have to be made, above all in the agricultural and livestock sector. Moreover, fresh opportunities were expected to emerge within the various areas of Spanish foreign policy. One of these was Latin-America. For the members of the negotiating team, the desire to join the Common Market would not lead to any break in ties with Latin-America; quite the opposite, it would serve to strengthen them. Spain could become the bridge between the EEC and Latin-American countries which, in turn, would also open up new possibilities for Spanish businesses. In a similar vein, the last of the recurring themes to appear in the arguments put forward by the ministry was the boost which accession would give to trade. The free movement of goods could not only improve the possibilities of obtaining supplies, but also the chances for exports; supply, competition, and product quality.[9]

## 14.4 The Position of the Businesses

"No one is a prophet in their own land". This was the title Leopoldo Calvo-Sotelo gave to the chapter in his memoires dedicated to recalling his relations with the business world (Calvo-Sotelo 1990, p. 157). In the same section, he evokes one of the phrases that accompanied him on many occasions during his time as negotiating minister: "Membership of the EEC yes, but not at any price".

This phrase summed up business sector concern with how the negotiations for accession were being conducted. The desire expressed by Spanish negotiators to conclude the process during the first term in office (in other words, in 1983) only served to heighten industry's misgivings. Businesspeople were worried that politicians would negotiate a good political agreement with the EEC, but without weighing up the economic repercussions: in other words, that they would sacrifice certain sectors,

[9] ALCS, Relations with the EEC. 79, 8. Note for the Minister for Relations with the EEC: possible ideas for the Study Meeting "Implications for the trade sector of Spain's entry into the Common Framework", 16 November 1978.

which would no doubt be forced to undergo major restructuring, in an effort to achieve political success that would lead to strong electoral support in the following elections.

The difficult political and economic situation, at both an EEC as well as a national level, with which Spain faced the challenge of negotiation should not be forgotten. Firstly, as mentioned previously, the country was being shaken by the delayed effects of the oil crisis. It was the first truly modern crisis to hit the Spanish economy, and affected mainly industry and the service sector, in a context of growing economic freedom and in which a monetary problem, in the shape of inflation, came very much to the fore and was to have significant repercussions for the financial system (Comín and Hernández 2013, p. 307).

The EEC was also going through a prolonged period of political instability which had been heightened by the three-fold application to join put forward by southern European countries. Faced with the lack of any common direction and the difficulty involved in managing an ever-growing group of countries, certain member states, and notably the French president, began to publicly defend the need to first deal with the problems in hand and then to address the issue of enlargement. The matter of French agriculture in all of this question was very much at the front of his thoughts when considering such an approach (Acuña 1986; Sánchez 2016).

This was the context, between 1978 and 1980, which helps to understand the position of Spanish businesses. As did the arguments put forward by the ministry, the number of issues raised by businesspeople during their meetings with the negotiators varied enormously. Some of the points which were of particular concern are highlighted below.

There was no shortage of what were referred to above as "theoretical" questions related to the EEC's situation, its future, the stages of negotiation, or what role France would play. Nevertheless, these were far fewer in number and always took a back seat compared to issues which directly affected the future of their businesses. It is worth noting that in the case of the negotiating team it was exactly the opposite. First and foremost amongst the latter were references to tariffs. One representative example may be found during a trip made by Leopoldo Calvo-Sotelo to Valencia, on 26 June 1978.[10] In this case, the problem concerned misgivings over the competition that would emerge with the economies of the major

[10] ALCS, Relations with the EEC, 72, 7. The visit to Valencia by the Minister for Relations with the EEC, 26 June 1978.

European countries and their large businesses, and which could lead to a rise in unemployment. Once again, the desire to ensure that the government would sign a "good" economic agreement, and one which was not subservient to political interests, was evident. Concerns regarding agriculture and the impact on small and medium enterprise, who feared they would suffer as a result of competition from the EEC, were also likewise raised. The negotiating team's response always tended to be one of optimism and reassurance, highlighting that in the long run the advantages would outweigh the drawbacks. Nevertheless, they repeatedly pointed out that Spain's position as a candidate country was to a certain degree unusual, but that for the moment the country could not aspire to anything more. As a result, a process of adaptation to face up to the competition and the removal of tariffs would be needed.

Another concern voiced by businesses involved what would happen in the period leading up to accession; namely, the situation at that particular time. The question was related to new EEC legislation which, mainly in the case of the fishing industry, could affect Spain's position as a candidate. In other words, negotiators were asked about what possibilities there were of reaching various preferential agreements by sectors in order to be able to face, with some degree of assurance, the period leading up to accession and the period immediately afterwards. Another major issue, therefore, concerned the transition periods. As pointed out, the core of the negotiation involved agreeing the timeframes each sector would have to adapt to EEC legislation. The conflicting interests of certain sectors of the Spanish economy meant that the subject arose again and again. Yet the negotiating team's position on the matter always remained particularly firm: no partial sectorial agreements could be signed, and there would be no differing transition periods.

The third major concern revolved around the role of imports from the Third World.[11] Questions of this nature arose because of the possibility that the trade agreements which the Common Market had with countries whose production costs were lower (and who therefore also offered lower prices) might damage Spanish business, particularly small businesses. A further worry involved the uncertainty concerning whether this kind of small business might actually benefit from Spain joining the EEC, and that it might be only the larger companies who would gain anything from it.

[11] ALCS, Relations with the EEC, 72, 5. "Official visit by the minister to Barcelona". 22 November 1978.

However, the possibility that Spain, once it had joined, could influence member countries to break such agreements with third world countries, was again constantly ruled out by ministry representatives.

Further, there was the matter of industrial reconversion.[12] In a somewhat pessimistic tone, the fear was voiced that Spain's competitive situation at the time, given its adequate work/product relation, might weaken over the years. This might lead to the loss of productivity in traditional industrial sectors who would be forced to undergo a process of reconversion, with the outcome being unclear. The standard response given by the negotiators was the same as mentioned above: the changes, sacrifices, and adaptations which businesses would need to make in the face of Spain's entry into the EEC were exactly the same as those that would be required when dealing with the economic crisis.

Finally, there was the matter of taxes. This was another of the major concerns expressed by businesses during a number of meetings with the negotiating team.[13] The question was raised on two fronts. The first was Spain's having to accept Value Added Tax and when this would be applied. Businesses often voiced their disapproval that EEC requests for Spain to speed up the introduction of the tax, as a sign of good will vis-à-vis the rest of the negotiation, might pressure the government into taking measures in this regard, and so make an economic sacrifice in order to achieve earlier entry into the Common Market. The second front concerned future taxes, not EEC ones but domestic taxes; in other words, whether the government was contemplating raising taxes once Spain had joined the European Economic Community in order to offset the loss of income that would result from the reduction in tariffs.

A concern could be felt amongst businesspeople not only for their region and their sector but also with regard to what direct impact Spain's entry would have on their product. Coupled with this, however, was also the optimism, anticipation, and opportunities which they believed accession would bring.

[12] ALCS, Relations with the EEC, 72, 7.

[13] ALCS, Relations with the EEC, 79, 8. Study meetings "Implications for the trade sector of Spain's accession to the Common Market", November 1978.

## 14.5 The Same Objective, But Two Strategies

The negotiating team, led by Calvo-Sotelo, viewed the meetings with the business sector as an "all-in-one". In other words, they felt it necessary to merge all of the theoretical arguments with the practical issues that would be brought to the negotiating table. This is why in many of the meetings with businesses not only were sectorial matters dealt with but indeed the whole context of Spain's application to join was put forward: why now was the right time, what steps would need to be taken, when it could be achieved. Questions concerning these matters also emerged in the meetings with businesspeople who, nevertheless, focused to a far greater degree on the material reality of the consequences of Spain's entry. One might interpret a division of roles between, on the one part, politicians in whose hands lay the future of the country, but whose personal wealth was not at stake and, on the other, representatives of the economic sector—in which SMEs were well represented—and who mistrusted their leaders because they felt that their livelihood was being threatened. The slogan of "membership yes, but not at any price" clearly exemplified this view. Yet, one should not oversimplify the interpretation of the situation, given that the vast majority of businesspeople who took part in the activities promoted by the ministry or at which the ministry was represented, were in fact in favour of joining. They were simply interested in gaining a clearer understanding of the risks involved in the process, how it was to be implemented and what direct consequences it would have for their businesses. Their main concerns were not therefore the future development of the EEC or what stance Spain would adopt in the federal-intergovernmental debate, but rather the negotiation of tariffs, the impact of competition from large EEC companies, or the transition periods involved.

A certain sympathy on the part of the negotiating team towards the issues which were important to business is in evidence. They were aware of what was important and why. To what extent this understanding influenced the negotiations is, however, quite another matter, although it can be seen by how firmly they responded to some of the questions raised during the meetings with businesses: a clear and determined response on some matters, whilst cautious and wary in others.

In the matter of EEC economic policy, for instance, some degree of consensus was evident, since at various moments during the negotiation the possibility was explored that Spain, as a candidate country, might enjoy a special status and be represented by being granted the right to speak, if not to vote, on any new economic matters which the EEC might approve.

Spain's proposal was not accepted by the EEC countries and the country had to remain in the uncomfortable position of being only a candidate. It wanted to play an active role in shaping any new EEC policies, but until it actually became a fully fledged member it would have to make do with maintaining its position as a third country.

Businesspeople were also constantly worried about the new tariff barriers that were being introduced. Nevertheless, the Spanish negotiating position afforded little room for manoeuvre since the country was merely a candidate for accession and one which had to be ratified when the time came by the countries that were already members.

The fishing sector proved to be a particular case in this regard (Bassols 1995, p. 170), since Spain could only forge its future position as a member country if it came to terms with the reality of the 200 mile law, and which placed severe restrictions on Spanish fishing vessels operating in EEC waters and which over the years of negotiation sparked countless conflicts between Spain and some of the EEC member countries.

When defending the Preferential Agreement of 1970, a certain degree of consensus was apparent between the position adopted by Calvo-Sotelo's team and the stance taken by businesspeople. This was the legal relationship which Spain maintained with the EEC until the country's accession to EEC bodies became official. Despite the request made by certain EEC countries to Spain to renounce the agreement so as to facilitate the country's entry, the Spanish negotiators stood firm, and used it as a bargaining chip.

Finally, there were the transition periods, which could prove to be more problematic. The interests of Spain's primary and secondary sector were not the same and nor was the EEC proposal. Although it seemed that Spanish industry would benefit from a long transition period, and the agricultural and livestock sector from a short one, the EEC advocated just the opposite: a short period of transition for industry and a long one for agriculture. For its part, the Spanish government always expressed its desire not to overstate the country's agricultural capacity, which would be offset in other sectors. It therefore established a single transition period, which was neither short nor long. When doing this, it drew on the previous experience of the first enlargement, which was used as a constant benchmark during Spain's negotiating strategy.[14]

[14] ALCS, Relations with the EEC, 62, 5. Opening act of the negotiations between Spain and the EEC. Brussels, 5 February 1979. It was also later to serve the experience of Greece, when granted admission in 1981: a single five-year period, with certain exceptions, three or seven years.

## 14.6 Conclusions

The last third of the twentieth century brought with it substantial changes in the political and economic history of Spain. As in other areas, democracy saw the emergence of the role of businesspeople as actors in the country's public life. This presence was particularly notable during the EEC accession process. Such a negotiation would not have been possible without the democratisation of the country, but was one which took place in the midst of an international recession that was to hit the Spanish economy. The history of Spain's approach towards the EEC contained a mixture of hope, fear, opportunity, and difficulties. For the first time since the Treaties of Rome, the very real possibility of achieving a goal that had been so long sought-after by society, the economic sectors, and the Spanish government, was confronted with a reality check in the shape of the long negotiation process which lasted, officially, from 1979 to 1985. Political assurances that Spain met the requirements for admission were confronted with the statistics, and the economic figures, which in certain sectors and with certain countries, seemed to offer more competitive than complementary aspects. This is why the shadow of France and its agricultural sector remained a constant throughout the process.

Although it is true that negotiations were conducted between governments, since it was the Spanish government who was negotiating and it was the governments of the nine EEC member countries who were setting the pace of the negotiation, other actors in one way or another also played their role and made themselves heard. Prominent amongst these were Spanish businesses. It has been quite rightly pointed out that, unlike membership of the Atlantic Alliance, accession to the EEC enjoyed a wave of unanimity and even enthusiasm. The case of Spanish industry, whilst not challenging this general image, did once again serve as a reality check. Businesses were in favour of joining the Common Market, but not at any price. They were afraid that the government's desire to score some political points might mean, in certain cases, having to make economic sacrifices that could prove detrimental to their interests.

It is therefore interesting to see the strategy devised by the Spanish negotiating team to initiate a campaign to persuade, amongst others, businesses. It was not merely a case of conveying to them the information concerning the EEC and how negotiations for accession would be conducted but also of trying to understand their ideas, concerns, and wishes. Between February 1978 and September 1980 (which saw the last of

Adolfo Suárez's cabinet reshuffles and changes to the original negotiating team) over 50 meetings with businesspeople are documented.

An analysis of these meetings, and of the initial positions of the representatives from the ministry together with the businessmen and women involved provides an insight into the views, starting points, concerns, and certainties of a historic process of enormous economic importance. The bottom line seems clear: there was certain consensus vis-à-vis the core issues: tariffs, transition periods, and taxes, although it is true that members of the ministry were not on occasions able to express their opinion as a result of not having closed the deals at the negotiating table. Other principles, in contrast, such as unity during the negotiations themselves or the transition periods, were very much in evidence. As a result, ministerial members' primary concern for the more theoretical issues did not reflect any disregard for material matters, and nor did industry's misgivings mean that they rejected accession. They were simply each on different levels, and each defended their own positions. Ultimately, the issue of timing is one that must inevitably remain unresolved. We shall never know whether, had circumstances been otherwise, the negotiation might have been different and swifter. Whatever the case may be, the opportunity arose when it did and Spain did not pass up the chance to position itself, politically and economically, at the heart of Europe. Here we have examined the role of a new set of actors, businesspeople, who were to play a key part in the economic preparation that led up to accession and, subsequently, to adapting to the new requirements of an EEC member country.

## References

### Archive of the Spanish Ministry for Foreign Affairs (AMAE)

### Leopoldo Calvo-Sotelo Archive (ALCS)

Acuña, Ramón Luis. 1986. *Como los dientes de una sierra (Francia-España de 1975 a 1985)*. Barcelona: Plaza & Janés.

Bassols, Raimundo. 1995. *España en Europa. Historia de la adhesión a la CE, 1957–85*. Madrid: Política Exterior.

Cabrera, Mercedes, and Fernando Del Rey. 2011. *El poder de los empresarios. Política y economía en la España contemporánea (1875–2010)*. Barcelona: RBA.

Calvo-Sotelo, Leopoldo. 1990. *Memoria viva de la Transición*. Barcelona: Plaza & Janés/Cambio 16.

Comín, Francisco, and Mauro Hernández. 2013. *Crisis económicas en España, 1300–2012: lecciones de la historia*. Madrid: Alianza.

Díez Cano, Santiago. 1991. Los empresarios y Europa. *Studia Historica. Historia Contemporánea* 9: 153–163.

García Crespo, Guillermo. 2019. *El precio de Europa. Estrategias empresariales ante el Mercado Común y la Transición a la democracia en España (1975–1986)*. Granada: Comares.

González Fernández, Ángeles. 2004. La representación de los intereses empresariales en el franquismo: los Consejos Provinciales de Empresarios, 1965–1975. *Pasado y Memoria. Revista de Historia Contemporánea* 3: 1–54.

———. 2012. Una esperanza acongojada: los empresarios españoles y portugueses ante el ingreso en la CEE. *Hispania* 72 (242): 699–722.

Gutiérrez Álvarez, Secundino. 2001. *Las organizaciones empresariales en la Transición: 1975–1985*. Madrid: Fundación CEIM.

Hernández Andreu, Juan. 2006. La transición centrista. In *Historia Económica de España*, Coordinated by Agustín González Enciso and Juan Manuel Matés Barco, 781–794. Barcelona: Planeta.

Lafuente del Cano, Jorge. 2017. *Leopoldo Calvo-Sotelo y Europa*. Madrid: Sílex.

Maluquer de Motes, Jordi. 2014. *La economía española en perspectiva histórica*. Barcelona: Pasado y Presente.

Sánchez, Esther. 2016. Francia y la España del tardofranquismo y la transición. Sinergias económicas en un marco de cambio político. *Hispania* 76 (254): 847–882.

CHAPTER 15

# The Automotive Equipment and Components Industry of *Castilla y León* in the World Automotive Market: The *Lingotes Especiales* Group

*Pablo Alonso-Villa and Pedro Pablo Ortúñez-Goicolea*

## 15.1 Introduction[1]

The car industry is one of the most characteristic sectors of twentieth century European industrialisation, although there have been enormous differences between countries in terms of the scope the industry has reached. Germany and France undeniably led the way throughout the twentieth century, yet since the early twenty-first century it has been Germany and Spain who have headed the European car market in terms of production

[1] We are grateful for the help and information provided by the company and, in particular, its current CEO. A more extensive and detailed first version in Alonso and Ortúñez (2019).

P. Alonso-Villa (✉) • P. P. Ortúñez-Goicolea
University of Valladolid, Valladolid, Spain
e-mail: portunez@eco.uva.es





M. Vázquez-Fariñas et al. (eds.), *Companies and Entrepreneurs in the History of Spain*, Palgrave Studies in Economic History,
https://doi.org/10.1007/978-3-030-61318-1_15

and exports (according to data from the 2018 report issued by the International Organisation of Car Manufacturers OICA). Whatever the case, the manufacture of cars and car parts is a strategic industry for the European Union economy since—directly and indirectly—it employs over 13.8 million people, which represents 6.1% of the total working population (European Automobile Manufacturers Association ACEA).

Despite Spain having suffered a considerable delay compared to some of its neighbours in terms of gaining a foothold and consolidating its position in the sector, the country has gradually risen to become the ninth largest producer of vehicles in the world and the second largest in Europe. If we add industrial vehicles, Spain has been Europe's leading producer and exporter for over 20 years (OICA, annual reports, 1998–2018). Today's car industry is a key element in the Spanish economy, since it carries significant weight in terms of GDP (8.6% of the national total), employment (9%), and exports (12.5%), according to data from the National Association of Car and Truck Manufacturers (ANFAC, annual report, 2018). Nonetheless, at the regional scale there are clear differences in terms of the industry's level of implementation and development. It is in Castilla y León and Cataluña where the industry is currently at its most dynamic. Between them, the two regions account for over 40% of national car and car component production.

The car industry in Castilla y León has achieved a solid position in international markets. Iveco, for example, which has been in Valladolid since the early 1990s (Fernández de Sevilla 2013) is the seventh largest exporting firm of automotive equipment in Spain, and Renault Spain the second. The latter is also the fourth largest at the national scale in absolute terms. For its part, the ancillary industry, as has the rest of Spain, has also experienced a period of increasing internationalisation since the country joined the EEC. This opening out was based on exports and direct investments abroad. Today, the car equipment and component industry in Castilla y León represents 23.4% of all the industry's exports at a national level, and the region ranks second only to Cataluña. Prominent examples of this dynamic are the *Grupo Antolín*—the sixth largest exporter of car equipment in Spain—Gestamp, which is present in 20 countries and a world leader in sheet metal stamping—and Lingotes Especiales—which exports over 80% of its production.

The relevance of the automotive sector in Castilla y León on the national and international stage, as well as its importance for the region's economy, highlight the need to delve more deeply into its history. This chapter aims to explore this issue by examining one of the few firms whose capital is entirely regional, and which has also managed to be enormously competitive both at home and abroad, Lingotes Especiales (hereinafter, LE). This firm, whose history is one of business success, has grown from being a small company to being a multinational that is present in a number of countries. It is currently the third largest iron foundry in Spain (*El Economista*, May 4, 2019). It accounts for 9.5% of national iron production and 13.5% of production destined for the automotive sector. It is also strongly involved in exports in this field, accounting for 11.2% of the total and 16.5% of those destined for the car industry (according to 2017 data from the FEAF). It is a regular supplier to over 60 production plants throughout Europe, thanks to which its production of disc brakes, its main product, represents 12% of the European market for these products.

The birth of LE came about when the Spanish automotive sector was at the height of its expansion according to Catalan (2000), the Spanish car industry expanded between 1950 and 1973, as was the white domestic appliance industry (De la Torre 2017), who soon became its main clients, which is why the company's growth is linked to the evolution of the two sectors.

## 15.2 Creating a Business Idea: The Advantage of Having FASA-Renault Nearby

In the mid-twentieth country, Valladolid already boasted of a long tradition of metal—mechanic and casting activities dating back to the late nineteenth country. This industrial base, together with other advantages—specialised labour, training institutions, metallurgical companies offering a wide range of products, stemming from the existence of a metallurgical area, was able to bolster, if not the arrival of FASA, at least the subsequent development of the automotive industry, not only in Valladolid but throughout the region as a whole. From the 1940s, there was a transformation in the supplies provided by companies in the metallurgical field towards manufacturing products aimed at the material transport sector. As a result, it can be said that industrial activities linked to the automotive industry have existed in the city since the arrival of FASA in 1951. However, it was not until the said company arrived that the sector began to grow in the region (Alonso et al. 2019).

The focus on the automotive industry in Valladolid was boosted as a result of two initiatives undertaken after the mid-1950s. The first was the creation, by Francesco Scrimieri, of Mundial Pistón Española, SA, in 1955, under licence from the Italian company Mondial Piston, Co. The second, also thanks to this businessman, was the setting up of another company to build three-wheeled vehicles, *the Sociedad Anónima de Vehículos Automóviles* (SAVA), which had its own patents and technology (Alonso et al. 2019). In 1968, SAVA was taken over by the national industrial vehicle company (ENASA), and in 1991 this was in turn taken over by the Italian group Iveco, who maintained the Valladolid plant where Pegaso trucks are manufactured.

In the early 1960s, three vehicle manufacturers were already operating in Castilla y León; FASA and SAVA in Valladolid, and FADISA[2] in Ávila. During those ten years, the industrial policy implemented by the Franco regime helped to boost the region's automotive industry. The government decided to bolster the industrial development of the Duero basin area by declaring Burgos and Valladolid to be "poles", and by including Aranda de Duero in the Madrid Decongestion Plan (Moreno 2006; Cebrián 2009).

These were the years that witnessed the start of mass production in FASA. The company management decided to invest heavily in means of production in an effort to expand its size and level of vertical integration. This strategy resulted in the enormous increase in its production, which grew from manufacturing 8400 vehicles in 1960 to nearly 170,000 in 1973 (Fernández de Sevilla 2013). The economic advantages to emerge from having Valladolid designated as a pole of development was able to provide FASA—which after 1965 became FASA-Renault—with the creation of important production units. That year saw the setting up of the subsidiary companies FAMESA and FACSA, which were responsible for manufacturing engines and bodywork, respectively (Fernández de Sevilla 2013). This was how the idea first emerged of what was later to become LE.

Juan José Villegas, who worked as an engineer at FAMESA, had the idea of using the iron shavings (or swarf) left over from machining the engine parts at the company to make metal ingots or blocks. The advantage was the low cost of the raw material, which was usually thrown away. Together with some friends and acquaintances—José Oliveri, Vicente Garrido and Eduardo Martín—, who later became partners in the company, they agreed that the idea might prove to be profitable, but that rather than obtaining iron blocks, it would be interesting to manufacture metal parts, which would have added value and which would thus yield a greater profit (Alonso and Ortúñez 2020).

[2] It started by manufacturing vans under licence from Alfa Romeo in 1956 (*ABC*, August 18, 1962; *El Norte de Castilla*, February 3, 2015).

It was the proximity of the flow of raw material from both FAMESA and FACSA, coupled with the possibility of selling the parts back to FASA-Renault itself, that led to the company being set up in Valladolid. Since 1957, the city had also been home to another vehicle manufacturer, SAVA, and in the nearby province of Ávila there was FADISA, both of whom would be potential clients.

These entrepreneurs had come up with a business project, but needed to raise the capital to get it started. They lacked the necessary financial resources, so that they were forced to look around amongst acquaintances and businesspeople in Valladolid in order to raise the capital required. It took them a few months to secure the money they needed, but finally on July 20, 1968 the 35 founding partners signed the public deed setting up the *Lingotes Especiales* limited company. The initial social capital was set at 25.7 million pesetas, represented by 2570 nominal shares to be split among the founding partners. The company's initial aim was to "manufacture, transform, sell and export all kinds of metal blocks and parts, of both iron as well as non-iron materials".[3]

## 15.3 Consolidation During a Period of Turmoil: 1970–1990

Once the facilities had been built, the next step was to provide them with the key element required in foundries, the furnace. In late 1968, two AJAX Guinea electric furnaces—the most efficient on the market—and one Disamatic moulding machine were installed and put into operation. This machine model had arrived on the market in early 1964 and was the only one capable of making sand moulds automatically.

For the first few months, the company still did not have any specific contracts to manufacture parts. As a result, they only cast iron to turn it into blocks. Even though this was not their aim, obtaining those first steel blocks and bars provided the plant's new workers with experience. Between 1969 and 1973, and once the first supply contracts had been won, four more furnaces, which were also low frequency AJAX models and Disamatic machines were installed. In 1975, as a result of the positive reception given to the parts manufactured by LE, it was necessary to construct another plant to house four further furnaces and two moulding machines.

[3] Lingotes Especiales Archive (hereinafter L.E.A.), public deed setting up the company.

Although machines were brought in to speed up the processes, the production lines in the early years were labour intensive. The company workforce grew during the 1970s at an annual rate of 20%, which meant that in 1979 the total number of workers stood at 268.[4] This number remained the same until the mid-1990s, when the subsidiary company responsible for metal machining (*Frenos y Conjuntos*, S. A.) was set up. Coupled with a constant increase in production, this reflected the solid labour productivity performance, particularly during the 1980s. Over this period, this grew at an annual rate of 9% as a result of the more intense use of machinery and the subsequent increase in the capital/work ratio.

The production strategy—investment in means of production—ran parallel to commercialisation and diversification; in other words, attracting clients in different sectors. In the automotive industry, one of the first companies to purchase L.E.'s parts was FASA-Renault, such that they became both a supplier of raw material—the iron shavings or swarf—and a client at the same time. Getting a foot in the door of this company was by no means easy. LE had no experience, as a result of which clients were at first reluctant to purchase the company's parts. FASA-Renault finally agreed to purchase the vehicle components manufactured by L.E. The first batch rolled out of the company's premises in the summer of 1969, a year in which production stood at the modest figure of 1029 tonnes.[5] Sales were also made to other vehicle manufacturers, SAVA—who had been manufacturing three-wheelers in Valladolid since 1957—and Barreiros, located in Madrid since 1954. Between 1970 and 1976, the number of clients from the automotive industry continued to grow. These companies were joined by Fraymon, the manufacturer of clutches—later taken over by the French firm Valeo—, SEAT, Chrysler, Talbot, Citroën and, finally, Ford.

Clients were also sought and found in sectors other than the automotive industry. LE signed supply contracts with firms involved in the household appliance sector as well as others engaged in construction machinery. Prominent amongst the former were Carsa-Kelvinator, located in Getafe, and a manufacturer of refrigerators and washing machines; Ibérica de Electrodomésticos S. A. (Ibelsa), the fourth largest manufacturer in the Spanish household appliance sector, who had been operating in Madrid since 1965 (De la Torre 2017); and Unidad Hermética, S. A., set up in

[4] L.E.A., board meeting minutes, 1969–2016.

[5] L.E.A., board meeting minutes, 1969.

1962, and specialising in compressors for cooling equipment. Leading companies amongst the latter included Imenasa, who manufactured cranes for construction. As the number of clients increased, so did the range of products made by LE. The firm was able to produce a wide variety of metal parts—disc brakes, camshafts, gear boxes, refrigerator compressors, and so on—and to supply to a large number of sectors: the automotive industry, domestic appliances, agricultural machinery, railways, and civil engineering, amongst others.[6]

LE's development during those first twenty years (1970–1990) cannot be explained with taking into account the dynamics of the principal sectors it supplied; the automotive industry and the "white goods" household appliance industry. Sales to these two sectors represented over 80% of the total. Supply contracts with the firms in these sectors were gradually adapted to their needs. The automotive industry underwent substantial growth during the 1960s—its production increased at a mean annual rate of 24% (rate calculated using data from the EU KLEMS 2009 database)—thanks to the rise of the two main vehicle manufacturers in Spain: SEAT, which went from building over 30,000 vehicles in 1960 to over 93,000 in 1970, and FASA-Renault, which manufactured 7824 vehicles in the late 1950s and 98,720 in 1970 (Catalan 2006; Fernández de Sevilla 2013). This situation remained steady until the mid-1970s, when there was a drop in the growth rate that was triggered, amongst other reasons, by the 1973 oil crisis. Certain authors feel that after that point, and virtually up until Spain's entry into the EEC, the sector plunged into a crisis (Situación 1980; Castaño and Cortés 1980; Portillo 1982). Other authors, however, believe that the Spanish automotive industry scarcely suffered the effects of the international crisis, since it coincided with the arrival of American manufacturers and a major increase in exports (García 2001).

A look at the production figures of manufacturers in Spain shows that they did not all follow the same pattern. SEAT and Citroën cut their production of vehicles between 1976 and 1978 by 18% and 19.5%, respectively. In contrast, others such as FASA-Renault and Chrysler increased production during those two years; 10% in the case of the former, and 43% in the case of the latter (Castaño and Cortés 1980). Overall, the growth in the sector's production in Spain stood at an annual rate of 3.9% between 1970 and 1980 (percentage calculated with EU KLEMS 2009 data). This reflects a significant reduction in the growth rate compared to the

[6] For the various parts the company has manufactured, see Alonso and Ortúñez (2020).

previous decade, although production did not in fact fall off. Nevertheless, the sector was by no means going through its best moment. Despite the successive rises in the price of the vehicles authorised by the government, the increased cost of living meant that, in real terms, cars were actually getting cheaper, such that manufacturers' profit margins were actually going down (Catalan 2007). Moreover, the increased fiscal pressure which the sector was coming under, together with the rise in fuel prices, led to a substantial drop in domestic demand for vehicles between 1974 and 1979 (Castaño and Cortés 1980). This made it necessary to resort to exports, which were able to provide some comfort for Spanish companies. Exports were favoured by the preferential agreement signed in 1970 with the EEC (Fernández de Sevilla 2013). Overseas sales grew spectacularly from late 1973 until late 1979 at a mean annual rate of 105% (percentage calculated using automotive industry export data from Situación 1980). FASA-Renault and Ford experienced the greatest increases in the years following the oil crisis (Castaño and Cortés 1980).

During the 1970s, the Spanish automotive industry was, in general, able to weather the crisis by resorting, as we have seen, to exports. Yet this was to change in the first half of the 1980s. The arrival of American manufacturers—Ford and General Motors, with their European subsidiary Opel—onto a Spanish market that was experiencing stagflation and falling demand, made things complicated for car manufacturers in Spain. Between 1981 and 1985, the production of SEAT, FASA-Renault, Chrysler-Peugeot and Citroën-Peugeot fell (Catalan 2000). It was perhaps SEAT, who had formerly come to be known as the "national champion" who came off worst. Since the mid-1980s, the firm had been racking up huge losses (Catalan 2007). In the early 1980s, LE decided to cut back the supply of parts to the factory at Martorell because of non-payment of some orders. The ups and downs of the automotive industry during those years had a major impact on LE, since these firms accounted for over 60% of the firm's sales. Some of the company's clients experienced serious financial difficulties whilst other were forced to cut back their production, which affected their demand for parts. As can be seen in Fig. 15.1, LE's production stagnated during the first half of the 1980s, and in 1981, for the first and only time in its history, it posted a loss.[7]

Yet it was not only the automotive industry that was having a hard time. LE's other main sector-client, the household appliance industry, also

[7] L.E.A., board meeting minutes, 1981.

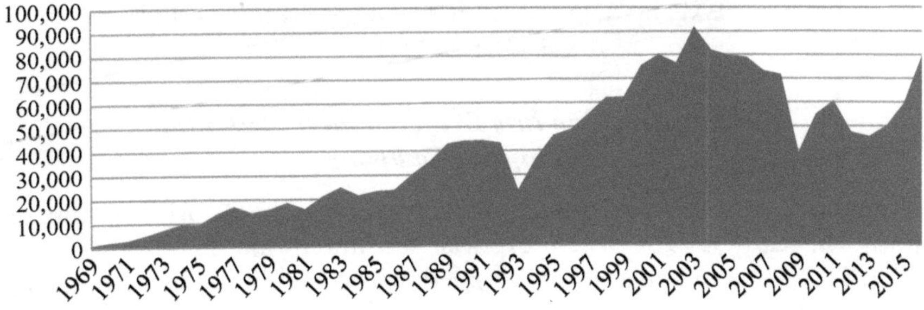


**Fig. 15.1** Evolution of LE production (Tonnes). (Source: Authors, based on *LE*, board meeting minutes, 1969–2016)

suffered the effects of the crisis after the late 1970s, coinciding with the second oil crisis. Families' disposable income stagnated and consumption plummeted. Some companies started to accumulate losses, since they kept up their plan for investing and increasing production even though disposable income had ceased to grow and consumption had slowed down (De la Torre 2017). Faced with this situation, in the early 1980s the Ministry of Industry and Energy began to develop an industrial reconversion plan for the sector, which was primarily aimed at restructuring companies and encouraging mergers (Navarro 1990). The goal was for firms in difficulty to invest in modernising their facilities and so make them more efficient and profitable (De la Torre 2017). Two of LE's clients in the sector were in financial difficulty; Carsa-Kelvinator and Ibelsa. The former, which had run up losses of 2600 million pesetas, suspended payments in 1980 (*El País*, February 14, 1980) and did not therefore renew the supply contracts it had been signing up to that point, while the latter, which was also making a loss, negotiated a state aid scheme after being taken over by the Italian company Zanussi in 1980 (*El País*, July 2, 1985).

Despite these ups and downs, LE continued to receive orders and so continued to grow, thanks to the wide portfolio of clients—from different sectors—it had managed to acquire since the early days of the company. Production increased substantially in the 1970s (Fig. 15.1), at a rate of 30% per year. In 1980, production stood at over 18,000 tonnes, a figure which ten years later had reached 42,000 tonnes a year.

## 15.4 Exports and Direct Investment Overseas: 1990–2018

### *15.4.1 Breaking into Exports, and the Subsidiary Machining Company*

Even though LE did not consolidate its position as an exporting company until the early 1990—when exports accounted for 22% of all sales (Fig. 15.2)—the first parts were shipped from Spain in the first half of the 1980s. The difficult situation facing the domestic automotive industry during those years led LE management to consider selling abroad. The firm had achieved a strong position in the domestic market after having been operating for a decade and a half. In addition, it had the necessary technology and production techniques required to provide competitive components abroad and had the experience needed to supply them to the various plants in a timely and flexible manner.

The volume of exports during the early 1980s was very small but helped to establish initial contact with European vehicle manufacturing plants. In addition to the huge amount of red tape demanded from companies wishing to buy and sell abroad, there was also the difficulty involved in selling to large European manufacturers for the first time. Given the ever-increasing competitiveness in the world automotive industry, manufacturers required any companies who sought to form part of their list of suppliers to have wide experience in the European market. Thanks to

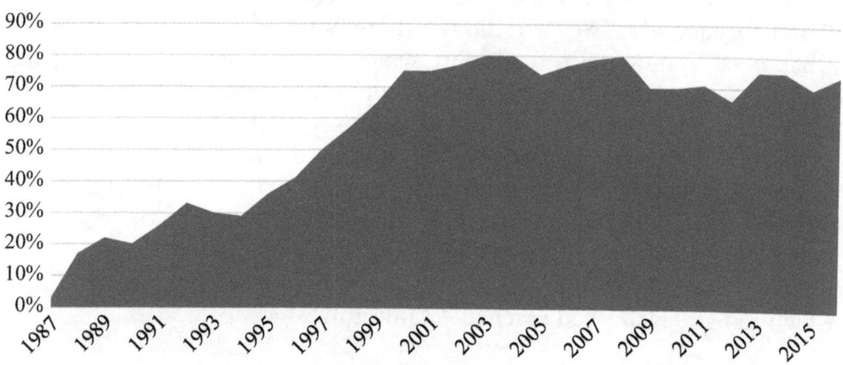


**Fig. 15.2** Percentage of LE exports out of total production. (Source: Authors, based on *LE*, annual reports, 1987–2016)

intense negotiations, and by being able to meet the extremely demanding quality standards required by manufacturers, LE managed to break into the overseas market.[8] Between 1981 and 1984 it was able to sell some batches of parts to the Opel plant in Germany, to plants in the PSA group, to Renault plants in Douai (France) and Cacia (Portugal), and to the French Valeo factories.[9] The flow of exports became constant and grew after 1987, thanks, in part to the easier trading terms which came about as a result of Spain joining the EEC.

The new relations which the company had started to forge in the European market led it to consider the possibility of going public. In such a competitive setting, it was essential to project an image of robustness and transparency, which is exactly what becoming a listed company would provide. In September 1988, preparations began for the company's venture into the stock market, and in November of that same year, the shareholders meeting ratified the agreement. At the end of the year, it was agreed to increase the social capital from 600 to 900 million pesetas.[10] 100% of the social capital was admitted for the official listing and on March 30, 1989 LE began its journey in the stock market. At the end of the financial year, its sound management had led to it becoming the eighth most profitable firm in terms of own resources of all the companies listed in the Madrid stock exchange, with a value of 63%. In 2006, it began listing in the Spanish Continuous Market, and since 2015 it has formed part of the IBEX SMALL CAP.[11] If Campofrío's joining the stock market in 1988 heralded a landmark in the business history of Castilla y León (Moreno 2006), no doubt so did LE's a few months later.[12]

The crisis that affected national industry in 1993 hit the automotive industry particularly hard. LE saw its orders cut, leading to a significant drop in sales, which fell below 27,000 tonnes (Fig. 15.1). Faced with this situation, the management implemented a number of tough measures such as laying off workers—cutting the workforce by 36, some 12%—and

[8] The ratings obtained by L.E. in the quality controls were comparable to those obtained by other European suppliers (L.E.A., board meeting minutes, various years).

[9] L.E.A., board meeting minutes, various years.

[10] L.E.A., 1988 board meeting minutes and 1988 annual report.

[11] L.E.A., annual reports, various years.

[12] Currently only three companies with their headquarters in the region are listed on the stock exchange: Europac (Palencia), Nicolás Correa (Burgos), and L.E. (*El País*, January 10, 2018).

drastically adjusting production in an effort to avoid excessive costs.[13] These measures were joined by others aimed at keeping operating expenses in check, in accordance with the zero-based budgeting model the company had been implementing since the mid-1970s (Alonso and Ortúñez 2020). Despite the fall in sales, applying this system allowed for lower, yet still positive, results.

This setback did not prevent the company from continuing to grow, both in the domestic as well as the European market. By the late 1990s, its sales represented around 33% of the Spanish market in disc brakes,[14] both machined and blanks, and its total production represented 9% of nationally cast iron.[15] It also strengthened its trade relations with its European clients, particularly with Renault, the PSA group and Opel, and the firm also won major supply contracts with new clients like General Motors, Volkswagen, Ford, Valeo, Delphi Automotive, and Bradi. LE's exports grew considerably during the 1990s and by 1995 it was selling 36% of its production abroad, a figure which was to reach 75% by the end of the decade (Fig. 15.2).[16]

The new relations which LE established with a leading supplier in the European automotive industry soon gave rise to a flourishing business project. Its new client, Bradi, purchased parts from the company, mainly disc brakes, which it then machined and sold to vehicle manufacturers. LE management weighed up the possibility of teaming up with this client —who had long-running experience in machining—and setting up a firm to machine the parts cast in Valladolid. In late 1996, it established a technical cooperation agreement—a joint venture—to engage in a project to machine iron parts. In April 1997, the new company, Braling Conjuntos, was set up with a capital of 200 million pesetas. LE disbursed 40%, Bradi another 40%, with the remaining 20% being provided by Sodical (Castilla y León industrial development company). The first board meeting of Braling Conjuntos, SA was held in October 1997 and was made up of five members from the three parties involved in the project. The distribution was as follows: two seats for LE—including the presidency—a further two for Bradi and the last, the secretariat for Sodical.

[13] L.E.A., annual report, 1993.

[14] Its main product in the automotive industry sector. Up until the creation of its machining subsidiary in 1997, it only made blank parts. From then, it started to machine the parts it cast.

[15] L.E.A., annual reports, various years. FEAF, sector data, 1999.

[16] L.E.A., annual reports, various years.

The technology with which the first machine line was equipped was imported from Germany, where technicians from LE went in order to learn how to work the new machines. As the number of orders grew, so did the number of production lines, until they reached the present figure of 11. In 2002, given the good results, LE bought out its Italian partner's stake. This deal led to the firm now owning 80% of the limited company and changing the name to Frenos y Conjuntos, SA. Two years later, Sodical left the limited company by selling its 20% stake of the capital to LE, the parent company.

As vehicle manufacturers gradually increased their demand for more finished products and, therefore, of greater added value, suppliers began to adapt to these demands. Over the whole period analysed, LE has devoted an average of 2% of its turnover to investments in R&D in an effort to enhance processes and obtain new products. It has added paint to the discs, manufactured all the components of the brake drums, and is currently making ABS systems.[17] After setting up the machining subsidiary and obtaining the new product, machined disc brakes, LE's exports grew considerably, and by 2003 these accounted for 80% of its sales. Current production stands at four million machined disc brakes and, together with blank discs, represents 12% of the European market share and 3% of the world market.[18]

### 15.4.2 *The Globalisation of the Company*

In 1999, at the *Foro Internacional de Fundidores*, the Danish firm DISA presented a new model of machine for moulding which was able to produce aluminium parts. This international meeting was attended by some of LE's managers, who contacted representatives from the American corporation, Alcoa. The automotive division of said company had for years been trying to develop and manufacture aluminium structural parts for vehicles.[19] Despite having obtained components of the metal, they needed to team up with a company who had experience in the casting and machining of car parts. For its part, LE had for some time been seeking to expand its range of products by obtaining parts made of a lighter material,

[17] In 2016, this company obtained the patent for the light disc brake, which reduced the weight by 30% (L.E.A., annual report, 2016).

[18] L.E.A., annual report, 2016 and 2017.

[19] L.E.A., board meeting minutes, 2000.

aluminium.[20] That meeting between representatives of the two companies heralded the first step in the project they were to develop jointly.

The business opportunities that could emerge through an agreement with a multinational company of Alcoa's calibre were vast. With its automotive division—Alcoa Automotive Casting Unit—Alcoa provided LE with access to an American car market that in 1999 had manufactured over 13 million vehicles (According to OICA data). After a number of meetings in Pittsburgh and Valladolid, representatives from the two firms reached an agreement to set up a company to make aluminium parts for vehicles. Before the end of 2000, the company Alcoa Lingotes Casting (henceforth, ALC) had been created with a 60% share of the capital for Alcoa and the remaining 40% for LE. The board was made up of three representatives from the former and two from the latter, with the latter two, nevertheless, having the right to veto, which balanced out the distribution of seats.[21]

The greater difficulty involved in machining aluminium parts as opposed to iron parts meant that the project was designed to be carried out in two stages. During the first stage, manufacturing tests were conducted, which—in an effort to speed up the process—required acquiring a fully operational industrial plant. ALC purchased Alloy Technologies Limited, located at Leyland, whose facilities included machine lines. The aim during the second stage was to manufacture those parts which had obtained the best results in the quality tests during the first stage. April 2001 was set as the deadline to commence the second stage of the operation. After intense discussion within the board, it was decided to set up a factory in Spain as close as possible to LE's facilities so as to thus receive technical assistance. Despite having all the required licences and the go ahead from the American company, construction of the facilities was delayed.[22]

In the first quarter of 2002 doubts began to emerge concerning the viability of the project, since some of the parts manufactured during the first stage had not had the expected reception in the market and had also created serious problems during the machining. In general, aluminium

[20] From the late 1990s, vehicle manufacturers began to demand lighter parts and components in order to reduce the total weight of the vehicles and so cut fuel consumption. This is why L.E. sought to develop new products using aluminium.

[21] L.E.A., board meeting minutes, June 2000.

[22] L.E.A., board meeting minutes, various years.

products had little impact in the European automotive market. In early 2004, LE announced it was leaving the company by selling its shares to Alcoa, who kept the Leyland factory operational in order to honour the supply contracts that ran until 2009. Even though the project proved unsuccessful, LE did gain vital experience in machining techniques for aluminium parts and components.

During those years, the European automotive market went through a period of stagnation. Faced with dwindling sales, European manufacturers undertook major changes in production in an effort to adapt to demand (Bueno 2010). As can be seen in Fig. 15.3, production of automotive vehicles, both in terms of cars as well as commercial vehicles, fell after 2004, in Spain and France and in the UK, LE's main export destinations. As of 2008, the stagnation the industry had been going through was aggravated even further by the crisis which began that year. It should be remembered that a very high percentage of vehicles are purchased on credit (Aláez et al. 2009). Vehicle production fell sharply in the main European producing countries (Fig. 15.3). The number of orders on LE's books tumbled as did company production, which declined considerably over the period 2003–2008 (going from just over 90,000 tonnes to 70,000) and spectacularly in 2009, when it plummeted by almost 50% compared to the previous year (Fig. 15.1). From the point of view of costs, the period was also characterised by an increase in raw material and electrical energy costs. All of this led to losses amounting to one million

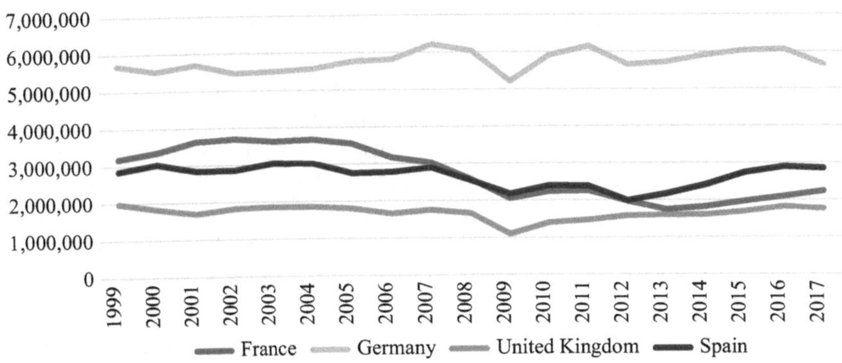


**Fig. 15.3** Progression in the number of vehicles produced in the main manufacturing countries in Europe. (Source: Authors, drawn up with OICA data)

euros in the first quarter of 2009, although results were back in the black by the end of the year. This was possible thanks to the rapid application of measures designed to revert the situation such as adjusting shifts, reviewing and adjusting all of the company's internal costs—applying the zero—based budget model—and by engaging in an intense commercial policy aimed at winning back orders as quickly as possible.[23] However, it was not until 2013 that the firm once again found itself on the growing curve that had been its hallmark.

Even though vehicle sales have picked up in Europe since 2013, the market is yet to return to pre-crisis figures (according to OICA data). Moreover, the European automotive market is clearly oversized, which could well trigger a fresh crisis (Bueno 2010). Faced with this situation and given the need imposed by manufacturers on their suppliers to become global suppliers, LE envisaged the possibility of accessing emerging markets, such as Asia, by producing abroad. It was decided to opt for India, a growing market whose vehicle production exceeded 3.8 million in 2014 (OICA), which in terms of disc brakes amounts to over 15 million. The country also offers a privileged location for getting a foothold in major markets such as China and South Korea (Gil 2011). Another advantage the country affords is its mercantile legislation, which is Anglo-American based, thereby making it easy to set up businesses, when compared to its neighbouring countries.

In May 2014, LE signed a joint venture with Setco Automotive Limited to manufacture machined parts for the automotive industry. Said agreement was drawn up in May of the same year through the creation of the Lava Cast limited company. Given the lack of knowledge of the Indian market, it was decided to team up with a firm that was already supplying automobile manufacturers. Setco is the number one manufacturer of clutches in India and has four production plants—two in India, one in the UK and another in the USA—and is a supplier to the leading western and Asian carmakers. The project was designed to be carried out in two stages. During the first stage, involving an anticipated investment of 25 million euros, a foundry was built and put into operation in the city of Kalol, in the state of Gujarat. It has a capacity of 25,000 tonnes a year and another machine facility with technology used at Frenos y Conjuntos. Following on from the good test results in quality, the first parts were shipped out to clients in mid-2016. In the second stage of the project, which is still

[23] L.E.A., annual report, 2009.

underway, another casting line and another machine line are planned, which will take Lava Cast's production capacity to 50,000 tonnes a year.

## 15.5 Final Notes

The equipment and component sector for the automotive industry emerged in Spain during the first third of the twentieth century, although it was not until the 1950s and 1960s that it really took off and established itself. Since the 1970s, it has undergone major changes, as a result of having modernised its companies and thanks to its internationalisation (Ortiz-Villajos 2010). As we have seen, LE has followed this dynamic, as it has gradually adapted its facilities to technical requirements and has become competitive in the world automotive market. In its internationalisation—which began after it had achieved a strong position in the domestic market—it has followed three well-defined stages. During the first, which commenced in the first half of the 1980s, it began with occasional exports. During the second stage, in the 1990s, it established itself as an exporting company. During the final stage, since 2000, it has made direct investments overseas through joint ventures with multinational firms.

We have seen how the factors which determined the setting up of L.E. and its location in Valladolid were the existence of partners who displayed a willingness to invest, and the nearby FASA-Renault factories. Since then, the firm has made the most of the advantages afforded to it by its environment-important clients nearby, specialised service centres, training centres, a specialised labour force; advantages which all the firms in the automotive industry cluster, to which LE has belonged since 2004, the year it was set up, can benefit from. These economic agents, together with the firms who supply equipment and components for the automotive industry, maintain important and highly varied collaboration and cooperation links with vehicle manufacturers in the area which, thanks to the externalities created, favours the regional sector's national and international competitiveness.

## References

LINGOTES ESPECIALES ARCHIVE (L.E.A.)

Aláez, Ricardo, Javier Bilbao, Vicente Camino, and Juan Carlos Longás. 2009. Reflexiones sobre la crisis de la industria española del automóvil y sus perspectivas. *Información Comercial Española* 850: 41–56.

Alonso, Pablo, and Pedro Pablo Ortúñez. 2019. De PYME a multinacional: el caso de Lingotes Especiales, 1968–2017. In *Empresas y empresarios en España. De mercaderes a industriales.*, coordinated by Juan Mnuel Matés–Barco, 369–387. Madrid: Pirámide.

———. 2020. El proceso de internacionalización en la industria española de equipos y componentes de automoción: *Lingotes Especiales, 1968–2018. Revista de Historia Industrial* 78: 115–154.

Alonso, Pablo, Montserrat Álvarez, and Pedro Pablo Ortúñez. 2019. Formación y desarrollo de un distrito metalúrgico en Valladolid (c.1842–1951). *Investigaciones de Historia Económica* 15 (3): 177–189.

Bueno, José Antonio. 2010. Crisis global y automoción ¿la tormenta perfecta?: la reciente evolución del sector a escala mundial. *Economía Industrial* 376: 37–50.

Castaño, Cecilia, and Gonzalo Cortés. 1980. Evolución del sector del automóvil en España. *Información Comercial Española* 563: 145–157.

Catalan, Jordi. 2000. La creación de la ventaja comparativa en la industria automovilística española, 1898–1996. *Revista de Historia Industrial* 18: 113–155.

———. 2006. La SEAT del desarrollo, 1948–1972. *Revista de Historia Industrial* 30: 143–196.

———. 2007. La primera crisis de SEAT: el veto a General Motors y la compra de AUTHI a Bristish Leyland (1972–1976). *Investigaciones de Historia Económica* 9: 141–174.

Cebrián, Mar. 2009. ¿Industrializar Castilla? El caso del polo de desarrollo de Valladolid (1964–1975). In *Entre el mercado y el Estado. Los planes de desarrollo durante el franquismo.*, coordinated by Joseba De la Torre and Mario García, 261–296. Pamplona: Universidad Pública de Navarra.

De la Torre, Joseba. 2017. Auge, quiebra y reconversión de la industria de electrodomésticos en España a la luz del Grupo Orbaiceta, S. A., c. 1950–1990. *Investigaciones de Historia Económica* 13 (1): 26–37.

Fernández De Sevilla, Tomás. 2013. *El desarrollo de la industria del automóvil en España: el caso de FASA-Renault, 1951–1985.* PhD diss., University of Barcelona.

García, José Luis. 2001. La evolución de la industria automovilística española, 1946–1999: una perspectiva comparada. *Revista de Historia Industrial* 19–20: 133–163.

Gil, Mario. 2011. Factores clave de éxito para una implantación de negocios en India. *Boletín Económico del ICE* 3006: 31–42.

Moreno, Javier. 2006. Factor empresarial y atraso económico en Castilla y León (siglos XIX y XX). In *Historia Empresarial de España. Un enfoque regional en profundidad*, coordinated by José Luis García and Carles Manera, 315–336. Madrid: LID.

Navarro, Mikel. 1990. *Política de reconversión: balance crítico.* Madrid: Eudema.

Ortiz-Villajos, José María. 2010. Aproximación a la historia de la industria de equipos y componentes de automoción en España. *Investigaciones de Historia Económica* 216: 135–172.

Portillo, Luis. 1982. La industria del automóvil en España: crisis y perspectivas. *Información Comercial Española* 587: 17–30.

Situación. 1980. Cambios en la industria del automóvil. *Servicio de Estudios del Banco Bilbao* 5: 2–33.

# Index[1]



[1] Note: Page numbers followed by 'n' refer to notes.



M. Vázquez-Fariñas et al. (eds.), *Companies and Entrepreneurs in the History of Spain*, Palgrave Studies in Economic History,
https://doi.org/10.1007/978-3-030-61318-1

**F**

T

Kolibri 360 GmbH
Ferdinand-Jühlke-Straße 7
99095 Erfurt, Deutschland
produktsicherheit@kolibri360.de